THE

HIBS GO

MARCHING UP

www.twitter.com/hibsmarchingup

www.facebook.com/thehibsgomarchingup

Braidwood Books

Also by Sandy Macnair

CARSPOTTING: THE REAL ADVENTURES OF IRVINE WELSH

'An outrageously funny, readable and very accessible book for anyone who's a fan of Welsh. There's a whirlwind of weeks, months and years squandered away mindlessly in bars and dirty nightspots, with an assorted cast of freaks, junkies, tramps and whacked-out teenage girls. A wild and punk storytelling that propels the reader forward.'

THE EDINBURGH BOOK REVIEW

GROWING UP IN GREEN: HIBS SUPPORTING THROUGH THE SEVENTIES

'A nostalgic trip back to the 1970s when flares were flares and Hibs were good! A coming-of-age tale with some crazy capers thrown in. Very well written and full of laughs – many at the author's expense.'

THE SCOTSMAN

Growing Up in Green was selected by The Scotsman for their 'Best Scottish Sports Reads of 2014' list.

MOONSHINE ON LEITH: HIBERNIAN'S 2015/16 SCOTTISH CUP-WINNING SEASON

'I enjoyed the jokes about Mark Warburton, less so the ones about myself. Rest assured comrades, when I finally fire a nuclear missile at the Famous Five Stand one Saturday afternoon at 3:00pm, it will be aimed directly at the seat allocated to this character Macnair, a running dog of the Imperialist capitalist decadent enemy if ever there was one.'

KIM JONG-UN, TOP GADGIE, NORTH KOREA

THE

HIBS GO

MARCHING UP

Hibernian's 2016/17 Championship-winning
season

SANDY MACNAIR

Published by Braidwood Books
4 Nellfield Gardens
Braidwood
Carluke
Lanarkshire
ML8 5GX

ISBN 978-0-9931012-2-9

Printed and bound in the UK by Witley Press Ltd
www.witleypress.co.uk

In memory of Alistair 'Ali' Tait, 1964-2016
and Colin Dobson, 1971-2017

Two Hibbies taken far too soon

CONTENTS

ACKNOWLEDGEMENTS

Thanks to Braidwood Books and Graham Ewing in particular for all invaluable assistance, up to and including cover design. For general help, sales and marketing of my previous books, a big ta to Roanna at Blackwell's Bookshop, Steven, Amanda and staff at Football Nation and Six Yard Box and John Urquhart (mainly in the Cask & Barrel). Cheers too, to Mark and Stu at Hobs Repographics. Thanks also to Colin Leslie for granting permission to quote directly from his work, to Lisa McGregor for not suing me (yet) and Jimmy Colvin and the girls at the Iona for keeping those pre and post-match pints pouring big style.

Cheers, y'all!

G G T T H

BACK COVER: the author with the Holy Grail.

INTRODUCTION

Like my previous book 'Moonshine on Leith', this one was written as the season progressed, which is really the only way to go about the task, if you want the finished article to hit the bookshops and other outlets by the start of the new campaign. It also helps if you're a lazy bastard who can't be arsed revising it too much on completion. So opinions, hopes and fears conveyed within are generally how I perceived them at that specific time, without any grand overview of what awaited us at the final dēnouement.

G G T T H

1.

JULY: HIBS AIM HIGH, BUT SHEEP CAN'T FLY

Greetings my fellow Hibbies – were the cup final hangovers from May 21st starting to wear off a bit then, by this, the seventh month of the Year of Our Lord, 2016? I know mine was still raging on, well into June. What an ending to the previous season though. I was as high as a kite for about a month afterwards and not just as a result of what I'd imbibed either. A wonderful once in a lifetime experience, *so far.* Let's just hope we don't have to wait one hundred and fourteen years for the next one.

The only downside in the aftermath of such a great day was losing our much-loved gaffer Alan Stubbs, who chose to take the highway south to Rotherham United. Disappointing as it was to bid farewell to him, his reasons for leaving were understandable. For how on earth could you ever hope to top an achievement like that? Stubbsy went on his way, secure in the knowledge that his name was now written very large in the Hibernian history books, right up there alongside Dan McMichael of 1902 vintage. (Maybe one of these days we'll win the Scottish Cup with a *Scottish* manager; now wouldn't *that* be a novelty?) But the likeable Scouser's family had remained domiciled in England when he'd taken up the Hibs job and his ambition was always likely to be found in eventually trying his luck at successful management south of the border. Commendably, despite all the euphoria understandably generated by the terrific cup runs, both League and Scottish varieties,

Alan never lost sight of the principal goal – promotion to the Premiership. That of course had floundered in the cruellest of circumstances, losing a fateful goal at Falkirk well into injury time in the second leg of the second Play-Off double-header. The huge sense of anti-climax that followed was mercifully obscured by events at Hampden on May 21st, but once the joy had dissipated somewhat from that, reality had kicked in sharply again. Alan Stubbs had succeeded in a manner that no other Hibernian manager in living memory had done, but the brutal truth was that he'd failed in his ultimate objective, namely returning Hibs to the top flight. So the hunt was on immediately, to find a suitable successor.

The usual fairly uninspiring names were duly trotted out, the ones that always seem to come to the fore when a managerial vacancy down Leith way comes along. Yogi, Stuart McCall, Gary Locke(!) et al. The only one of the crop that I thought in any way might measure up was Malky Mackay, but it looked as if he was always going to be second favourite at best. Iron Rod was reading a Hibs history book by the light of a guttering candle one dark and stormy night, when he came across passages pertaining to a legendary Hibernian manager from the first half of the previous century. A light-bulb suddenly went off in Rod's brain – which was just as well as the candle had burned right down – and he paused reflectively.

"Mmm," he mused, "McCartney, eh? Well if it was good enough for him, I suppose there's no reason why I shouldn't follow that up by appointing Lennon."

However, Danny of that ilk was not available (it was his bath night), but the Hibs chairman was something of a tenacious tiger with the bit between his teeth when he'd just had an idea. Vladimir Ilyich was long dead, so it would just have to be that other bloke with the same surname instead.

I must admit that I was not overly enthusiastic on hearing the news. To be blunt, I didn't like Neil Lennon in his playing days with Celtic and I didn't much care for him during his managerial tenure there either. That had nothing to do with his tactical nous or the way he applied himself to the playing side of things in general; I just wasn't impressed by the way he all too often conducted himself. Impetuous and undignified, he seemed to me to lack the qualities that a manager expecting to garner respect should embody. But that had been when he was a fair bit younger and we could only hope that he'd matured in the intervening years. Of course he was also subjected to dreadful experiences at the behest of lunatic bigots, culminating in failed bomb-plots and death threats, something that most right-minded people would not wish on their worst enemy. Certainly, no-one deserved what he'd had to endure in the cauldron of hatred that was the Wild West (of Scotland, shamefully enough.) He'd spoken courageously and openly about his battles with depression, which had not unnaturally been exacerbated by living daily with very real danger to life and limb. So he obviously wouldn't have been my first choice, but the die was cast now. I was prepared to at least give the man a chance.

Neil's first task was to strengthen his new team's attack, something that was clearly a priority after the departure of Anthony Stokes. Grant Holt was the first to put pen to paper – not a name I was familiar with – and Scott McDonald looked to be joining him, but that deal soon collapsed with recriminations flying in both directions. Lennon claimed that it was he who pulled the plug on the Australian striker's proposed move to Easter Road, after McDonald had failed to show up for a standard medical assessment. That was only part of the story though, as Hibs' initial offer had apparently been beneath the player's original expectations – as is so often the case – but negotiations had continued. Before long, the deal appeared to be back on again, but after the usual shit-stirring input from the agents involved, McDonald looked to be still holding out for more. By that stage Neil had had enough, accusing the player of being 'economical with the truth' over what he'd said publicly and decided not to pursue it any further. All along it seemed as if McDonald just wanted to get back to his old stamping ground of Fir Park, Motherwell anyway.

A more positive acquisition was that of Jordon Forster, returning to the Hibernian fold after a forgettable loan-spell at Plymouth Argyle. It had been unclear whether or not the big defender would ever retrace his steps to Leith, as previously the excellent form of his team-mates looked to have consigned him to the substitutes' bench at best, long before he departed from Easter Road. But he'd also struggled with niggling injuries which had clearly hampered any return to his top form. He'd got along fine with the amiable Alan Stubbs and had never ceased to speak extremely highly of all at Hibs, including the supporters.

"I'm still 22," said Jordon, "but I think it's an age where I really need to get some games. That's obviously what I did when I went to Plymouth."

So at least some positive aspects could be attributed to his tenure on the south coast of England and hopefully he'd returned in better nick overall.

Also hoping to be back playing on a regular basis was young Lewis Allan, who had spent most of the previous season out on loan at Forfar Athletic. The aforementioned Jordon's medical problems had been very awkward and highly frustrating for him obviously, but they somewhat paled into insignificance when set aside those of Lewis. Troubled with a sore back during his initial loan-spell, he'd returned to East Mains where the doctor had first suspected a trapped nerve. But the symptoms were peculiar – while out for a run the player had the oddest sensation where he couldn't feel his feet actually touching the ground.

"The weirdest feeling I've ever had," said Lewis.

A scan followed and an instant summons back to the Western General Hospital followed hot on the heels of that.

"I went in and saw a nurse – it was scary, she told me it might be cancer," he went on.

What the scan had revealed was a growth 'like a big cauliflower'. It turned out to be a blood-filled cyst, which had been growing inside him for so long it had calcified and was now pressing on his spinal cord. It was so serious that one knock might have left him totally paralysed for life. A gruelling nine and a half hour operation followed, which mercifully appeared to have been successful and remarkably Lewis was back at East Mains to hopefully resume training by the turn of the year. But devastatingly for the youngster, another cyst then formed. The procedure to remove that took even longer but Lewis showed astonishing resilience and bravery in coming through that too and once again tried to focus on getting back into action on the training pitch.

"As they say, time is a healer," he remarked stoically. "I don't want any special treatment. I haven't been clattered on it yet, but I know I can run and that's what you want for peace of mind."

The 35 year-old Grant Holt made his debut in the friendly encounter away to Berwick Rangers on July 5th and Neil was impressed with the form of his one-time Nottingham Forest team-mate. He must have been even more impressed with Jason Cummings – it's doubtful whether the live-wire Jase will ever score a quicker goal. Only twelve seconds had elapsed before he had the ball in the back of the net, without a single Berwick player even getting a touch on it. He was assisted by another returnee to the ranks, Alex Harris, as well as new boy Holt, whose exchange of passes set up the opening for him. The visitors also hit the bar twice and looked capable of really going to town on their lowly opponents, before they struck back with an equaliser from Michael McKenna.

The second half saw the usual 'friendly' scenario whereby a non-stop revolving door of substitutes make an appearance and while it is unwise to base any serious assessment on such matches, it was a generally bright start.

"It's all about fitness levels," said the new gaffer, "and this game will benefit. A few of them need a bit of work by the look of things, but that will come."

He added that he had got into the unfortunate habit of usually losing pre-season friendlies when with Celtic, so this made a nice change.

"I was very happy with the work-rate – everyone got a run-out which was important."

The day after, it was announced that Ross Laidlaw had agreed a one-year deal, the keeper most usually associated with Raith Rovers having been a bit of a Conrad Logan-style nomad of late, with loan spells at various soccer outposts. With the departure of the effervescent giant who'd enjoyed such a uniquely rewarding window of opportunity with Hibs late in his career, this was another area of the park that required bolstering. Neil also revealed that he intended to take a serious look at West Bromwich Albion keeper Alex Palmer, as Oxley prepared to move to Southend United.

That followed on from the second friendly of the week, a local derby no less, against Edinburgh City at Meadowbank. Shades of East of Scotland Shield days, for those of you old enough to remember the late lamented 'local' trophy of high renown. The newest kids on the block were effortlessly swept aside by their near neighbours, as Hibs pumped four past them in twenty-six minutes. A tough one for the City slickers to take, but Hibs fans knew only too well what it was like to lose such a number of goals within half-an-hour in a friendly – however that *had* been against Barcelona at Murrayfield a few years ago. McGregor,

Cummings, Boyle and McGeouch were the four Hibs men of the apocalypse in the first half, before the usual substitution merry-go-round took place at the interval. The SPFL virgins popped their collective cherry late on in the second period, which Hibs had continued to dominate, although without the sharpness in front of goal they'd exhibited earlier. They still managed another couple before the end though, as firstly Keatings and then the long-absent Danny Handling wrapped it up 6-1 for the visitors.

"Excellent," asserted Neil with evident satisfaction. "We got six and it could have been a lot more. The attitude of the players was excellent, considering they had played only forty-eight hours earlier."

The fine run continued with the last game in the series of warm-ups, before the real thing just up ahead – the Europa League clash with Brondby four days hence. Premiership side Motherwell were the Sunday visitors to Easter Road and their early lead on the third minute was instantly cancelled out by a goalbound reply from the man who'd scored a few on the four-minute mark the previous season, Jason Cummings. His team-mates Grant Holt and John McGinn would add to the tally, putting Hibs a highly satisfactory 3-1 up at the interval, over their supposedly superior opponents. James Keatings rounded off a good afternoon's work with a lovely curling shot after the break, as assistant gaffer Garry Parker expressed himself well-pleased, although cautioning, "Let's not get too carried away – this was a friendly and Thursday (against Brondby) will be a different test."

He'd assumed command for this one, as Neil was away back to France, fulfilling his Euros punditry commitments. The team selection against the Steelmen was pretty much the one which would be likely to feature in Hibs' opening Europa League game, with the exception of trialist keeper Alex Palmer. It looked as if Otso Virtanen would at last make his home debut facing the Danes. It had been a toss-up from the outset whether Hibs would line up against them or Valur, as those two sides had fought it out in the first round for the honour of taking on the mighty hun-humping cup-winning cavaliers – but there had been little doubt as that tie got under way. Brondby had crushed the Icelandic side 6-0 and 4-1, giving them a whopping 10-1 margin on aggregate.

Scottish clubs got off to their by now traditionally woeful start against lowly European competition who no-one's ever heard of, the jambos looking on shaky ground against Infonet (*who?*) before turning it around in the second leg, the Sheep took a dip of unprecedented proportions against a team of deejays from Radio Luxembourg but managed to scrape through – *just* – and Celtic saved the very worst for last. Yes, the laconic Lincoln Red Imps from Gibraltar made a monkey out of the green chimps from Parkhead, in surely one of the most embarrassing results the latter had ever endured in European competition. They were beaten 1-0 by a team of butchers, bakers and candlestick makers, some of whom had actually been working at their 'proper' jobs earlier the same day. New Hoops gaffer Brendan Rodgers declared however that he wasn't embarrassed at all. I'm not quite sure if that's a good thing or a bad thing – if that genuinely doesn't shame you, then very little else is likely to bring a flush to your cheeks in the future. Caught by a tabloid newspaper indulging in cocaine-fuelled orgies with rent boys? Stroll in the park, mate. Revealed as the secret cross-dressing lover of Boris Johnson? Hey, no biggie. But Brendan was just carrying on a Celtic tradition of presiding over ghastly European debuts – Gordon Strachan was still waking in the dead of night with the cold sweats after dreaming of his less than auspicious start – getting humped 5-0 by Artmedia Bratislava. (As I mentioned in my last book, they were still talking about that in the bars and cafes when I visited the Slovakian capital two years later.)

So Hibs undoubtedly faced a far sterner test than their countrymen had done in the same competition so far. As expected, Neil Lennon went with the side who'd roundly defeated Motherwell four days earlier, apart from one enforced change as Dylan McGeouch stood in for Fraser Fyvie, sidelined with a knock. Virtanen was in goal as expected and got off to the worst possible start, by gifting the opposition a goal with a howler virtually straight from kick-off. Like many others I failed to see it, as I was still waiting in line at the turnstiles – maybe just as well, as I might have turned on my heel and walked right back out again. Mortifying memories of Malmo were still bubbling away beneath the surface, as Fenlon (mis)guided Hibs to their personally most embarrassing outing in European competition, three years before. Now, the jittery young Finn looked to have set the scene for Brondby to go to town right from the off. He spilled a Martin Albrechtsen effort straight into the path of striker Kamil Wilczek and he gleefully smashed it into the roof of the net. It was a dreadful start, but the Hibees could take a lot of credit for not allowing their heads to go down and were soon proving themselves very much the equal of their loftier visitors. 'Loftier' in the true sense of the word, as height-wise most of the Danes wouldn't have looked out of place in a basketball team. Jason Cummings, the man described by his new gaffer as 'a rascal' and somewhat insultingly as 'not the brightest' was soon in the thick of it, rasping in a stinging shot which Brondby keeper Ronnow was forced to punch away, before McGregor headed inches wide from a McGeouch free-kick. There was certainly much that was pleasing about Hibs' performance during the first half-hour. Then, on the thirty-first minute, a McGinn pass sent Boyle off motoring down the right. He clocked Jason making a run and sent over a perfectly placed ball for the irrepressible striker to slide home past Ronnow. Mass exultation in the stands – but only briefly, as the linesman had wrongly flagged for offside. He'd clearly failed to keep up with play and wasn't best positioned to make the call, but did so anyway. The Spanish officials were very poor overall, proving that it's not only domestically that they're to be found wanting. Referee Munuero acted like a prize prat throughout, over-fond of imperious gesturing and grandstanding that indicated he'd have been better off in the matador role down his local bullring. It was a bullshit decision and no mistake. But the upshot of that was Neil Lennon losing his rag and being sent to the stand by the main official. Neil's reaction was understandable, but we could only hope that this wasn't a foretaste of things to come, regarding his lack of self-control. So Hibs could justifiably feel aggrieved in going in one down at the interval.

Former Celtic man Teemu Pukki made his appearance as second substitute of the night for Brondby just after the break, whilst Hibs waited until nearly twenty minutes had elapsed before putting on Keatings and Fontaine to replace McGeouch and Bartley respectively. This was achieved by shouted instructions being conveyed between Neil and assistant Garry Parker, as apparently the phone connection between the Directors' Box and the dug-out had been severed. Or maybe Rod had just skimped on paying the bill again. However, Hibs continued to look lively but also had a couple of scares at the back, principally when Paul Hanlon was obliged to make a fine block from another attempt by danger-man Wilczek. Then came the second major flashpoint, when our own imposing big felly Grant Holt took a tumble in the penalty area after being fouled by Brondby's first substitute Hjulseger – but the referee immediately waved play on. Possibly Grant made slightly too much of it, but it still looked like a clear trip. Jason had a frustrating second half, during which he protested too vociferously over being ruled offside again (the officials got that one right, at least), receiving a predictable booking and then when captain David Gray tried to pick him out but unfortunately the ball rebounded back off his heel. The main task was now to ensure that the visitors didn't sneak another, as that would surely have put the tie beyond Hibs, who still continued to search for an equaliser, while endeavouring to keep the back door shut. But it finished with a solitary goal for Brondby and still a wee chance of progression to the next stage, with the return in Denmark one week hence. The most surprising fact was that it concluded with the full complement of players still on the park after the card-happy Munuero had flashed five yellows, some for utterly innocuous misdemeanours. Plus, he'd recently gone crazy in a Barcelona v Espanyol match, by the end of which he'd virtually run out of players to penalise and looked perilously close to embarking on issuing cards to select members of the crowd as well. A bad day at the office for him, but the Hibs manager was going to have to learn to take these numpties and their daft decisions in his stride, as it would be unlikely to be the last below par performance from officialdom he'd have to face over the piece.

"We've had a brilliant goal disallowed," he fumed. "Jason was onside. I was angry because the linesman was not up with play. I remonstrated with him and the next thing I am sent to the stand for no reason whatsoever. It's the first time I've been sent to the stand in Europe. It looked like he wanted to be the star of the show rather than the players."

Well, the gaffer was spot on with that assessment, although I'm sure the claim about making his own personal debut in Europe regarding viewing from the stand would surprise a few.

"When you see it again, Jason at the very least is in line with the two defenders," he reiterated. "It was a perfect goal, a brilliant ball by John McGinn, brilliant ball by Martin Boyle and brilliant goal."

Pure dead brilliant (by the way) is what I think Neil was getting at there. Unsurprisingly, he was less than impressed with the official's handling of the other main talking point either.

"He's not going to fall over on his own," he remarked, of Holt's penalty box tumble.

He acknowledged that Hibs needed to get on the scoresheet in the return leg at the very least, but felt that the tie was far from over.

"I'd like to think we can do it. There's nothing we did not expect."

He loyally refused to have a go at Virtanen, while conceding that his blunder was 'avoidable'.

I only hope that he avoids dropping the ball invitingly in front of an opponent so readily again and whilst it's early days the harsh truth is that he looked far from comfortable over the ninety minutes. Hibs do not have the luxury of time to experiment with who might prove most suitable between the sticks, certainly not once the race for the Championship gets under way. They paid a very heavy price for poor starts in the previous two campaigns and firing on all cylinders further up the park is of little use if the back door remains ajar. Those of us with memories stretching back to the tail-end of the previous century still shudder at the antics of Ole the Goalie (*sic*). The giant Icelander of yesteryear really *was* a basketball player in some strange parallel universe and cost Hibs an untold number of points through his gaffes when brought in as a replacement for Jim Leighton. We don't want to go down *that* particular road again.

Meanwhile, the Hearts players were spewing up big-style after their punishing encounter with the Maltese team apparently named after some virulent tropical disease – Birkirkara.

"Having watched the videos we know what Birkirkara can do," claimed Robbie Neilson, after viewing footage akin to that on 'Most Embarrassing Bodies'. The most likely reason for the mass vomiting outbreak was the sight of the sign outside the ground – 'HIBERNIANS STADIUM'. Well, at least they were only throwing up this time. On the last two occasions they'd faced Hibernians in a stadium they were full-on shitting themselves. (Firstly they blew a two-goal lead at the Pink Bus Shelter and then lost the replay at Easter Road.)

At Fort Ibrox, Warby started off the new season in the same manner as he'd finished up the last one – by moaning his box off. This time his ire was focused on the Right Said Fred Cup as Rangers would be obliged to play too many games for his liking and the fact that they'd only had one pre-season warm-up game in which to prepare. Well whose fault was that then, eh? This was in the USA when they'd played against the splendidly-named Charleston Battery, during which the grumpy Ibrox gaffer almost caused a major diplomatic incident. Finding suspicious crystals of white powder underneath the seat he'd just vacated, the FBI immediately launched a probe. They discovered that Warby had been munching on his favoured Smith's Crisps and had inadvertently dropped the wee blue salt-bag within on the floor. He was charged with committing salt in Battery and fined a packet before being unceremoniously deported.

In seemingly no time at all the second leg against Brondby was looming up; they don't waste time getting the diddy qualifying games in Europe out of the road, that's for sure. I became aware of this on the Tuesday, as Platform 5 opposite Haymarket Station was hoatching with Hibbies in excitable travel mode, their bags spilling out everywhere and blocking up the route to the Gents'. I'd been offered safe passage by a couple of acquaintances who were heading for Denmark and had been cajoling me into joining them; but with memories of my last visit to Copenhagen still fresh in mind, I had swiftly declined. It had been a good few years ago, but I was unlikely to forget it in a hurry.

When I arrived, they were still picking up the pieces in the aftermath of what became known as 'The Great Nordic Biker War', during which two of the world's largest outlaw motorcycle gangs had fought a brutal five-year long conflict across Scandinavia. The Hell's Angels and the Bandidos had battled it out with machine guns, bombs, rocket-propelled grenades and anti-tank weapons and body parts were still turning up in the picturesque waterways of the Danish capital.

"The mentality of the players is good. Our physical levels surprised me. The game was played at a ferocious pace and tempo – particularly in the first half – but we finished the game well. They'll feel the benefits of it. We're massive underdogs, but it's not beyond us."

The stark statistic remained though – which showed that Hibs had *never* survived losing an opening tie at home in European competition.

Former full-back David Murphy recalled his tenure at Easter Road ten years ago, when Hibs had faced Odense in the Inter-Toto Cup and narrowly lost by a single goal in the first leg away from home. So that left them with still a reasonable chance of progression – but the visitors struck first at the Leith San Siro too, leaving Hibs with a three goal mountain to scale, just for starters. They scored almost immediately through Rob Jones and added another one courtesy of Paul Dalglish later on, but still lost out over the piece.

"Being knocked out on the away goal rule was really tough to take," reflected David. "Hibs need to start tight tomorrow night, not give Brondby any encouragement at all and look to grow into the game. They have to remember they've got ninety minutes to turn it around – there's no need to go for it from the first whistle."

David was back in town and looking forward to viewing another of his previous clubs – Birmingham City – who'd take on Hibs in a friendly at Easter Road three days after the Danish jaunt.

Martin Boyle – who would have had a first half assist to his name in the first leg if the linesman had been paying attention – was in bullish mood.

"No way is the tie over. We can take a lot of positives from the first leg. We played very well considering we were only a couple of weeks into pre-season and trying to find our legs. There is nothing to fear – we'll give it a good go and attack them. This is a great experience. This is the stage we need to be playing on and if we play the way we did at Easter Road then there could be plenty more nights like this."

Marvin Bartley was quick to emphasise how the camaraderie developed under Stubbsy's tutelage would stand them in good stead.

"We have a togetherness, very good players who play well as a team, we work hard for each-other and belief is massive. Look at football, on paper there are games people don't expect teams to win but they do, look at Portugal in the Euros, no-one would have thought it, but they had the belief."

The big man was careful however not to draw *too* many parallels between the Euro-winners and the Big Cup-winners.

"I watched a few matches but not Portugal until the final because they were boring the life out of me," he admitted. "I'd watch for ten minutes and that was it for me. I think that when Cristiano Ronaldo went off people thought that was it, game over. But they had that belief."

He referred briefly to that never-to-be-forgotten afternoon at Hampden, exactly two months before.

"I didn't realise how absolutely massive it was until afterwards. It was hard to put into words – but we enjoyed the next few days, it was brilliant. The cup was memorable, brilliant, but it's gone now, we move forward into this game and want to go through, it would be an achievement to do that."

The cup's gone already has it? Typical, just after I was photographed with it on the Famous Five stand concourse too. Well, if it's been nicked it wisnae me, Rod, honest. Too heavy by half. Best send for Pickles…

Hibs took to the field in Copenhagen with Laidlaw replacing Otso Virtanen between the sticks and although Ross (like Conrad Logan making his spectacular debut a few months before) hadn't played a competitive game for a good old while, he looked anything but rusty and lacking in match fitness. Indeed, he didn't actually have a great deal to do over the piece, but when called upon he coped admirably with whatever Brondby could throw at him. He was confident right from the off, positioned himself well for free-kicks and made a terrific last gasp save to deny Johan Larsson in time added on.

Initially though, it seemed as if the home team might simply sweep the plucky visitors aside, such was their dominance in the opening spell. As at Easter Road they weren't shy in employing the physical stuff to gain advantage either and the Romanian referee was far too hesitant in clamping down on their overly aggressive tactics. The first real chance came when the man in black judged that Bartley had fouled Pukki just outside the penalty area, but Larsson's subsequent free-kick slipped narrowly over the bar. Laidlaw didn't look too troubled by that and then did well to push a far more dangerous effort courtesy of Norgaard over the crossbar too. Hibs' best opportunity came when a cross from McGinn picked out his captain, but David was unable to direct the free header accurately enough to worry Ronnow in the Brondby goal.

However, he made amends for that and more on the sixty-second minute as McGregor stabbed the ball through to him following a McGeouch corner and David did exceptionally well to strike it with the outside of his right boot. That was just enough to propel it past Ronnow and into the left-hand corner of his net. It was no less than Hibs deserved as they'd turned the tables on their opponents after the interval, which had the vociferous home fans momentarily silenced. That was in sharp contrast to the wall of sound created by the jubilant travelling support, numbering well in excess of a thousand. Few –if any – in the media had given Hibs much of a chance beforehand, but now the men in green had levelled the tie on aggregate and looked well capable of causing a major upset. It was inevitable that their somewhat shellshocked opponents would resort to even more rough stuff as they grew increasingly frustrated and goal hero Gray was to pay the price as he was forced to make way for Martin Boyle thirteen minutes before the end of regulation time. This was as a result of a nasty foul by Norgaard which caused the Hibs captain to fall heavily and injure his shoulder and earned the culprit a well-deserved yellow card. (Remarkably, their first such award of the evening.) Assistant referee Valentin Avrum was then on the receiving end of a mini-barrage of water bottles from the clearly rattled home support, which would surely land the Danes in soapy with UEFA in the near future. Hibs had a late scare when McGregor brought down Pukki which gained the Hibs man a booking but the referee wasn't interested in the former Celtic man's histrionics. He followed that up by rather amusingly failing to award Brondby a corner after Laidlaw had done well to nudge a Larsson shot to safety. Howls of protest from the home fans extended into the added-on period when McGinn went in heavily on substitute Rezan, but the Hibees rode their luck until the conclusion of the full two hours, finishing strongly and defying the majority of pundits who had written them off before a ball had even been kicked.

So a penalty shoot-out was going to be required to separate the teams and those of us harbouring memories of the previous season's Scottish Cup semi-final were probably relieved that Jason had already vacated the field, to be replaced by James Keatings. Dinking in Denmark was not on the immediate menu, at least. However, it's a finish that no-one really wants and always something of a lottery. (Anyone who witnessed the laughably inept spot-kicks at the conclusion to the Germany v Italy Euros quarter-final will surely vouch for that. I've seen better in Saughton Park on a Sunday afternoon.) And so it proved, as John McGinn missed the first one for the visitors after Brondby had already netted their opener. It was an uphill task now and although Hanlon, Holt and Boyle all confidently converted, the home team were in the driving-seat and put all five away in a relatively clinical manner.

Frustratingly, Ross Laidlaw got a hand to a couple of them, but not enough to keep them out. It was a very disappointing and cruel way to lose, but Hibs could take huge credit for turning in such a plucky and brave performance overall.

"He had a superb game," said Neil Lennon, of the former Raith Rovers stalwart. "He dealt with everything very well and was unlucky not to save one or two of the penalties."

Referring yet again to the events of a week previously, he declared, "I feel we were the better team and but for a horrendous goalkeeping error and scoring a perfectly good goal that wasn't allowed – and clean sheet tonight – we deserved to win and we should be heading to Berlin."

That wasn't a case of Neil making like Joseph Stalin circa 1945 there; Hertha of that city would have awaited in the next round, if only we'd had a wee bit more of a rub of the green.

"We showed tremendous character," concluded the manager. "Paul Hanlon in both games was head and shoulders above, absolutely outstanding."

Wait 'til Jason finds out he's been dipping into his shampoo – it'll be a case of wash 'n' go for Paul.

'SO CLOSE TO BRINGING HOME THE BACON' stated Friday's Evening News, reminding me yet again of Danish Pride and homo parades, but they went one better with their reportage of the jambos' utterly unexpected capitulation at home to Birkirkara. 'HEARTS CHOKE ON MALTESERS!' screamed the banner headline. Ho ho ho. Life wasn't too sweet in the Gorgie Suite, on another hideously embarrassing night for a Scottish team in Europe. At least Hibs could hold their heads up high after running a 'name' side so very close over two physically punishing encounters.

Elsewhere on the continent, the Sheep came perilously close to being fleeced by UEFA, after it emerged they'd be struggling to meet the deadline for arrival in Latvia to face Ventspils. Regulations decreed that the visiting team must be in place twenty-four hours before kick-off and the prospect of a substantial fine had the Aberdonian top brass running around distractedly like headless chickens, shouting "Fit like, quine!" and similar imprecations. It would of course be unfair to play up to the stereotype of northern tight-wads, but last time someone accidentally dropped a ten pence piece in Union Street at least a dozen people were killed in the ensuing stampede to pick it up. But what had caused the Sheep to be so very nearly sheared? A bloody seagull, that's what. It had flown into the plane's engine causing the entire aircraft to shut down. Hardly reassuring for your nervous flyer, but the most important thing immediately was to implore UEFA to accept that this was out-with the club's control.

"It was an act of God," said the Dons chairman, with some measure of desperation.

You'd have thought the omnipotent deity would have better things to do than kill our feathered friends in such a gruesome manner, but the explanation was apparently accepted, to huge sighs of relief all round. The prospect of a monetary penalty and shameful coverage in the notoriously parochial local print media had been narrowly averted. The misfortunes of those in that vicinity in particular had always featured prominently in the Press and Journal. (Who could forget their reporting of the sinking of the Titanic with the loss of 1,500 lives, via the headline 'ABERDEEN MAN LOST AT SEA' ??)

On the penultimate Sunday of the month, Hibs were back in action at Easter Road, although the team on display bore no resemblance to the one of three days earlier. Indeed, Liam Fontaine was the only survivor from the outfit who'd competed so valiantly in Copenhagen. English Championship side Birmingham City were the friendly visitors this time, featuring former Hibee Clayton Donaldson up front and also Jonathan Grounds who'd had a brief loan-spell back in Colin Calderwood's day. The result was a satisfactory 1-0 win for the home team with James Keatings the scorer and it could well have been more. Neil Lennon declared himself "really pleased" which was justified, as the Brummies had fielded arguably their strongest side, although the usual plethora of substitutes appeared during the second half. (Five on the hour mark alone.) Three minutes after that Hibs took the lead, as youngster Callum Crane laid it off for Boyle who in turn picked out the former Hearts man in space and he crashed it high into the net. Few would have been surprised at an 'all change' approach after the effort expended by those who'd taken the field against Brondby, although perhaps not anticipating quite such an overhaul. But the manager certainly had cause to be happy with the performance of the young dudes in particular, with Scott Martin restored to the midfield and Sam Stanton and Alex Harris lasting the full ninety minutes.

"I thought Hibs were bright and looked a really good side," said Birmingham boss Gary Rowett. "I know they had several first-teamers absent and it looks like they have a really strong squad."

There was disappointing news though, with the revelation that Danny Handling was crocked again, as he was spotted in attendance on crutches. Poor Danny had had a wretched time of it, missing the whole of the previous season with a damaged cruciate ligament and only recently had looked to be capable of making a comeback. However, he'd taken a knock in training on the same knee, although this time it didn't appear to be quite so serious. Still, he'd be facing another spell on the sidelines, for possibly up to six weeks.

Rangers' latest acquisition Joe Dodoo was then quick to put his foot in the doodoo, by stating, "We can definitely win the League." Which one, though? Not the Human League anyway, that's for sure. Or the League of Gentlemen either, come to that. Referring to Ibrox, he added, "I can't wait to see this place erupt!" which could be construed as something of a threat, given the terroristic times in which we live. After all, that's exactly what the gadgie in Paris said the year before, just prior to trying to blow up the Stade de France. Luckily in that case he only succeeded in erupting his own body. Suicide bombers carry out their actions in the belief that they'll go straight to Paradise – he still got some shock when a few seconds later he found himself getting kicked to fuck by the Green Brigade inside Parkhead.

One man who was mightily relieved to have pulled on a Hibs shirt again was Jordon Forster, confessing that he was something of a nervous wreck coming on as substitute right at the tail-end in Copenhagen. It was little wonder really, given the topsy-turvy couple of years he'd endured. His previous season had been cut short almost before it had really started, as the Petrofac cave-in to Rangers had been his solitary appearance. Injury and then being deemed surplus to requirements as his able-bodied contemporaries strung together a dazzling run of results under Stubbsy had kept the big felly well and truly confined to the sidelines. Then the move south to Plymouth had had a spanner chucked into the works almost immediately by another serious injury, although he did go onto feature in the League Two Play-Off final at Wembley, albeit on the losing side.

"Coming on against Brondby I was more nervous than playing at Wembley," he stated. "I think that had a lot to do with how much the club, the supporters and the boys in the dressing room mean to me."

Jordon had made his debut late in 2012 / 13 season at Tynecastle and was then thrust into the Scottish Cup final against Celtic only a few days later. (Yes, I know it's hard to believe now, but this was still in the bad old days *before* the Big Cup finally came home to Easter Road after a trifling absence of one hundred and fourteen years.) He'd not regarded himself as being a particularly nervous individual and hadn't been overly fazed by that or, indeed, his Wembley outing, but this was different.

"It was the first time that I had felt those butterflies for a really long time. I went on, tried to keep things simple, as going on at that stage of the game as a defender you can only be the villain. Although going out was disappointing, it was a really positive performance. All the boys would have loved the chance to play against a big, big side in the next round – but we can take a lot of confidence from it."

Meanwhile, there was excitement across the city, with the announcement that Fleetwood were due at the Pink Bus Shelter the following weekend. Fans were soon snapping up tickets by the thousand, in anticipation of a fantastic one- and- a- half hour's worth of entertainment, given the calibre of the veteran outfit. However, that soon turned to disappointment, when it became apparent that it wasn't Fleetwood Mac after all – it was Fleetwood Town. But worse was to follow, with the news that 'ELVIS HAS LEFT THE BUILDING', as the former jambo sour-puss did do walking away and left the Lancashire club in the lurch. So they wouldn't be turning up either. A statement on their official website said that after a meeting with Pressley it was agreed that, "It would be best to take the club in a different direction." Er, that'll be east then. About bloody time – have you seen where it's situated geographically? Any day now the whole town's gonna cowp into the Irish Sea.

"Rumours," said Annie Budge firmly, when asked if there had been any substance to reports of the other Fleetwoods appearing at the PBS. Did she have any words of consolation for scarf-twirlers who felt they'd been deceived into buying tickets?

"If you wake up and don't want to smile, if it takes just a little while, open your eyes and look at the day, you'll see things in a different way. Don't stop, thinking about tomorrow, don't stop, it'll soon be here, it'll be better than before, yesterday's gone, yesterday's gone," advised the Hearts owner cheerfully, before adding, "You can go your own way, you can call it another lonely day…"

She then took a bow and put the microphone down, to a thunderous round of applause. Truly, karaoke night at Dickens' had seldom felt so good.

At Easter Road, club safety officer Rob 'Roy' McGregor was clearly hoping to hear singing of a different sort – that more associated with the canary or stool-pigeon – as those suspected of being on the pitch at Hampden on May 21st were invited in for a wee chit-chat. The letters sent out to an unspecified number apparently read, "I am in possession of information which infers that you were on the pitch at Hampden Park at the end of the match.' (I say 'apparently', just in case you think he sent me one too.) Rob was soon swamped, as fourteen people confirmed right away that they were guilty of just such an infraction; but it turned out that he'd posted the letters to the Hibernian *players*, rather than the fans, by mistake. Jason later retracted his statement, saying that in retrospect he couldn't remember what he was doing that day, but he might have been at the hairdressers.

It was quite something that the Glasgow polis were so inept that they now needed Hibs to do their dirty work for them, although if the safety wallahs were working from the photographs supplied by the weedjie constabulary, they were unlikely to be very successful. You'd have more chance of identifying the Loch Ness Monster, the Beast of Bodmin Moor or the Abominable Snowman than of picking out individuals from some of the laughably blurred out-of-focus indistinct snaps. In fact the aforementioned three mythical creatures might well have actually been in them, but it was impossible to tell.

Paul Hanlon was looking forward to the weekend, partly with a view to reacquainting himself with former colleagues Ryan McGivern and Gary

Deegan, now of Shrewsbury Town, in Hibs' final friendly. Both had looked fine prospects at Easter Road after being signed by Pat Fenlon, but quickly faded from the picture. McGivern often excelled during an initial one-year spell on loan from Manchester City, but failed to impress the following season. (Being 'managed' by Terry Butcher can't have helped there.)

"It'll be good to catch up with them, it was the same with the Birmingham game, seeing Clayton Donaldson and Jonathan Grounds," said Paul. "I got on well with Ryan and Deegs. They were both good guys – good players as well."

It had been an eventful summer for him; holding aloft the Scottish Cup, signing a new contract and getting married.

"For a couple of weeks after winning the cup everyone was so high and fans were coming up and thanking you, saying how amazing it was. It really was incredible. The parade on the Sunday was a lot bigger than I'd expected. It was a great weekend but we need to put it to bed now. It's time to forget about the Scottish Cup for now – I can enjoy that when I retire. As soon as pre-season starts again, you need to refocus."

In the event, both ex-Hibees lasted the full ninety minutes against their former club, who turned in another very impressive performance. Despite missing four first team regulars in Gray, McGeouch, Fyvie and Bartley, the visitors romped home with a 4-1 victory, the first two goals coming in the opening six minutes as Liam Fontaine got the first from a header deflected in off the underside of the bar following a Keatings free-kick and ex-Shrews man Holt notching the second. Former Dunfermline and Motherwell man Jim O'Brien pulled one back, but that only briefly interrupted the flow of play in the opposite direction. Jason was quick to accept a gift as Gary Deegan slipped and gave away possession in the middle of his own half and ran on unchallenged to slot home. A mere two minutes after that James Keatings completed the rout with a looping shot over the keeper's head.

"It was another quality performance," said the manager. "We got off to a good start and played with a real intensity and quality. We could have won the game by more, but to come here and play so well shows we are at a good level at the minute."

Ross Laidlaw had another satisfactory afternoon between the sticks, but it looked as if Neil was now prepared to sign up Israeli international goalie Ofir Marciano on a loan deal. The name Brian Murphy had also been in the frame for the same position, but surely he was getting on a bit – he was hardly a spring chicken when he played George Roper in seventies' sitcoms 'Man About The House' and 'George and Mildred' was he? The gaffer had also taken time out the previous week to watch Ross County's Brian Graham in action against Alloa, another big man with a proven goalscoring record at all levels with various Scottish clubs.

The month was rounded off with the draw for the second round of the League Cup, pitting Hibs at home against Queen of the South. The Radio Scotland announcer first slipped up by referring to the Dundee United v Partick Thistle tie as an 'all Premier' one, then reiterating the gaffe after failing to pick up on a corrective aside from Mark Burchill. However the latter proceeded to put his foot in it as well, by remarking of the fifth tie to be drawn, "I think I'm correct in saying that Queen of the South won there (at Easter Road) last season." Unfortunately, Mark, you're talking pish. Hibs won both their home League games against the men from Dumfries. Sometimes it was hard to hear what was being said over the peculiar rumbling sound in the background, presumably being made by the rotating drum used to conduct the draw. Is such a contraption really necessary in this day and age? Mind you, the previous season the Blazers made a total arse of the televised big cup draw, by failing to operate the uncovered goldfish bowl properly. Maybe they're better off with a big twirly machine instead.

So, all in all, it had been a very promising start to Neil Lennon's tenure in the hot seat. Sixteen goals had been scored in five warm-up games and he'd had a good opportunity to assess the many different players who had featured wholly or partly throughout. There was disappointment obviously with losing out so narrowly in the 'proper' encounters against Brondby, but Hibs had turned in two very commendable performances there, particularly in the second leg. It was as good a build-up as we could have hoped for, really.

2.

AUGUST: JESUS WALKS ON WATER, JASON WALKS ON EGGSHELLS

The new month dawned with the good news that the majority of those sidelined through injury should be restored to fitness in time to face Falkirk in the opening Championship League encounter. Hibs' previous campaign had of course been hampered by an extensive injury list, but this time David Gray (shoulder), Marvin Bartley (back) and Dylan McGeouch (hamstring) were well on the road to recovery. However Fraser Fyvie and, inevitably, Danny Handling could expect to remain absent for a good few weeks yet.

Another player plagued by injury throughout 2015 / 16, Dan Carmichael, was hoping to be back in the thick of it too. He'd been a more or less constant member of the Queen of the South line-up for a fair old while before his move to Easter Road, which then saw him make only nine appearances in fifty-four games.

"It was embarrassing. When you arrive at a new club you want to hit the ground running and show everyone what you can do. But instead, I was getting treated rather than playing."

Dan had had on-going abdominal and groin problems and resorted to some 'alternative' remedies before an operation was finally deemed necessary.

"It was a niggle that wouldn't go away, it felt as if it never would. I got the operation but it took longer than expected and the outcome was not what we wanted it to be."

As well as hoping to get those who'd been crocked back into contention, Neil Lennon also revealed that youngsters Scott Martin and Callum Crane were very much in his thoughts too. Both had undergone lengthy loan-spells the previous season, with Forfar and Berwick Rangers respectively.

"I like what I am seeing. Their attitude has been exemplary," said the manager. "They are good footballers, they need a bit of physical development but that will come."

Meanwhile, Hampden hero of May 21st vintage, Liam Henderson, made a wonderful gesture by signing and donating his No. 3 shirt from that day to the charity behind much of the fundraising for the Sick Kids Hospital. He dropped in to visit the young patients in the company of his brother Jamie, who'd been treated there several times in the past.

"It's a charity close to both our hearts," said Liam.

His shirt would ultimately be auctioned off at a Spartans FC event the following month.

Towards the end of the first week of the month, it was announced that Hibs had finally got their man, in the shape of Ofir Marciano, the giant Israeli international goalkeeper. Neil was reportedly 'delighted' at the coup, less so understandably over the five-match touchline ban imposed by UEFA over his Brondby strop with the officials.

"A piece of nonsense, really," asserted the manager, adding that the wording of the charge was "ridiculous". As UEFA cited the reason for the punishment as 'acts of violence against a referee' you could understand his frustration. If shouting at incompetent numpties in black is now deemed a violent act, there's going to be a whole lot more managers sitting twiddling their thumbs in the stands throughout the season, that's for sure. Neil was so shocked that he spat his coffee out when George Craig broke the news to him. Just as well he didn't spit it out over his head of football operations, as then he'd have been up on a charge of violence against George too.

The annual Edinburgh Arts Festival was now under way and Peterborough made a small yet significant contribution towards the comedy programme by offering a million quid for Jason Cummings. There were also reports of mysterious 'add-ons' if the deal had gone ahead.

"Six extra tins of Harmony isn't enough to sway me," said Jason loyally. "I could have opened up a tin of beans with a million pounds though, in fact I could have opened up an entire chain of supermarkets selling *only* tins of beans with that. But my hair's staying put and so am I."

Doing the Festival for real was Grant Holt, who was making the most of life in his new adopted home. The big striker had taken in a few shows already and knew his way around, having been a regular visitor to Edinburgh over the years. He was also radiating positivity about the main challenge now just up ahead.

"When you are a good team and have two sides like that you always end up going head to head," he remarked, with the Falkirk game on the horizon. "There is always rivalry because you both want to achieve the same thing. Unfortunately last season neither team did it and they are here to do it all again and I am here to make sure that this year we come out top of the bill."

He was also aware of the scenario that his new club had been faced with, time and again the previous season.

"It doesn't come easy and there will be teams who come to us and try to sit in to try to get points and it is their right to do that. But I think we need to get over that quickly and show them how strong we are and how resilient we are and when we get the lead we have to hold onto it and see games out."

On the Thursday, I'd been plastering flyers advertising my book 'Moonshine on Leith' around the hot-spots of Easter Road, while half-heartedly endeavouring not to get too plastered myself while doing so. I dropped in at Middleton's, a pub I'd always liked and after ordering a pint asked the barmaid if it was OK to stick up a few.

"Sure," she said, proceeding to closely scrutinise the picture thereon, a copy of the book's cover depicting the victorious cup-winning team atop the bus coming down Leith Walk on May 22nd. "I can't see my brother there, though."

"Eh? Who's your brother?" I asked.

"Darren McGregor," she replied.

Wow! Small world. Sadly Darren had been blocked from view in that particular photograph, partly due to the giant Liam Fontaine looming over everyone with arms outstretched like the Christ the Redeemer statue in Rio. But Daz had of course featured in other pictures proudly holding the trophy aloft on that never-to-be-forgotten day.

"He's got a huge *head* you know," she informed me confidentially. "Me and my mum used to try and put a tape measure round it when he was younger, but we couldn't get it to stretch all the way round. That's why he's no' bad at headers – the ball can hardly miss!"

Fantastic stuff, I thought, scrabbling around for a pen and piece of paper. If you don't want your family secrets to appear in print, don't reveal them to me in the first place! However, Daz undoubtedly deserves it. After all, it was he who first broke the news about Jason's out-of-control hairspray addiction to the Press the previous season.

Lisa kindly bought a copy of my book (I'm always packing) for her brother's upcoming birthday, which I duly signed to him with particular thanks for his contribution towards events on May 21st. Just then a portly regular customer approached the bar, causing her to exclaim, "He'll buy a copy too." Hardly, I thought, clocking the Hearts crest tattooed on his arm. But he did, explaining it was for his ninety year-old Hibbie stepdad. Then, after money had changed hands, he added, "He's blind now." I didn't have the heart to tell him that unfortunately 'Moonshine on Leith' wasn't in Braille. Not yet anyway... A sale's a sale, though. My evil ruthless business streak had reared its ugly head – but at least it wasn't as big as Darren McGregor's.

Hibs finally got down to the real thing at the Falkirk Stadium on August 6th, with expectations high in the sold-out away end. This was – on paper anyway – arguably the toughest League fixture of the lot, facing the same outfit who'd cruelly denied them at the same venue not long before, in the Play-Offs. But the visitors got off to the absolute best of all possible starts, as the man everyone was talking about put them ahead after only eighty-eight seconds. Jason, whose worth on the open market had apparently now climbed to £1.7 million, was on hand as Bairns' keeper Rogers pushed out a James Keatings effort into his path and he had no trouble finding the net from sixteen yards. However it wasn't long before the home side were right back in it with a twenty-five yard blaster courtesy of Craig Sibbald. Like jambos in the past, Houston's team always seemed to save these sort of sensational-looking efforts from distance for games against the Hibees.

"You can't give Sibbald that amount of time," observed the Hibs manager. "It's a fantastic goal and you have to hold your hand up sometimes, say "well done, son." Our reaction was OK. Although we looked more of a threat first half, I thought we managed the game a lot better second half."

Indeed, that got off to the most satisfactory of starts too, as this time a mere three minutes had elapsed, before the on-form Hibs hot-shot struck again. Grant Holt provided the pass and Jason tore through on goal, holding off Falkirk defender Luca Gasparatto as he did so, before rifling a sizzler into the top corner. Neil was right to be very pleased indeed with his team's overall performance – Ross Laidlaw looked a calm presence in goals again and the backline of McGregor, Hanlon and Fontaine held up well. In the previous two seasons Hibs had paid a very high price for poor performances at the start and losing to inferior opposition; there never seemed any chance of that happening here as they held on for a fine 2-1 victory. It was a proper team effort, but inevitably one player's name was on everyone's lips, before, during and after.

"He won the game single-handedly," said his manager, of the mercurial Cummings. "He scored two goals and was the best player on the pitch. It's brilliant to have someone like that in our team. You are guaranteed goals so I do not know what price you can put on that. But as long as he is here scoring goals, I am sure he will be happy. He enjoys playing with us and we enjoy playing with him. We don't want to lose him. I know from my own experience that everyone has their price, but there are not many clubs who can meet our valuation of Jason."

That valuation may well be around three times the original figure offered by Peterborough, he hinted, such was the importance of the player to the club, particularly in a season of such magnitude. It seemed like a touch of deja-vu, hey-ho, we've been down this road before, as memories of the Scott Allan saga of twelve months previously came to mind. However the major difference there (apart from the disparity in potential sums of money involved) was that ultimately Allan had *wanted* to leave. There was certainly no indication of that where Jason was concerned, just the opposite in fact. He may be able to open up a tin of beans, but he couldn't boil an egg, he revealed. How could he possibly survive in the alien environment of Peterborough, lacking such essential culinary skills?

"He is getting better all the time," asserted John McGinn. "To have scored fifty goals already is good going, but hopefully Jason continues doing that. There's no limits to where he can go. A goal nearly every other game is what he gives you but he's added another few things to his game – he can take the hits, he links in and he'll keep improving."

On the more general front, the midfielder was evidently very satisfied with the opening League performance. He'd been well-aware of the slip-ups at the same stage before, even prior to his joining Hibs.

"I remember playing at Easter Road two or three seasons ago with St. Mirren and the mood was completely different. Now it is a nice environment and hopefully that continues," he said. "Falkirk is always a difficult place but we have dug in and come out with the win. It's nice to get off to a flyer against a good side which will be competing at the top end this season, there's no doubt about that."

Even the usually dour and ungracious Falkirk gaffer Peter Houston took time out to praise the man of the moment and for once omitted to make claims that his team had been hard done by. They'd changed their system around to try and deny space to the Hibs attack, but, "We just didn't get it right. In other games you might get away with that, but we didn't because of the class of Cummings."

The following day came proof positive that Tynecastle was indeed haunted by a particularly muscular poltergeist, as Jamie Walker suddenly collapsed like a ton of bricks in the penalty area during the Hearts v Celtic game. As no-one was near him that could be the only explanation surely, as the player claimed, "I felt contact, so I went down." Spooky stuff, eh? Ex-Hibee nutcase and Celtic captain Scott Brown was not so willing to accept that supernatural forces were at work however.

"He is really good at that, he should be at Rio," said Broony, with reference to the spectacular diving on show at the Olympics. "There's no place in football for cheating and that has been a couple of times here now."

This was another laughable day at the office for Scottish refereeing, as in a never overly physical contest John Beaton booked seven Hearts players and four from Celtic. On the hour mark, Hearts were leading 6-1 on yellow cards, an impressive feat in itself. Of course, if the official had been applying consistency throughout, he'd have been obliged to start sending 'em off too, after original miscreants committed further infractions. Predictably, Broony himself was most culpable here and should by rights have been heading for an early bath. The fact that he remained on the park until the end had the scarf-twirlers foaming at the mouth well beyond the final whistle.

A couple of days later it was time for Hibs to finally get going in the League Cup, having enjoyed a bye in the group stage due to their Europa participation. The awkward squad from Dumfries were the visitors, although for most of the first period it looked as if it was just a matter of time until the home team wrapped it up altogether. Hanlon opened up proceedings halfway through when he got on the end of a terrific Keatings free-kick, diverted on its way by the outstretched foot of Fontaine. Paul had the easiest of finishes to prod home from close in and only a couple of minutes later Grant Holt had a great chance to double the lead but failed to capitalise on it. It was all Hibs at this stage, as Marvin Bartley (restored to the team in place of Scott Martin) then threaded it through to Keatings, but James couldn't get enough power on it to convert. He had a good game throughout though, deservedly scooping Man of the Match award and going close again with another fine free-kick before the interval. Jason was not nearly so effective as he had been at the weekend, partially due to being tightly policed by the Queens' defenders, although he did exhibit some lovely close control skills. However, probably the best chance of the lot fell to Fontaine, but big Liam headed wide with the goal at his mercy.

You could imagine that the manager would have been slightly concerned that his team were only one up at the interval when the lead should certainly have been more substantial, but there seemed little to worry about until former Hibee Stephen Dobbie took to the field. Back at Queens for a second spell, he came on to replace the injured Dale Hilson and we all know from bitter experience what's all too likely to happen when an ex-player puts in an appearance. Sure enough, he got on the end of a Brotherston cross on the sixty-sixth minute, just the latest in an interminably long line of returnees coming back to haunt us. Especially in cup-ties it seems, dating back as far as Colin Stein in the late sixties at the very least – is there *any* team who have suffered as much as Hibs from their former charges coming back to bite them on the bahookey, usually with fatal consequences? I very much doubt it. Even then, James Keatings might have put Hibs in front again almost immediately, but keeper Robinson did well to get the tips of his fingers to that curling effort. Holt followed up by missing an absolute sitter, comparable to Fontaine's before the interval, when a free header on goal was wasted and he was replaced by Martin Boyle. Ross Laidlaw then erred in allowing his former Raith Rovers team-mate Grant Anderson to show how it should be done, as he nodded it home into the far corner of the net. Five minutes later Dobbie again made his presence felt, setting up midfielder Dykes to strike a decisive and ultimately match-winning shot past the Hibs keeper. It was a shock result certainly – one of several on a night where Alloa, Dundee United and Morton all progressed at the expense of Inverness CT, Partick Thistle and Hamilton respectively – and no doubt leaving Neil with much to chew over.

"It's disappointing. I'm annoyed at the way we defended, particularly in the last third of the game," said the manager. "Their third goal was academic and we were chasing the game then. We have to do better than that. We have to be more resolute. We peppered their goal all night long but I've been in the game a long time and you can see it coming. There is always that nagging worry at 1-0. We encouraged them by keeping it at 1-0. (At half-time.) Queen of the South are in our division and there looked to be a gulf between the teams, but they have come away with a win and congratulations to them."

For his part, Queens' gaffer Gavin Skelton admitted that the only saving grace from his point of view as regards the first half was that his team went in a mere 1-0 down at the interval. The second period had been a very different story however, particularly after the introduction of Dobbie.

"Credit to the players. They showed good character. It was a good night for them and the club."

And it was goodnight for Hibs as far as their League Cup campaign was concerned, rather earlier than we might have hoped.

My enjoyment of the match had been compromised anyway, by the appearance of three hugely overweight American tourists who'd taken their seats in front of me, just on kick-off. Resplendent in brand new Hibs scarves – no doubt just purchased from the stall on Albion Place – they lost little time in living up to every negative stereotype associated with Yanks abroad. Having some good friends from the Land of the Free, I'm aware that they were about as representative of that fine nation overall as the CU Jimmy-style ginger wig brigade are of Scotland, but unfortunately these are the ones that always stand out. Despite clearly having a very tenuous grasp of the rules of *sakker*, this did not serve as an impediment to making their views known loud and clear over every incident on the park. One in particular never shut his mouth for the entire ninety minutes and kept making whooping noises like some mentally retarded frat-boy at the college basketball tournament. Amusing though this was initially, most Hibbies within earshot soon tired rapidly of their club's newest and most enthusiastic supporters. One who had the misfortune to be seated right next to them pointedly moved to several rows down before very long.

"ONE...TWO...THREE...FOUR...GODDAM IT REFEREE! I MEAN, WHAT THE HECK, HUH?!" yelled Fat Bastard No. 1, counting out aloud every second the Queens' goalkeeper wasted in the second half, prior to taking a bye-kick.

"WHAT THE HELL'S GOIN' ON NOW??" wailed Fat Bastard No. 2, the female lard-bucket, every time play was halted for some infringement.

Her enormous buttocks wobbled alarmingly in front of my unwilling gaze, as the outsize leisure-wear 'pants' rode down to reveal her arse-crack in all its Grand Canyonesque glory. There was a brief respite at the interval when they waddled off towards the concourse, most perhaps hoping that they'd had enough of this strange outdoor Festival Fringe show they'd stumbled upon and were now back on the official tourist trail. It was a forlorn hope though. They all re-emerged fifteen minutes later, absolutely laden down with pizza slices, pies, colossal cartons of chips and cans of Coke. There can't have been much of anything left for the starving locals unfortunate enough to have been in the queue behind them. That of course had the effect of attracting the unwelcome attentions of the dreaded Leith seagulls, some of whom were now almost as obese as their unwitting foreign targets below. They swooped savagely out of the skies, screeching like the feared *Nazgul* from 'The Lord of the Rings'.

"GODDAM IT TO HELL! AH'M BEIN' FRICKIN' DIVE-BAHHMED!" screamed Fat Bastard No. 3, trying in vain to shield his chips, sorry, *French fries*, from the winged terror overhead.

I half-expected him to pull out a Magnum .44 and start blasting away at this unexpected threat, whilst taking the Fifth Amendment. When I left on the eighty-sixth minute I could still hear their distressed cries from afar.

"YA JUST GOTTA BE KIDDIN' ME, REFEREE! SHEEIT..."

By this time, Hearts had ridiculously backed up Jamie Walker's claim of unseen forces being at work in the game against Celtic and gone to bat on his behalf against the SFA judicial panel. To no-one's surprise, their appeal against a two-match ban on the player was then thrown out. Hot on the heels of that, Jamie's invisible assailant had then apparently followed the team to Perth for their midweek League Cup-tie against St. Johnstone and shoved Callum Paterson in the back too. Again a penalty was awarded, again it was converted, again it made no difference to the overall result as Hearts this time lost by three goals to two. Saints fans responded to the ghostly goings-on in much the same way as Scott Brown had done, three days previously.

"We can't stop people calling us cheats," lamented Paterson.

Aye you can – just stop cheating!

The same day, a bouncer called Zahid Harris appeared in court on a charge of biting Jason Cummings, as the player and his team-mates celebrated their historic Scottish Cup win back in May. Who does he think he is – Luis Suarez?

"That must have been very painful," said the Sheriff sympathetically. "Where did he bite you?"

"In George Street," replied Jason.

"I mean, which part *exactly*?"

"In Shanghai," confirmed Jase.

"That's not in George Street, it's in China," retorted the beak. He turned to address the alleged culprit. "Why did you make such a meal of it?"

"I thought he looked like a tasty geezer," said Harris.

"There's no such thing as a free lunch," warned the Sheriff. "Certainly not in George Street and probably not in China either. Next time you want to swallow a Foxy Blonde I suggest you go to the bar and buy one."

With the opening League game against the newly-promoted Pars just up ahead, Neil Lennon was admitting to frustration over the bureaucratic red tape that was holding up Ofir Marciano's debut at Easter Road. It had now been revealed that the keeper would have to return to Belgium to complete some paperwork. Have these Flemish fuckwits never heard of fax machines? The manager had grown so exasperated he claimed that it "was akin to dealing with the Mafia."

"How so, Neil?"

"They made as an Ofir we couldn't refuse."

He remained tight-lipped over the possible addition of any other new recruits for the time being, but declared that he was "still a striker and a midfielder short."

Nellie was also still ruminating over the League Cup reversal, while observing that Hibs "are good at playing against Premier teams." One glance at the previous season's results against those in the top tier would certainly have confirmed that for him. But he knew from his own experience as a player how the so-called 'lesser' teams could frequently raise their game against more illustrious opponents, whether subconsciously or otherwise. Then the performance would tend to drop off somewhat in the following game.

"I'm not saying they weren't up for the Queen of the South game, because there was no real complacency but there were lapses in concentration that they wouldn't make in other games. This is a big club and they have to develop that big club mentality."

Lewis Stevenson, although Kirkcaldy born and bred, was now resident in Dunfermline and had been impressed by the progress of his new hometown team.

"They'll be on a high having won the League last season. I'm sure they'll have come up looking to finish in the top four."

Hibs' longest-serving player was now on course to reach another milestone – our club's sole joint holder of a Scottish Cup Winners and a League Cup Winners medal was about to make his 325th appearance in green and white, the same total as that of Jimmy O'Rourke.

Meanwhile, Liam Fontaine was eager to get back on track against the Championship new boys, while holding his hand up to his midweek header.

"I was getting pulled, but it is what it is. I missed a chance and I won't miss again."

The big man would have been aware that his lapse contributed to the manager's stated dissatisfaction with both defending at one end and chances passed up at the other, although the tip of his boot had certainly contributed to the Hibs goal.

"Last year we had a lot of ups and downs and showed great character to finish on a high. Now we have a new manager and a new style about us and we all want to learn – and he's a great manager and person to learn from because of what he has achieved in the game and the levels he has played at."

He revealed that he'd actually played against his gaffer, in his debut game in Scottish football. Liam had been a callow youth farmed out on loan to Kilmarnock from his parent club Fulham when Jim Jefferies pitched him in to face Celtic at Rugby Park in January 2005. That had ended in a narrow 1-0 win for the visitors, a game he still clearly remembered. The ability to grind out such results without conceding was something that Neil was trying to drum into his present day charges, if – like Celtic then – they hoped to entertain a realistic chance of ultimately topping their particular division.

So it was the Championship new boys up next, who'd doubtless have a point to prove regarding their exalted League status this campaign. The way the Pars had tumbled out of the second tier initially by losing over the Play-Offs to close rivals Cowdenbeath had been a similar shock to their fans as that experienced by Hibbies with the Hamilton horror-show of 2014. But now they were back and most pundits were tipping them to be in hot contention at the top end of the table, rather than struggling to compete at the higher level. The sense of anticipation was certainly high, as some 1,200 crossed the Forth Bridge to contribute to an excellent attendance of 16,477, the biggest turn-out of the day north of the border.

However, as against Queen of the South, Hibs' undoubted superiority overall was not satisfactorily converted into actual goals. In many ways the first half was almost a carbon copy of the League Cup encounter, but with extra frustration engendered by Hibs passing up even more chances than they had in midweek. By the time they'd trooped off at the break only one goal to the good, there was a certain sense of deja-vu apparent. Even that was in some way fortunate, as it came courtesy of Richards-Everton who headed past his own keeper. David Hutton had done well to keep out two McGinn efforts, but Grant Holt should have done a hell of a lot better with the couple of opportunities that came his way, woefully misdirecting one header in particular.

Into the second half and there was something of an air of inevitability about the equaliser, coming as it did after more sustained pressure from the home team which failed to pay dividends. Twelve minutes in and on-loan Hearts man Gavin Reilly beat Ross Laidlaw to generate ripples of unease radiating out around Easter Road. Here we go again, was the thought uppermost in the home fans' minds. Neil opted to replace the largely ineffective Holt with Martin Boyle ten minutes after that and he instantly made an impression with his lightning pace down the flank. Martin seems to be one of those destined to forever fulfil the 'super sub' role (think Gareth Evans, perhaps), but there's no doubt that on his day he can virtually turn a game on his own. That was the case here as his remarkable tenacity and no little skill resulted in the ball skimming across the goalmouth as he chased it down the bye-line before flashing it over. Unfortunately for the Pars fans, they were about to witness their team's second major blooper of the afternoon as central defender Callum Fordyce made a right hash of it. Only just returned to the side after a lengthy absence through injury he failed to react and the ball ran onto Jason Cummings. The latter had recently confessed to the Press that he couldn't boil an egg, but there was nothing wrong with his poaching ability. Lurking just behind the hapless Fordyce, he gleefully took advantage. Cue sighs of relief around the stadium, although there were still twelve minutes left on the clock. The Pars were a spirited outfit and did have a real go – indeed, in the period between the equaliser and the introduction of Boyle they looked the team most likely to score. On this showing they certainly appeared capable of giving the majority of contenders in the Championship a run for their money, although they lacked a decisive killer instinct up front. Ultimately, it was a hard-fought and extremely valuable three points for the Hibees, especially given the fact that they were already five points ahead of Falkirk and Dundee United after only two games played.

"I have to say I'm very happy. Two wins out of two – I have to be happy with that," said the manager, whilst reflecting that – again – they could well have been two or three up at half-time, perhaps more. He was clearly delighted with the performance of Man of the Match McGinn especially, saying, "John was outstanding."

Pars boss Allan Johnston observed that, "A lot of teams will come to Easter Road and park the bus, but we had a real go and I'm disappointed not to have got anything from the game. Hibs and Dundee United are the favourites to win the League, but if we put in a performance like that every week, we are not going to be far away from the top of the table."

Club captain David Gray was looking at the bigger picture, in comparing the bleak outlook when he first signed on the dotted line to the current situation. David had been Stubbsy's first signing and of course no-one then had any idea of how things would pan out, in the aftermath of the Butcher/Malpas fiasco.

"Back then was the lowest point," reflected the full-back. "We only had six or seven players so where we were then to now is a massive difference. The fans have come back in their numbers. We know the fans are there. We have to make sure we keep doing the right things and I am sure they will keep coming back. We know the expectations are to win the League. The League is difficult – if you are chasing you can't slip up, if you are out in front they have to beat you. We want to put a string of results together and to start with two is very encouraging."

He was correct in that assessment and as Lennon had cautioned that his team would perhaps take a few games to properly gel, it could scarcely have been a better opening to the campaign. Two tricky hurdles had been overcome and two of our main challengers had but one point apiece. Very early days for sure, but a highly positive contrast to the previous two seasons' stuttering starts.

Neil was still intent on bolstering his squad and his attention had turned to former Inverness Caley midfield man Andrew Shinnie, currently surplus to requirements at Birmingham City. He'd been out on loan at Rotherham the previous season and the Hibs gaffer was hoping to secure a similar arrangement.

"We have made contact with Birmingham and we are waiting to hear from the player. He's a player I have liked for a long, long time. We've made the approach so we'll see how it goes."

Over the past few years, we have grown accustomed to a minute's applause reverberating around the stadium on occasion, in tribute to some member of the Hibernian community who has passed away. Unfortunately, as I stood up to participate on the fifty-second minute of the Dunfermline game, this time for me it was personal. A few weeks earlier I had received the shocking news that Ali Tait, a stalwart Hibbie and good friend to many, had died suddenly as a result of a heart-attack. He'd been cycling to work in Atlanta, Georgia (where he'd lived since moving to America and remarrying over a decade before), when the fatal moment occurred. I'd last seen Ali when he came over for the League Cup final in March and it was hard to believe that we'd never see that cheery smile and share a laugh and a drink ever again.

The venue on that occasion was The Windsor; an appropriate choice as Ali had been a leading light on the committee of the Hibs Monthly / Mass Hibsteria fanzine and that had long been our rendezvous point for editorial meetings (or piss-ups, to be strictly accurate.) Despite living abroad for many years, Ali still continued to send back 'Leon Cropley's Letter From America' which always featured prominently in the 'zine, his alias derived from a combination of the Christian name of his favourite Russian revolutionary and the surname of his favourite

Hibs player. When a starry-eyed laddie just embarking on a lifetime career as a Hibs supporter, he'd been out with his older brother John in town one day and they'd come across the Hibs star. Too shy to speak up for himself, Ali had prompted his sibling to approach Alex for an autograph and had never forgotten how the great player had not only obliged with his signature but had taken time out to have a lengthy chat with an impressionable young admirer.

On the morning after the Dunfermline game, his widow Tina (how strange it feels writing that, pertaining to a pal of long standing, a good few years younger than myself) had taken his ashes down to Easter Road. There they were scattered behind the goals, as everyone's favourite Chinese/Malaysian Fifer Andy Chung strummed his acoustic guitar and sang 'Caledonia' and 'Sunshine on Leith'. When occasionally troubled by pangs of homesickness those were the two songs that Ali always turned to, for solace when he felt far away from Scotland.

Later that evening there was a celebration of his life at the Hibs Supporters' Club and it was apparent just how many friends from diverse walks of life he'd acquired throughout his lifetime. There were former workmates from his time in the Civil Service and others who'd got to know him through his tenure conducting literary sightseeing tours during the Festival. There were those who'd known him through his involvement with the Trade Union movement and those he'd known from his love of music and attendance at numerous gigs and aspiring thespians he'd known through participating in (very) amateur dramatics. I ticked two of these boxes, having originally known him as a workmate of a pal then employed by the Scottish Office and through running into him many times at concerts, even before elevation to the giddy heights of the Hibs fanzine committee brought us together in another context.

He was the kind of mate you might occasionally get into heated debate with – Ali lived by Voltaire's maxim whereby he'd maybe disagree violently with what you had to say, but he'd defend to the death your right to say it – especially on matters of politics or music. Where the latter was concerned, he had an unstinting love of Pink Floyd (particularly Syd Barrett era), the Incredible String Band, The Clash and The Fall. As an unreconstructed old hippy, I shared his passion for the first two; I even wrote for the ISB fanzine as well as the Hibs ones. But I didn't have much time for The Clash and absolutely none whatsoever for the last-named, especially that belligerent little twerp of a front-man (I can't bring myself to refer to him as a 'singer'.) So we might have not seen eye to eye on that, but were happy to agree to disagree on the merits or otherwise of Mark E. Smith.

Likewise with politics, where the sound of Ali making his socialist views loudly known in a busy pub was always likely to draw unwelcome attention from strangers who did not necessarily take kindly to being subjected to the Che Guevera of Wallyford's strident opinions. But the one subject dearest to his heart that you could never find fault with was his undying love for and commitment to Hibernian FC. He'd spent thousands of pounds travelling back to see them from his adopted homeland, usually for it all to end in tears. The unmentionable Scottish Cup final of 2012 and now the let-down against Ross County. Sadly, the expenditure of yet another final so close after that was just too much to bear and Ali never would see his beloved Hibees lift the Big Cup. But although he couldn't make it in person on May 21st there was never any doubt that he was there in spirit. Then of course he had to endure good-natured slagging via text message and email for being silly enough to have picked 'the wrong final' to return for. (In fairness, not many of us would have countenanced the likelihood of Hibs reaching the ultimate stage of the Scottish Cup, particularly after the League Cup disappointment.)

Ali certainly wore his heart on his sleeve where Hibs were concerned. Many moons ago he'd been caught out by an enterprising Evening

News reporter who had been canvassing opinions from fans leaving Easter Road. This was a regular slot at the time and the hope was that, naturally, some supporter would blurt out something controversial in the heat of the moment. Many managers had learned from bitter experience to curb their tongues when facing the media in the immediate aftermath of an emotionally-charged game, but the fans were not quite so circumspect. Ali was not one to disappoint there, his post-match tirade in the wake of a poor performance capped by the assertion that Stuart Lovell was one of the *worst* Hibs players he had *ever* seen, or words to that effect. Naturally, the reporter who captured this on microphone scurried back post-haste to the North Bridge office and gleefully transcribed it, with possibly a few embellishments of his own added. When the piece duly appeared in the paper, Ali was of course utterly mortified. He'd said what he'd said in the white heat of the moment, with no time for calm reflection. He'd over-reacted, he hadn't meant it anyway…

A letter of contrite apology was quickly despatched in Mr Lovell's direction with a couple of priceless enclosures, a fact that he was quite happy to keep secret from his family and friends. However, this was blown wide open when Hibs released an end of season video, part of which featured Stuart Lovell ruminating in his usual articulate fashion about the campaign just concluded. He emphasised that he hadn't been best pleased to hear that someone had deemed him simply the worst, after one particular match, but had been mollified by the resulting apologetic missive. Enclosed with the letter were two complimentary tickets for Ali's latest amateur dramatic performance of one of Shakespeare's works, which the player had very wisely omitted to put to use. Being a gentleman he neglected to mention my pal by name, but those of us viewing the video screened on the telly in the Four-in-Hand were in no doubt at all as to the identity of Mr Lovell's unfortunate critic. Needless to say, Ali was even more horribly mortified to learn that he'd been 'outed' so to speak, although massively relieved that Stuart hadn't actually revealed his identity. Not that it mattered much; anyone who knew him and subsequently watched the video had a very shrewd idea as to who the midfielder had been referring to.

So all in all, a very poignant night at Sunnyside, where proceedings were rounded off in the only way possible. As the shutters came down on the bar in the Stanton Suite, everyone formed a huge swaying circle with glasses held aloft, preparing for an almighty roof-raising sing-along. Then Andy Chung took up his guitar again and from his position right in the middle carefully picked out the opening bars.

"My heart was broken, SORROW, SORROW..."

A fitting conclusion to an evening of reminisces, laughs and inevitably a lot of tears. Farewell old pal, you made the most of life and will be sorely missed by many. Alistair Tait, 1964 – 2016, R.I.P.

By the start of the following week, Birmingham City boss Gary Rowett – who had been so complimentary towards Hibs after the pre-season friendly – indicated that he was amenable to the Shinnie move.

"I hope that if he goes to Hibernian, probably the biggest club in the Scottish Championship, it would be a really good move for him. I would like to think they would dominate quite a few games and he would get lots of opportunity in the final third to show his undoubted quality."

Back at base, Ross Laidlaw was enthusing about the positive atmosphere, aided by 10,800 season tickets having now been sold and sell-outs in the away end likely to be a feature when Hibs were the visitors. Ross, who'd been keeping goal for Raith Rovers when they won the Scottish Cup-tie at Easter Road during Butcher's blundering tenure, was well placed to compare then and now.

"Obviously it was a huge surprise to everyone to see Hibs relegated, no-one expected it. But now there's been a real reconnection between the fans, the players and the club. This is a big club," he said, still on a high from the atmosphere generated by the crowd at the Dunfermline game. "I think the crowd showed everybody just how big. It was brilliant."

He also admitted to a sense of relief that apparently the majority of the Pars fans didn't recognise him – given his stint at Kirkcaldy he might have been in for a noisily negative reaction, particularly in the second half, if they had!

At Parkhead, Brendan Rodgers unveiled his latest 'family friendly' approach, regarding players' training commitments. This was to the effect that those who had children just beginning their scholastic careers would be given the chance to start later in the week, enabling them to escort their offspring to the school gates. The manager said that he recognised this was an important milestone in family life – "They are fathers, not just footballers." Well, some of them are a bit more, er, 'fatherly' than others, aren't they? Hardly fair on the childless Celts either. He's not going to be seeing much of Leigh Griffiths for a while, put it that way. Indeed, Leigh confirmed that he'd be walking young Rhys to his palace of education first, followed the next day by doing likewise with Kacie. He'd then take the rest of The Sunshine Band in on the Thursday and draw the names of his remaining children out of the hat to see who'd win the accolade of having daddy walk them to school on Friday. He'd then spread the process out over the following fortnight, to accommodate the rest of them.

Meanwhile in Brazil, former FIFA heid honcho Joao Havelange was havin' a farewell party as he died in a Rio de Janeiro hospital, aged 100. Only three years earlier FIFA Ethics Court Judge Joachim Eckert said he was havin' a laugh instead. He'd been responsible for appointing three of the biggest crooks to the Frankly Intolerable Fraudsters' Association, including his own son-in-law, as well as Chuck Blazer and Dixon of Dock Green himself, a.k.a. Jack Warner. "Morally and ethically reproachable," thundered Eckert, somewhat impotently. And that was *before* he allowed Blatter's patter to batter its way through the hallowed portals to stick his big fat Swiss snout in the trough. Havin'-a-laugh was also forced to resign from the International Olympic Committee just prior to being suspended for taking a million dollar kickback. He'd also boasted not long ago that when he quit the FIFA top office, he'd left "property and contacts worth over four billion dollars. Not too bad, I'd say." Fair play to him, it must have taken a lot of time and effort to stuff that amount of cash into separate brown envelopes before distributing them amongst his fellow thieves and chancers. Gary Linekar was quick to issue his own fitting tribute – "Joao Havelange has died. Football gave him so much. Yes, you read that correctly."

As the St. Mirren clash loomed on the horizon, Hibs finally got their man, as Andrew Shinnie agreed terms. He'd been frustrated at failing to establish himself as a first choice at Birmingham and – like his manager – had been impressed by what he'd seen at Easter Road pre-season.

"Hibs were an option and the one I have chosen," he said. Referring to the friendly encounter, he added, "Hibs played very well, the stadium is lovely and the pitch great and I got good vibes. This club should be in the top flight. It's been a few years out so it's time to get back in and I want to be part of the journey."

Also aboard for the ride was Brian Graham, signed on a two-year deal from Ross County and pitched into the fray with fifteen minutes left in Paisley. It seemed a sudden appointment, but negotiations had been going on behind the scenes for some time.

"I was glad just to get everything finalised and put pen to paper for such a massive club as Hibs. When you know a club of that stature is interested in you then it's a relief just to get it done. I know what I've got in terms of my ability and Neil obviously believes in me. I just want to do well for Hibs, help my team-mates, score a lot of goals and win promotion – that's our number one priority."

Indeed, he might well have scored on his debut too, but was denied by Saints' keeper Scott Gallacher near the end. The other new boy, Andrew Shinnie, also made an appearance, coming on to replace James Keatings for the last quarter.

By that time happily, Hibs were already well away over the hill, sitting on a comfortable two goal lead at half-time. The deadly Jason Cummings was the principal architect yet again, taking full advantage of a slip by Saints' defender Jack Baird. Jason was hovering with intent as the centre back fluffed a back pass, hitting it short and the Hibs man was on it in a trice to force it into the net from a tight angle. Ten minutes later he doubled his tally and his team looked to be coasting, even with two-thirds of the game left to play. It had looked a potentially tricky encounter beforehand, but the home team were very disappointing and didn't even manage a shot on target until seven minutes from the end. Hibs appeared very assured, the three-pronged attack of Cummings, Holt and Keatings being ably supplied by their team-mates further back. Captain David Gray had set up Jason's first, by firing over one of his deadly low crosses and Stevenson was equally effective on the other flank. In midfield, John McGinn was back to something approaching his best, blasting a long-range effort off the crossbar right at the death.

"He just cracked one off the bar from thirty minutes!" yelled BBC Sportscene pundit Kenny Crawford excitedly, which – if true – meant that the ball had been hovering magically in the air for about an hour.

The only justifiable criticism the manager could level against his team was still their inability to make the absolute most of all the chances accrued.

"We could have been four up at half-time," said Neil. "We had good control of the game."

A reporter asked Jason if he was yet again aiming to surpass his goal tally of the previous season. With disarming candour the striker explained that he wouldn't be aiming for any definitive total, outlining the reason why.

"I did that last season – but after hitting it I was terrible! So this season, no targets, we'll just see what happens." However, he was well satisfied with the afternoon's work. "Our victory was a credit to the way we played. I thought we were really good. The midfield was brilliant and big Marv played a massive part but a lot of people would not see what he does off the ball. I got two, but I did have other chances, although getting three points was the main thing."

There was no doubt about that and Hibs had now won three out of three in the League, the first time they'd managed such a feat at the start of a campaign since 1974. (That had been in the top division of course, during which they battered a total of ten goals past Aberdeen, Hearts and Partick Thistle, with two of those games away from home.) Raith Rovers defeated Dunfermline Athletic in the Fife derby the same day and held onto the top spot in the Championship thanks to a marginally superior goal difference; another wee reminder to the Hibees about the consequences of not making best use of all their goalscoring opportunities. For if they had, they'd be leading the pack already. But the good news was that Falkirk flopped again, going down 2-0 to Queen of the South, who looked more likely to put in a real challenge at the top end than Houston's huffers and puffers had done so far. They lay two points adrift of Hibs and Dundee United finally found some measure of form to defeat Ayr United by three goals to nil. However, their poor start might yet prove to be significant and there was still a five point gap between them and the top two.

The following week there was encouraging news for John McGinn, whose latent super-ness had clearly made an impression on Scotland gaffer Gordon Strachan. The latter had just picked his twenty-seven man squad for the first game of the World Cup qualifiers against Malta in September and John was the sole Hibernian player to be named. Little wonder really, as the midfield maestro had scooped the Man of the Match award in his international debut in Scotland's 1-0 win over Denmark in March. That was a great achievement in itself and with Strachan focusing on the youngsters for the fresh campaign – bringing five novices through from the Under-21s – the future looked bright for John. With Scott Brown having just announced his retirement from the international stage, it gave Super a great chance to step up and perhaps establish himself fully in Strachan's side.

His mentor at the lower level was sorry to have to dispense with his services, but clearly glad that he'd made his mark.

"As a player he has developed, physically he looks stronger, leaner. He has worked extremely hard," said Ricky Sbragia. "I miss him at Under-21s, but am really pleased he has gone up to the big squad – I would never want him back! He has got everything you could want from a midfielder and he's been playing first team football from an early age."

Jason would feature again for the wee Scots and the gaffer was well impressed too with his blistering start to the season.

"Week in, week out he's scoring goals and for a centre-forward that's the main thing. He's always worked hard – he has a wee edge about him."

However, there was disappointment where the other Hibs contender was concerned, as poor Danny Handling was ruled out for the time being due to his recent cartilage injury. The Under-21s coach clearly felt for a player who had also missed out so much the previous season with his cruciate ligament problem.

"I told him to be positive, that the main thing now is to get fit and get back in the Hibs first team."

Making his long-delayed debut in the first team in the new indoor facility at Riccarton was goalkeeper Ofir Marciano – the Under-20s first team that is. The wee derby took place on Tuesday the 23rd with Fraser Fyvie also getting a run-out after his lengthy spell on the sidelines due to injury. Jordon Forster and Alex Harris also featured for Hibs in a highly entertaining contest. It looked like life was a beach for the junior jambos as Gullan twice put the Hibees in front, but their opponents came back both times and it ended 2-2. Hibs had secured the use of the venue for the season, making it effectively another 'home' ground and Neil Lennon was also in attendance to keep his eye on his up and coming youngsters.

In Israel, Celtic squeezed through by the narrowest of margins in the Champions League qualifier – against a team ranked 284th on the continent. (Not that they're actually geographically on it at all, but you get my drift.) They lost 2-0, but had done *just* enough in the first leg at Parkhead to go through on aggregate. Fans of their opponents Hapoel Beer Sheva made their feelings clear over the pro-Palestinian flag protest by the Green Brigade in Glasgow, as about half of the home support appeared to be waving the Star of David. Some of them even resorted to wearing old nineties-era Rangers tops in a bid to wind up the opposition. Right enough, these folks will do anything to get their hands on the Gazza strip, one way or another.

The next day the sad news broke that the world's oldest Hibbie (and indeed Scotland's second oldest man) Sam Martinez had passed away from heart failure in the Western General Hospital at the age of 106. The wee man originally from Belize who'd pitched up in Scotland during the Second World War had become something of a latter-day celebrity to the Hibee Nation, none more so than when he travelled to Hampden in May to see his team lift the Big Cup at last. By good fortune, he'd arrived on these shores just in time to witness Smith, Johnstone, Turnbull, Reilly, Ormond and their cohorts at their absolute zenith.

"I sat behind the Directors' Box and the Famous Five were playing in those days. I had a great seat," Sam reminisced in later years. "They were all dressed in green and white and they are my favourite colours. I started to support Hibs and have been ever since."

Hibs issued a statement, saying "The club are deeply saddened to hear of Sam's passing. Sam was a lovely person and touched us all with his character and commitment to the club. He persevered longer than anyone else to see Hibernian lift the Scottish Cup and we were delighted that he was able to attend the game in May. Our thoughts are with his family and friends at this time. His memory marches on."

I recalled standing at the foot of Leith Walk on May 22nd, eagerly awaiting the approach of the bus bearing our Hampden heroes, as a couple of wee laddies in our company hopped up and down in excited anticipation. You lucky little *bastards*, I thought rather uncharitably, you've no idea of the historical significance of this occasion, you probably fondly imagine it's something of a regular occurrence! Have you any notion of just how long some of us have been grimly hanging on for, to experience such a moment?? But then I thought of Hibs' oldest fan and suddenly my own lifetime vigil of hope didn't look quite so interminable after all. I looked again at wee Lewis in front of me and couldn't help but reflect on the astonishing fact that Sam had waited patiently for precisely *one hundred years* longer than he had, to see the boys bring home the silverware! Truly, Sam's achievement through his incredible longevity seemed almost as noteworthy as that of the fabulous fourteen in green and white who'd made the dream finally come true on May 21st.

The last fixture of the month was now upon us, to find Ofir Marciano at last about to make his Big Team debut against Morton, after his midweek warm-up with the Under-20s. He'd had to pass an English test as part of his work permit conditions, but, "The English they speak here is different to the test!" he quickly noticed, with some bemusement. "They need to speak a bit slower for me, but it's OK. I hear Jason maybe wouldn't pass my English test but I like this guy, he is a good boy and I am trying to learn Scottish."

Jason had quite enough on his plate as it was – he was still hoping to pass his egg boiling test before the year was out. Whether or not he'd succeed was another matter, but Hibs had a crack team of trainers on stand-by, just in case. Gordon Ramsay, Marco Pierre White and Humpty Dumpty were all ready to help, confirmed Neil Lennon.

"Once Jason comes out of his shell he'll be fine."

"Are his brains not too scrambled?" asked a reporter.

"Is that some kind of a yolk?" retorted the Hibs manager. "Jason's no chicken, I can assure you. He is the egg-man, goo goo g'joob. Now get tae puk puk puk..."

Meanwhile, Hibs' new keeper revealed that it was his fellow countryman, Nir Bitton of Celtic, who recommended the move to him. Currently international colleagues, they'd grown up together and remained friends.

"The minute I told him it was Hibs he said – "You have to take this chance to test yourself in British football." He told me this was a good place to start."

Well, the man who the tabloids rather inevitably have chosen to refer to as 'Rocky' had a satisfactory enough start alright in the big boys' team, although with little to do over the ninety minutes. The reason for that was quite simple – a rip-roaring performance from his new club on a day of balmy sunshine on Leith – four goals from four headers from four different players, what's not to like?? The manager had alluded to the certainty that someone somewhere along the line was going to cop it big style due to his team's attacking prowess, which – up until now – hadn't quite translated into actual goals. But they made a significant leap forward on that front with this outing.

"I had no complaints, no complaints at all today," said Neil. "We had another fantastic crowd, it was a beautiful day. I think that's as good as it gets really. I'm happy – and it takes a lot to make me happy! Our two centre halves (McGregor and Hanlon) were outstanding and they made it easy for Ofir because they defended solidly."

Hibs did take a while to get going, but happily there never looked like any repeat of the previous season's shock capitulation to the same side. New boy Andrew Shinnie did well to latch onto a Fyvie cross and bullet it home past Derek Gaston for the first, just on the half-hour mark. He looked to be a terrific asset and a smart signing by Neil, slotting in comfortably to the team as if he'd been there for ages. OK, the odd pass went astray, but it was pleasing that he had the confidence to try, after quickly sensing any given opportunity. Grant Holt put in a decent enough shift too and clinched a second just before the interval, giving Hibs an extra wee cushion at the break. Too often, the single goal advantage at this stage had felt a bit precarious, as was proved in the League Cup reversal to Queen of the South. But few would have seen any realistic way back for the visitors, even your most optimistic Morton supporter.

So it proved, as the home team really found their rhythm in the second period, putting the game beyond doubt within ten minutes. I thought initially that it was Fraser Fyvie who notched this one (as did the folk sitting next to me), but the stadium announcer reckoned it was down to Grant Holt, before someone's moby info service declared that the indefatigable Jason had done the deed. This was most satisfactory, especially as he'd had a wild sclaff in the first half which brought to mind the Jase of old, where it would turn out to simply not be his day, no matter what he tried. But there were no worries on that score now. The blond bombshell does not lack confidence and that certainly didn't derail his eagerness to get stuck right back in at the next opportunity. He also made an integral contribution to the last – and best – goal, setting up the other newbie, Brian Graham, with a tremendous pin-point cross. Brian rose to it admirably and powered an absolutely stonking header into the back of the net. That one flew past the fingers of the hapless ex-Hibee Andy McNeil, who'd come on to replace the injured Gaston. Neil made very shrewd use of his own substitutes, as the former Ross County man had come on in place of Holt ten minutes before and then Bartley made way for Keatings. But the most significant replacement yet again was Martin Boyle (for Cummings) – in the twelve minutes he was on the park he could quite easily have had a hat-trick! That he didn't was in some way down to the valiant effort of McNeil, who observed afterwards that, "All four goals were from crosses and headers, all different types of headers and crosses. That shows the new manager has changed style slightly and I think that will pay dividends. Last year I felt that in some of the games we played against Hibs they were predictable. Now they still play good football, but have the aerial threat of Holt and Graham. That will make a big difference for them this year."

"We have to be honest and realistic and say Hibs have got a huge gulf in quality and that was shown," the Bald Eagle in the visitors' dug-out glumly conceded.

The month concluded with the news that Dan Carmichael had left Hibs 'by mutual consent'. The midfielder signed on a free transfer from Queen of the South had really struggled with injury, making few appearances and scoring a solitary goal in the process. (That had come just over six months ago, in a 3-0 victory over Alloa Athletic at Easter Road.) It's always a shame when these things don't work out, particularly as the player had been extremely enthusiastic about the move in the first place. But like poor Farid El-Alagui, he left with everyone – club, team-mates and fans alike – wishing him all the best for the future.

But it was fair to say that the aforementioned denizens and devotees of Hibernian FC saw the month out on something of a high. Barring the disappointment of an early League Cup exit, it had been better than anyone had a realistic right to expect. Neil had taken the wise precaution of stating beforehand that his new charges would take a few games to gel properly, which would surely have sent a shudder through the ranks of their opponents up ahead. Four straight wins in the Championship with ten goals scored and only two conceded – and that was the Hibees only 'warming up'? Oo-er! On the evidence of the last game things looked even more rosy regarding the latest acquisitions too, who would have a big and hopefully very positive part to play in the months to come.

3.

SEPTEMBER: GREEN TRAIN KEPT A-ROLLIN'

So the midnight hour was struck as August morphed into September, with the attendant CRASH and BANG and WALLOP that jerked the law-abiding populace of Auld Reekie wide-awake in their beds. But for once it wasn't the bloody fireworks in Princes Street Gardens, but the apocalyptic sound of the transfer window smashing shut. There were no further additions to beat the clock down Easter Road way however, although a couple of bodies were heading away from Leith instead. Jamie Insall for one, although he'd hardly put a foot in the old Port since arriving the previous season. It was back over the Forth to East Fife for him, while Sam Stanton went out on loan to Dumbarton for the remainder of the campaign. He'd last played for the first team in October 2015 and again looked to be surplus to requirements, despite trying to get his career back on track at Hibs. However, they would have the option of recalling him in January, if they so wished. The same applied to Jamie, who was realistic about his prospects of breaking into the first team, with so many now ahead of him in the queue. But he'd be operating at a higher level anyway, as East Fife had stepped up to League One and he certainly didn't lack an optimistic outlook or confidence in his own ability.

"I'm playing at a level now I couldn't have imagined eighteen months ago and I'm in better shape than I've ever been. I believe I'm good enough for Hibs now," he said. "I believe I'm good enough to be in or around the first team squad. I've trained with them every day and I don't feel I looked out of place."

On the first Friday night of the month, Jason Cummings turned out for the wee Scots at Tynecastle, as the Under-21s went down 1-0 in a disappointing match to their far stronger opponents from Macedonia. Many chances were squandered, including one by Jason in the first half, but the visiting keeper played his part with super-swift reactions to keep the Hibs man out. The Scots youngsters had virtually no chance of qualifying from the group, as they now lay seven points behind Macedonia and Iceland, albeit with a game in hand over the former.

His team-mate John McGinn was in Gordon Strachan's squad to face Malta in the big boys' World Cup qualifier two days hence, an accolade that pleased his club manager immensely.

"The fact that he's in the squad and getting recognition is fantastic," said Neil. "He's a really strong player. He's got bags of enthusiasm for the game. He's really good with both feet and athletically he's very strong and a good runner."

With Scott Brown having announced his retirement from the international stage there were more than a few pundits pontificating on the possibility of a ready-made replacement in the shape of Super. But the Hibs manager was having none of that, emphasising that McGinn was very much his own man.

"I think it is really unfair to make a comparison with Scott Brown. It is inevitable that people will compare both players but they are different types. John is intelligent for a start!"

So as a result of their international commitments both John and Jason were absent for Hibs' next foray into the wilderness, as their team set off to face Turriff United in the third round of the Irn Bru Cup. This was the rebranded version of the Petrofac – the trophy itself being made in

Scotland from girders – and as such pretty much a waste of time in my opinion. These tournaments have virtually no credibility and you have to ask if it is really worth risking possible injuries to valuable players who should be one hundred per-cent concentrating on winning promotion, with now only the Scottish Cup as a valid distraction. However the manager deemed it a useful exercise – although he probably felt obliged to say so – as it did give some of the up and coming hopefuls as well as those coming back from injury a competitive work-out in the sun. Neil made eight changes for the long trip north, from the side that had so comprehensively beaten Morton and of that lot the youngest dude on the park was one of the stand-outs in luminous green.

17 year-old Fraser Murray slotted in comfortably to a midfield alongside Fyvie and McGeouch and did not look in any way out of place. By the time he'd opened the scoring on the eighteenth minute Hibs had already hit the woodwork twice (within the first three minutes) and seen a long-range strike from Callum Crane dip just over the bar. Young Fraser kept calm as he took possession from a Martin Boyle pass and thumped a low shot past the generally impressive Turriff keeper from around fifteen yards. A few minutes later, big Brian Graham leapt to connect with a McGeouch cross and powered a header into the net and Hibs were already on easy street. Callum then made an excellent run, beating three men in the process, but goalie Main did enough to stop a third, prior to the same player in turn setting up Graham with a couple of good crosses. Martin Boyle looked like he was relishing being handed a starting berth for once and just shy of half-time fired a rocket in the direction of the Turriff goal. It was aimed too high to trouble Main but just at the right height to certainly trouble the unfortunate cameraman perched precariously on a plinth. The ball smashed off his forehead to induce much hilarity around the ground, an action luckily captured for posterity by another camera angle.

Alex Harris opened up the second half with yet another woodwork wobbler as his header hit the crossbar, before Marciano was called into action for virtually the first time at the other end. He acted decisively to deny Turriff's Polish striker Kleczkowski just after Alex's effort and then watched with relief as another sizzler zipped just past his right-hand post some ten minutes later. This was something of a flat period for the visitors and they seemed to ease off a bit, but as the game moved into the final quarter there was never any doubt about the overall result. Graham might have done better after a double-chance fell to him on receipt of a Fyvie corner – the first effort was blocked but a second opportunity on the rebound saw him sky it over the bar. However, a minute after that the lively Alex Harris picked out Boyle and Martin did well to finish from an angle. It was all over bar the shouting and Neil felt able to give another Murray his debut – 18 year-old Innes – with five minutes remaining.

"It was great for young Fraser to get a goal on his debut," said the gaffer. "We've watched him at Under-20 level and he's caught the eye, so we had him training with the first team on a number of occasions. He's a good footballer, very good with both feet. He could do with a bit of meat on him but that will come as he gets older."

"Neil's a clever manager – he was never going to put out a team that he thought might get done," observed Ross Jack in the home dug-out. "The Hibs team was strong and experienced with some quality young boys mixed in. We got the runaround in the first half especially, but we sorted things out a bit more in the second half. Our goalkeeper was outstanding. It was a great lesson for us but we didn't disgrace ourselves in any way."

That evening Scotland ran out 5-1 winners away to Malta, but it was a wasted journey for Super John McGinn, who didn't get a look in. Same old Scots though – after taking an early lead they were pegged back by a Maltese equaliser only four minutes later and ghastly memories of

Berti Vogts' blunderers from the past were briefly rekindled. But it evolved into a Mediterranean cruise ultimately, with Robert Snodgrass notching a hat-trick.

Another player that Lennon had been interested in, Polish full-back Filip Modelski, got a run-out with the Development squad, as they defeated Motherwell 3-1 at their new home from home, the Oriam facility at Riccarton. Both Murrays who'd featured in the tussle at Turriff played from the start, but it was a double from Ruari Paton that sealed it for the young Hibees, as well as a clincher from Ben Stirling.

Waxing lyrical about his recent return to his hometown was Jordon Forster, clearly relieved at being part of the Hibs family again, albeit only on the sidelines for the time being. His start in the Irn Bru cup-tie had been his first since he played against Rangers in the equivalent competition a year previously, before heading south to Plymouth. Jordon had got on OK with Stubbsy, but never felt that the Scouser had planned to make him an integral part of the set-up, whereas he'd got more positive vibes from the new man in the hot-seat. However he was realistic enough to appreciate that with the current crop in the middle of the park generally performing to a high standard week in week out he was going to have a tough task in making any lasting breakthrough. Jordon had been very fulsome in his praise of his contemporaries and said of Hanlon, "I made my debut beside Paul at Tynecastle and I trained with him before that and for me he's always been a great player. I've got massive respect for him. I think he should probably be involved in the Scotland set-up, which shows you how highly I rate him. Keeping Paul is probably one of the biggest signings the club have made recently. He's a great player who could walk into a lot of big clubs." He also reflected on the conflicting emotions that had led him to seeking pastures new and then eventually deciding to return to Auld Reekie. "When you come through the ranks at a club, you can maybe take it for granted. I'm honest enough to admit I probably did that before I went to Plymouth. But as soon as I went down there, I missed my family, I missed the club, I missed everyone. It was a good thing to get away at such an early age and experience somewhere else because it made me appreciate what I've got at Hibs."

Also keen to kick-start his career after a lengthy period of frustration was Ofir Marciano. He'd had a trying enough time with all the red tape that had delayed his move to Scotland and had been pretty much left out in the cold in Belgium prior to that. Up until leaving his homeland he'd spent his entire career with Ashdod (during which he'd established himself as first choice keeper for his country), but things collapsed in disarray once he'd signed for Mouscron-Perwelz. Although their first choice too from the outset, that soon changed as the team began a long losing streak, week in week out. Nothing to do with Ofir's efforts, but the club panicked and brought in a large number of homegrown players, including a keeper, who was soon getting the nod ahead of him. He'd had offers back in Israel, but felt obliged to try and stick it out in Europe for a bit longer. Happily, he instantly found the positive atmosphere at Easter Road to his liking, in marked contrast to that at his former berth. He revealed however that The Big Man Upstairs had had a hand in his fate.

"I'm very happy that God put me in this situation because if I had stayed in Belgium I might not have come to Hibs. God helps you keep balanced, which is good for life."

He added that he was currently living in Musselburgh. Was God responsible for that as well? He's a strange sense of humour, that omnipotent deity felly, right enough. Surely a penthouse pad in Albion Road overlooking the Holy Ground would have been more in order? All the upheavals had also seen him omitted from the Israeli squad for their opening World Cup qualifier, but he was determined to return to that particular fold as soon as possible. Macedonia and Liechtenstein awaited next and it was surely up to God to get the finger out pronto and have a word in the manager's lug.

"I hope that I will play well for Hibs and get back in the national team for the two games next month," said Ofir. "That is my target."

So the weekend choice was – watch Hibs face Dumbarton, or take the telly option and watch Celtic face dumb Barton, as the jackass known as Joey played in his first Old Firm derby for the huns. In the event, 'Dick' Barton made a right prick of himself, as his wind-up words directed against his opponents and Scott Brown in particular came back to bite his bum and boot him in the balls into the bargain. The cry was "go surrender, go surrender when it's five..." Final score in the lunchtime kick-off? Celtic 5, Rangers 1.

Visiting the other Dumbarton in the flesh was a no-no too, as you have to be pretty sharp off the mark to secure a ticket for an away game these days, especially at a stadium built to accommodate one man and a very small dog. Ah, the good old days, when you could just breeze along before kick-off and pay at the gate. The waves of nostalgia were washing over me, as I recalled a visit to Celtic Park with three Hibbie acquaintances, many moons ago. This was when the old Parkhead was falling apart brick by brick and as a result the capacity had been drastically reduced. So there still should have been room to house those wishing to view in person, but of course it helped if you'd purchased tickets in advance. Naturally, our quartet was far too disorganised for that and optimistically intended to just fork out on arrival.

We were imbibing in the Gordons' pub near Central Station where a couple of local worthies were making doubtful noises about such a course of action. Our Hibs scarves had attracted a degree of attention when we'd entered; you sensed a subtle change in the atmosphere right away. Like a small herd of wildebeest grouped together on the open savannah, just as the hungry lions on the horizon started to sniff out their presence, we began to wonder if this was an entirely *safe* environment. Negotiating the alien Glasgow hostelry terrain was always a tricky business for interlopers – were the natives hostile, or not??

However, all seemed reasonably OK, a neutral enough reaction overall, in a pub where we appeared to be the only ones sporting football colours. Then one of the worthies who'd been making pessimistic sounds about our chances of gaining admittance to the match, sidled up a bit closer. He had the unmistakable air of a traditional West of Scotland chancer / conman about him, I couldn't help noticing.

"Are youse interested in buying Stand seats?" he whispered in my ear.

Or at least that's what I *thought* he'd said. There was a hell of a racket all around so I got him to run it past me again, a bit louder. Mmm, tickets for the Stand, eh? It might be easier to purchase now after all, rather than face a possible disappointment on being refused entry if the stadium did fill up, I thought. Of course there was always the chance that they'd be forgeries, but surely there was no harm in taking a look? The faces of my compatriots had remained impassive when they'd heard his offer repeated, so I tentatively indicated that I might be amenable to some sort of deal.

"How much?" I enquired.

"Goat some at twenty, others mibbe at twenty-five like, totally legit, big man! Nae problems."

Now, bear in mind that this was donkeys' years ago. For such an outrageous price you'd be expecting the Directors' Box at the very least, or possibly the full complimentary hospitality package with half-time drinks thrown in. I was about to demur, when, sensing my hesitancy, he sought to reassure me.

"I'll jist go 'n' get them the now, goat them stashed through the back there. Then youse can have a look," he said helpfully. "Jist haud on a minute."

As he temporarily disappeared through the crowd of bodies, I could see my so-called chums regarding me with a collective expression of open-mouthed incredulity.

"What's the matter?" I snapped irritably. "There's no harm in taking a look, is there? Might make it easier to get in, surely."

There was a pregnant pause, before Tadge spoke up.

"How the fuck is it going to make it easier to get into the game, by buying satin sheets?" he demanded.

What?! I gaped at him stupidly.

"Eh? What are you on about? I thought he said he had Stand seats?"

"Naw, you deef daftie, he said he had *satin sheets!*"

Oh, Christ on a bike. At that very moment our new benefactor hove back into view, bearing several large bedroom accoutrements neatly wrapped in cellophane. He gave me an encouraging gap-toothed grin.

"Here you go, big man, straight aff the production line, like! Cheap at the price, man! Tap *kwality!*"

"Uh...no, sorry, mate. Wee communication problem..."

Seldom had the language barrier between two alien cultures led to such a sad misunderstanding.

"Whit? Whit are ye sayin' likes? Are youse no' wantin' them noo??"

"Eh...well..."

I didn't even bother pointing out that I'd never actually said I definitely wanted them in the first place. As it transpired, we had a fucking nightmare getting into the game after all, satin sheets or nae satin sheets, by the way. And then Hibs lost 1-0. Sheet happens...

So to the catchily-named Cheaper Insurance Direct Stadium, to face the team who'd chucked a major spanner in the works of the green machine the previous season. Dumbarton sought to make advantageous use of their notorious pitch, by omitting to water it or cut the grass – pity Ally McCoist was no longer 'on gardening leave' or he might have done it for a couple of steak pies and a Bovril. The surface had undoubtedly made things awkward for Hibs in the past, but there was a steely aspect to the team now, which hopefully would ensure that such tactics would prove little more than a minor hindrance.

The telling moment came just after the half-hour when referee Greg Aitken pointed to the spot as Sons' defender Gregor Buchanan appeared to obstruct Grant Holt in the area.

"I thought it was harsh," mumped home gaffer Steve Aitken (no relation to the man in black, or at least you'd hope not), in sharp contrast to Neil Lennon's appraisal as "a clear penalty. The boy has no chance of winning the ball but he goes right over the top of him."

Jason Cummings then proceeded to go from hero to villain within a matter of minutes. He converted the penalty assuredly enough, but missed two sitters before half-time. The first he struck over the bar after the ball had broken kindly for him in the clear and then he headed a Stevenson cross over too, with the goalmouth yawning in front of him.

Andrew Shinnie voiced a long-held lament by Hibs supporters when he observed that, "You never feel comfortable at 1-0." He added though that Jason had now scored in every game he'd played – "He could maybe have had a couple right after the penalty but it didn't come. We won and that's all that matters."

Indeed, Hibs saw out the second half without any real problems, but it was still a naturally tense closing spell for the visiting fans. Neil wasn't quite so casually accepting of the scorned chances as the Birmingham loanee had been however, remarking that, "Jason is always in the right place, but his finishing can be a bit sloppy. He has been away with Scotland and has come back rusty for some reason. You forget he is still young and he has scored seven goals already but there is a sloppiness about him at times. He needs to be more ruthless although I cannot tell him how to score goals as I wasn't exactly prolific myself."

Shinnie concluded, "It was a bit of a grind, but we knew it was going to be a tough game. The gaffer had been drumming that into us all week. It's a tough place to go, teams have been undone here this season, as we were last season, but we were up for the battle. We are not going to let teams back into games and that was maybe a criticism over the last couple of seasons. It's not going to happen this year."

The afternoon drew to a close with Hibs sitting atop the Championship table with a full fifteen points from five fixtures. That now made them the first Easter Road side in *seventy* years to win their opening quintet of League matches. They'd done it under McCartney and now they'd done it under Lennon. Already the bookies were cutting the odds on them doing it under Harrison and Starr too. With this fab four behind them they were two points ahead of Queen of the South, who had a fine away win against the already struggling St. Mirren and even at this stage the Dumfries dudes looked to have the makings of contenders. Third-placed Raith went down at home to Falkirk and Dunfermline did likewise against Dundee United and hopefully a 'dog eat dog' scenario would continue to be of benefit to the Hibees in the long run.

At the PBS, the jambos continued with their by now well-worn tactics; those that had Scott Brown sarcastically suggesting they'd be better off employed in the swimming pools at the Olympics. Firstly, Tony Watt took a dive that was so completely theatrically over the top the referee booked him, instead of pointing to the penalty spot as had been hoped for. By the start of the second half their visitors, Hamilton, had taken the lead and the result was already looking academic, but unfortunately they had a bit of a Want about them. Shaun Want that is, a teenager making his debut, who made the mistake of breathing out rather too heavily when Sam Nicholson was in the vicinity. Oops-a-daisy! The latter's acting ability as he sprawled to the surface was that worthy of an Oscar that it could have been mistaken for a performance by Jack Nicholson instead. This time The Joker *did* fool the whistler, who chose to award a spot-kick on this occasion and Walker duly converted. Hearts finally ran out 3-1 winners and could well have fancied pipping Celtic for the League title if their ducking and diving antics went on being rewarded in such a fashion.

Back at Easter Road, Neil Lennon revealed that he'd snapped up Neal Eardley on trial. The 27 year-old former Welsh internationalist had been released by Birmingham City and the Hibs manager clearly saw him as a possible stand-in if necessary for David Gray, after deciding not to pursue his interest in Filip Modelski. Eardley had played sixteen times for his country and spent three years at Birmingham, but had been sidelined after persistent injury.

The gaffer was pleased to be awarded 'Championship Manager of the Month' by Ladbrokes for August, whilst Jason scooped the 'Player of the Month' accolade.

"It's nice to get recognition, but it's down to the players," said Neil, coming over all modest. "It's not an award that's at the forefront of your mind, but I will take it anytime because it shows that the team are playing consistently well."

"The manager is keeping on my back to keep me on my toes," remarked Jason, which conjured up a rather peculiar picture of dual acrobatic machinations. "If there's nobody shouting at me I would just muck about," he added candidly, although admitting he attempted to hide on the opposite touchline if he'd buggered up, to keep out of earshot when Neil opted to let rip. A reporter then asked who his boyhood footballing hero had been. Jason said he didn't know, but he liked Van Nistelrooy, mainly because the name appealed to him. Apparently his former coach at Tynecastle had referred to him as such and he was keen to have that reactivated. "Ruud Van Cummings might stick, eh?" he pondered wistfully. "Hopefully it does. I like that!"

As the BBC screened the last part of their ultra-depressing 'Scotland's Game', which focused unblinkingly on the decline of said game over many years north of the border, Celtic rather validated its conclusions by suffering their worst ever defeat in European competition. It had been that long since they'd reached the group stages of the Champions League their fans had forgotten all about the timings of the games. "When are Celtic kicking off against Barcelona?" they asked, only to discover that would be at approximately ten minute intervals throughout the match. The score more commonly associated with Tynecastle Park on January 1st, 1973 was soon flashing up for all the world to see, driving another nail into the coffin of Scottish clubs' credibility in Europe. Yet it was another reminder that out of all the initial contenders, only Hibs could still hold their heads up high with regard to their performances.

Then there came dark mutterings down East Mains way that Neil Lennon was being a right pain in the arse, as a result of him barring mobile phones from the training facility. To deprive a person of a certain age access to their moby is akin to slicing off one of their legs in terms of incapacitating them these days and was unlikely to increase the gaffer's popularity.

"He wants us to be talking to each-other, not sitting on our phones," explained Paul Hanlon.

Well, sitting on your phone is also likely to cause a right pain in your arse, depending how you position it. An exception was made for Jason naturally, as he had to have his hairspray dealer on speed-dial, in case of emergency.

"The gaffer keeps us in check," acknowledged Marvin Bartley. "You see him on the side of the pitch – well, he's worse in training! He demands high standards at all times. I fall short of them sometimes and I hear "Marv! Marv!" It's like being back with my mum."

But the former Bournemouth and Burnley man was quick to emphasise the huge boost that they'd all received from Neil's winning mentality, which had them poised on the verge of a record-breaking run of opening League victories.

"I haven't had a start to a season like this before. I have been in some good dressing rooms before, but here, right now, everyone is delighted. We're all pulling in the same direction, even the boys who aren't playing, we're all in it together. Since May it's been brilliant – everyone is on the green train and it keeps rolling. We need to keep going and grinding out results and that starts all over again against Ayr."

Unfortunately though, the green train to which Marvin rather poetically alluded was to come off the rails after sixty-seven minutes, taking him with it. A red card saw the big man take the long, lonely walk, after apparently lunging at the ball rashly when surrounded by four Ayr players. I say 'apparently' as it was not at all clear from my vantage point – sometimes the Famous Five Stand provides more of a *disadvantage* point – and Neil Lennon certainly thought it was a harsh decision.

"The red card changed the game. But I am not convinced it was a red card. He's gone in low, he might have caught the boy, but there's no real malice in the tackle. There were more cynical things that were going on that went unpunished, so a red card was really harsh, to say the least. It looked pretty innocuous from where I was. It was not two-footed, so I'd like to hear the referee's interpretation."

However, let's not make excuses. Hibs were one up at this stage, against a side who had found it hard going since their promotion from League One, with a solitary win under their belt before this encounter. Even reduced to ten men, the home team should still have had enough in the tank to see this one out. They'd almost taken the lead after only two minutes, when a typically dangerous cross by Sir David Gray (Knight of the Hibernian Realm since May 21st) was met decisively by Holt. The crowd behind the goal all rose to their feet as there seemed no way his powerful header *wouldn't* end up in the back of the net, but goalkeeper Fleming made an exceptional save to divert it over the bar. The big green Hulk up front would be denied again later by the woodwork, but on this afternoon there would be precious few cross-balls equal to Gray's opening effort, to trouble the Ayr defence. Buoyed up by that early chance, Hibs looked lively enough for the first ten or fifteen minutes, during which it seemed likely that the floodgates might swing open at any moment, but it wasn't to be. The more the first half unfolded the more bogged down they became. There was a sense of understandable frustration rippling around the stands as they went in level at the interval.

The picture grew instantly brighter at the start of the second period however, as the talisman in the number 35 shirt suddenly made his presence felt. I had no sooner wondered aloud if Jason was actually still on the park when out of nothing he swept a terrific curling ball past Fleming from around thirty yards. As had already been demonstrated, it was going to take something special to beat the Ayr keeper and this undoubtedly fell into that category. The striker's left peg seldom lets him down, as his highly impressive scoring record showed, but a stabbing strike towards goal some time later would have had more chance of success if his right peg had been utilised instead. As it was, Fleming managed to block that effort. Then came the main turning point of the game as Marvin received his marching orders and the visitors took advantage within eight minutes. However, this was not down to the extra man, but a plain error, pure and simple. Marciano and Hanlon were equally culpable as communication broke down completely, with the latter giving away a needless corner. Ofir should still have cleared the danger and booted it into the Upper West Stand if nothing else; but instead a few heated words were exchanged between the pair before Gilmour lined up to take the kick. His effort was met squarely by the head of Balatoni and all of a sudden Ayr United were right back in it as the ball flew into the net. It was Gilmour himself who nodded in a second only five minutes later, an outcome that had seemed scarcely possible after Jason's sensational swerver. Hibs might have huffed and puffed a bit over the piece but they were still streets ahead in terms of possession and chances (fourteen shots, eight of which were on target). An old story sadly and it could have been even worse too. Another cross from the visitors' right sneaked across the goalmouth in the dying minutes and we might have been reliving the Queen of the South in the League Cup experience all over again, as the defence went to sleep. (Indeed, the Dumfries men were the main beneficiaries, as their win over Raith Rovers saw them leapfrog Hibs to claim top spot in the table.) Neil made full use of his substitutes – Graham, Boyle and Keatings – but to little effect in the end.

"We were in total control," lamented the gaffer afterwards. "What annoys me is that we conceded from a set play. That should not happen, we should be better than that. We've had fifty corners against us this season and defended them pretty well, so I am annoyed – really annoyed."

We believe you Neil, don't worry. When you feel the need to employ the word 'annoyed' three times in four sentences, we kind of get the picture. Sometimes it would be quicker if you just told us what *didn't* annoy you instead.

For his part, a delighted (although you'd never guess that from his glum-looking coupon) Ayr boss Ian McCall observed, "Fleming had an unbelievable save after two minutes which kept us in it and then they scored a wonder goal. We took our chances and for us to come here and win is just fantastic."

Which just about summed it up. Ayr had two clear chances and took both; Hibs had an absolute minimum of ten and took one. Suddenly, the following weekend's fixture against the new Championship leaders had the unmistakable look of a six-pointer about it.

"It's a different test for us now," said Paul Hanlon. "We have not experienced defeat in the League this season and that will test our character going into next week. But we have the squad for that and we'll pick ourselves up and be good to go next week. Queen of the South is always a tough one. Ever since we were relegated that has never been an easy game for us, but it's one to look forward to and shaping up to be a big game. We'll be back and full of confidence and looking to get the win."

Well, we all knew it was highly unlikely that Hibs' early winning streak would continue indefinitely, but the standard set by Rangers the previous season and the one set by Hearts the one before that had recently looked eminently achievable. Now the green train had somehow got sidetracked and hit the buffers en route. Hopefully it was merely a footballing equivalent of leaves on the line but the points were down and few would have imagined that the Championship new boys would be the ones doing the derailing.

But if the Hibernian railway network was temporarily malfunctioning, there was nothing wrong with the machinery at the rumour-mill, which appeared to be in danger of overheating. The latest one doing the rounds was the (allegedly) *real* reason why Stubbsy had purchased a second-class one-way off-peak single to Rotherham and scarpered from Leith faster than Jason Cummings heading for a half-price hairspray sale. The scurrilous allegations being bandied about in whispers across the Hibee Nation were to the effect that Stubbsy had had his hand in the Kitty, so to speak. And not just his hand either, some hinted darkly. No wonder he looked like the cat who'd got the cream, they muttered, the fur was fairly flying when Mrs Stubbsy got wind of it. A Pussy Riot was surely in the offing. The gossips were further galvanised by the fact that the fab-looking physio had also done a runner from Easter Road and hadn't been seen since, despite the fact that Iron Rod kept leaving a saucer of milk on the doorstep once he'd locked up every night, just in case she returned. I must admit there were times during last season during less than enthralling matches when I half-hoped some Hibs player *would* get injured, just for the pleasure of seeing the lovely Kitty purring onto the park like a sleek well-oiled machine of feline fabulousness.

Meanwhile, up in Perth, Robbie Neilson was in hot water (again). This was because he had the opportunity of taking an early bath when the referee at St. Johnstone v Hearts decided to send him packing. You'd have thought he'd had his fill of getting belted on the bahookey by the Blazers throughout the previous campaign, for persistently having a pop at the officials and then having to explain himself before the headmaster time and time again. So what was Robbie's crime this time, you ask. 'Clapping in a Sarcastic Manner', that's what. Normally it wouldn't have been a big deal, but unfortunately it occurred during a scheduled minute's applause for a Hearts fan who'd recently died – of boredom. He'd keeled over after reading Craig Levein's column in the

Hearts programme, entitled 'Why A Ten-Man Defence is the Best Way Forward' and couldn't be revived.

There was more sarcasm getting dished out in the east end of Glasgow, as Celtic Chief Executive Peter Lawwell stood up before a meeting of the club's shareholders and said with a straight face, "Fundamentally, Celtic is a Champions League club." This, hot on the heels of the most comprehensive European defeat in their history, surely he *was* being sarcastic –wasn't he?? Champions League, you're havin' a laugh...

Across town, Warby clearly had had enough of Joey Barton's antics and sought comfort by hitting the drink. As the ridiculous saga dragged on, with the eejit in question being barred from Ibrox for twenty-one days, the issue of what could be voiced openly and what couldn't was up for debate.

"The environment we create here for the players and staff is about giving respectful opinion," warbled Warby. "I never have a problem with a player knocking on my door to talk about a session."

Surely he wouldn't have dared to come out with an invitation like that, if Goram and Gascoigne had still been in the offing? He'd have been missing from Ibrox for three weeks himself if he'd gone out on the piss with that pair.

By the middle of the penultimate week of the month, Neil Lennon's assessment of the red card issued to Marvin Bartley had been wholly vindicated. Marv had been due to face a judicial panel at Hampden on the Thursday, but that was deemed unnecessary, after the SFA Compliance Officer viewed the evidence supplied by Hibs a day earlier and ruled that the referee had been in the wrong. So the red was downgraded to a yellow, freeing the big stopper up for the tricky trip to Dumfries, which was a relief at least. The gaffer was still not happy though, quite rightly so and was not slow in making his views known.

"I'm glad they have seen sense. We felt at the time that it was not a red card, that there were worse tackles in the game than Marvin's. Obviously we're happy to have Marvin available at the weekend, but there is a sense of injustice as the red card had a big influence on the game. We lost an important player and went down to ten men at a stage in the game when we were really on top. We were also looking to break the club record for the number of League games won at the start of the season, so while we are pleased that the red card has been rescinded, there is still a sense of annoyance that the decision cost us a point or all three."

Over in Gorgie there was excitement aplenty as Hearts opened their official museum to the public, with the top exhibit being a stuffed puffin. No, really. It had been presented to the somewhat bemused jambos by officials of IBV from Iceland when the teams met in the UEFA Cup back in 2000. Also on display was a stuffed Kenny Garland, who was even more immobile than the puffin when he played in goal on January 1st, 1973. Other items for eager fans to view included a dartboard with Chris Robinson's face embossed on it, Graham Rix's handwritten guidebook for grooming under-age girls, Vladimir Romanov's brain suspended in a jar of formaldehyde, Wallace Mercer's magic stretchy underpants and a selection of suicide notes penned by scarf-twirlers after Sir Albert Kidd's heroics led them to losing the League on the last day of 1985 / 86 season.

Particularly looking forward to the QoS game was Fraser Fyvie, one of Hibs' few stand-out performers in the disappointment against Ayr. Voted 'Man of the Match', it had only been Fraser's fourth start due to his persistent knee injury problems, which had disrupted his progress the previous season too. But hopefully he was now finally on the mend.

"The injury's all done, all fine now," he said. "It's great being back and getting a wee run in the team. I'm a really bad spectator. I'm moany when I'm on the pitch – but I'm a lot worse when I'm in the physio's room!"

Bet he wouldn't have said that if Kitty had still been there, running her claws all over him.

"It's tough being out, especially when there's a new manager coming in," he added. "But I've had four games, so I feel like I've put it all behind me now."

Queens had been comprehensively turned over in the League Cup quarter-final, going down 5-0 at Ibrox, but, "I wouldn't read too much into Tuesday," he cautioned. "That was a cup game and they can be different to the League. Rangers romped this League last season and going there can be tough."

He revealed that he was a fan of Stephen Dobbie and there was no doubt that the former Hibee was on fire, Queens' equivalent to Jason Cummings effectively, with nine goals to his name so far.

"There are similarities with what Dobbie has brought to Queens and what Grant Holt has brought to us. They're both experienced lads who have played at the highest level, so they both bring a lot of qualities to their teams, that ability and know-how."

Unfortunately, Grant's contribution had been nowhere near his rival's in pure scoring terms, with a measly single goal to his credit from the victory over Morton. But he already looked a good deal fitter than he had at the outset and he was starting to contribute a lot more regarding holding the ball up and providing service for the effervescent Jason.

However, Neil chose to dispense with his services altogether for the visit to Palmerston Park, opting to start with a front three of Boyle, Graham and Cummings. There was little to write home about in a stuffy first half, on a day of dreich conditions for both sides. Hibs also had to contend with a similar disadvantage to the previous week, as Lewis Stevenson received a second yellow card at the start of the second half and that was the visitors down to ten men even earlier than they had been against Ayr United. To their overall credit though, it didn't seem to knock them off-kilter to the extent that Marvin Bartley's dismissal had apparently done. Lennon adjudged the decision to be a harsh one and even former jambo Jamie Hamill (victim of the initial challenge which had earned Lewis his first yellow) was in agreement there. So Hibs seemed to cope with that fairly well, but unfortunately the old failings were well to the fore too; namely the failure to take their chances. They had a dozen corners and yet failed to overly trouble Queens' goalkeeper Robinson with any of them.

"I don't know how many we had in the second half that we should have scored from or made more of," lamented Lennon. "We do work on set-plays, believe it or not. So I need to find a remedy to put teams away."

Captain David Gray did his best with a shot from distance which was tipped just over the bar and Hibs' best player on the day, Super John McGinn, did likewise and put in an industrious shift in the middle of the park. But ultimately they were let down by the profligacy of their front men. As has been noted many times before, the over-reliance on Jason becomes even more apparent on days when it doesn't really click for him, as was the case here.

"Jason is a good goalscorer," emphasised his gaffer, "but when he is not scoring he doesn't bring much else to the team at the moment. We need to be better. We are dominating games, we are creating chances and the majority of them seem to fall for Jason. We need to look at some of the others and ask 'where are you, why are they all falling for him?' We can't keep relying on Jason."

Hibs certainly had the bulk of the play in the second half but the home team also had their moments, none more so than right at the death when Dale Hilson came within a whisker of nicking all three points. Marciano pulled off a good instinctive save to keep him out, while admitting that he'd found the conditions hard going throughout.

"It wasn't easy. It was a struggle, but, as a footballer, you have to adapt to any conditions. It shouldn't affect your performance. Here in the United Kingdom it's something you have to accept."

Ofir had also made a fine block to deny the same player as early as the second minute and could take credit for keeping the top team in the Championship out over the ninety minutes.

It was clearly no disgrace in view of their opponents' exalted position for Hibs to emerge with a draw, particularly in light of the underfoot conditions, but there was no doubt that the early momentum which had produced five straight wins had been somewhat arrested. They remained in second spot, but ominously Falkirk had now jumped past Raith Rovers on goal difference to occupy third, while Dundee United also picked up full points against Morton. Hibs had been fortunate really that those who had at the outset looked likely to be their main challengers had got off to very poor starts, but already their points advantage had been significantly cut. Alas, a mere point garnered from a possible six over the two most recent outings had seen to that, causing Mickey Weir to observe in his Evening News column, " I think every Hibs fan would have expected more than one point from our last two games." Mickey also expressed his concern about the problems up front – "I can see why the manager has taken a pop at the strikers" – and noted that the pressure was now on, with high stakes games against Dundee United and Raith Rovers just up ahead.

As the month drew to a close, it was revealed that Welsh full-back Neal Eardley had put pen to paper, on a short deal that would tie him to Hibs until January. He'd played three times for the Development Squad and Lennon had clearly seen enough to deem him worth of Sir David Gray stand-in status. As for the latter, he was furnished with further acclaim over his heroics on May 21st, as *that* goal was voted the 'Sporting Moment of the Year' at the Team Scotland Scottish Sports Awards. Sporting Moment of the *Century*, I think they mean. A line was finally drawn under the Hampden pitch hoo-hah too, with the SFA announcing that a judicial panel had thrown out notices of complaint over the event and that was Hibs effectively off the hook. About bloody time too, talk about a storm in a teacup. The panel dismissed it as 'irrelevant', which most normal people could have told them was the case, four months ago. Hibs said that the club had paid for the damage caused to the pitch and the posts – they should have stuck the polis with it, as if they'd been doing their job properly no-one would have got onto the pitch in the first place.

Meanwhile, the tabloids were having a field day with short-lived England manager Sam Allardyce's fall from grace. 'FIRED MAN SAM' offered The Sun's front page, after the bulldog-faced blusterer got the heave-ho, although that was arguably usurped by The Metro's headline writer, who opted for 'THREE LIONS IN THE DIRT'. You'd have thought by this time, in the wake of the 'fake Sheikh' stings and numerous similar stitch-ups, that even the dimmest mark would smell a rat when finding himself in a posh hotel somewhere, surrounded by people he hardly knows offering him cash-stuffed brown envelopes at the drop of a hat. Then comes the familiar self-pitying cry of "Entrapment!" when the shit hits the fan. We shouldn't feel sorry for slippery Sammy though. With a unique one hundred per-cent record on results as his country's gaffer and now a proven propensity for blind greed and stupidity, he has surely shown that he is eminently qualified for another top job in football. Yes, that's right – running FIFA. Sepp's bound to give him a glowing reference, just for starters.

4.

OCTOBER: SUNSTROKE ON LEITH

First, an open letter to the Chief:-

Dear God,

So you think you're the big man, eh? While I am aware that you are indeed The Big Man (Upstairs) so to speak, it ill behoves you, the Great Jehovah, to show off your powers quite as shamelessly as you did on this day, Sunday, October 2ⁿᵈ, the Year of Our Lord (that means YOU, Lord), 2016. In other words, while I'm worth my room on this Earth would you kindly desist in putting sunshine on Leith to the extent that you chose to do so here? Totally unnecessary behaviour, particularly for this time of year. It's OCTOBER, you big beardy radge! In Scotland that's practically winter-time. Yet the heat was such that after being baked alive in the Famous Five Stand for an hour and three-quarters, the sweat pissed out of me to such an extent that several of my tattoos slid off altogether. Even the enamel on my teeth got sunburned. Not big or clever, mate. So leave it out in future, eh?

Thanking you kindly,

Yours respectfully, etc., etc.

Well, I might have been boiling halfway to hothouse hell behind the goals, but it's a fair assumption that Neil Lennon was boiling on the touchline too and not just as a result of the solar fire frazzling his freckles from above either. Neil's old bug-a-boo had come back to bug him again, as Hibs lost another avoidable goal to a set-piece. Seemingly cruising against Dundee United at half-time through a lovely goal from Keatings (aided ably by Shinnie), they somehow contrived to throw it away in the second half. Excuse me, I think I've seen this one before…

Truly, it appeared that the deja-vu experience at Easter Road was repeating itself again in rather depressing fashion. It's got to the stage now where even when they're sitting on a one-goal lead, I fully expect them to drop at least two points and quite possibly three before the day is out. Yet there was much to admire about Hibs' play overall, with the gaffer forced into some measure of change due to Lewis Stevenson's absence through suspension. Jordon Forster came on to bolster the backline and Neil opted for the old guard of Cummings and Keatings up front, dispensing with the new boys for now (although Graham would come on as a late sub.) Keatings had already served notice of intent with a wonderful long-range free-kick which curled *just* the wrong side of the post, before getting on the scoresheet two minutes before the interval. Andrew Shinnie held the ball up well before slipping a peach of a pass through to James, whose raking left-footer gave Cammy Bell no chance of saving it. Their opponents had been decimated by injury and were clearly aiming for a 'damage limitation' exercise, contributing a measly *one* shot on target throughout the entire first half. Thus, although the lead was a narrow one, it *should* have been enough, but it's the Hibees we're talking about here… We all know that a two-goal cushion is the absolute minimum required, for you to have any real confidence of them grinding out all three points.

Inevitably, the Tangerine troops did rally somewhat in the second half and kept possession well in stages, but they were hardly an impressive looking outfit overall. Neil threw on newbie Neal Eardley to replace

David Gray, as the latter picked up a nasty knock in the first period. United weren't shy in dishing out some niggly fouls which referee Craig Thomson treated with utmost leniency; but the Gray incident occurred when play should have stopped altogether. On a very rare foray upfield, United players had been caught offside and, despite being well-aware of this, carried on, which led to the painful collision. Lennon had earmarked Eardley as a replacement for Sir David if the need should arise, but he probably didn't envisage giving him a run-out quite so soon. He seemed to slot in quite smoothly and had the confidence to have an early pop at goal himself. That followed a great chance which Jason did well to generate, for once managing to break free from the attentions of the giant Edjenguele at the centre of the visitors' defence. He turned quickly in a tight space, but his shot although well-angled scraped over the bar. However, Hibs also had a scare from a United corner when Van Der Velden went very close and might well have scored, if not for the slightest of deflections. They failed to heed the warning from that effort though and it was little surprise really when the big defender who'd given Jason a torrid time of it throughout rose above everyone to thunder another Scott Fraser corner into the net past Marciano. Hibs regrouped and largely dominated the remainder of the game with Paul Hanlon wasting one great chance when he pulled his shot just wide of the target. As so often in the past, the inability to put away gilt-edged opportunities would be the undoing of the Hibees. They had a further couple of scares at the other end though and it was a nervier finish than it might have been. An almighty stramash in the visitors' goalmouth ensued in the three and a half minutes of time added on, with everyone and their granny seemingly hell-bent on getting an outstretched toe to prod the ball into the net. But somehow United got enough bodies in the way to keep it out. So it ended 1-1 and the Arabs would be far happier with the draw than the hosts.

A frustrating afternoon – again – tempered with the realisation that due to the way the other results went, Hibs at least had not lost any further ground. But a win would have propelled them back into top spot; as it was they'd have to settle for second place to Queen of the South for the time being.

"We should be doing better," stated the gaffer bluntly. "We want to get out of this division and players have to deal with the opposition. It's not a major problem at the minute. Overall we are playing well enough, but I think our game management has to be better. We were totally comfortable. Paul Hanlon had a great chance and we would have deserved it."

Neil was rightly displeased at the unnecessary injury to his captain, due to the tardiness of the officials, pointing out that if the linesman had put his flag up to signal offside earlier, the play would have already stopped. Thomson should have taken firmer action too, at the time.

John McGinn, one of the better performers on the day, rued the fact that, "We did have chances. Not as many as we would have liked and with the players we have we have to be creating more, scoring more. We are not doing that at the minute but it shouldn't take one set-piece to mean we don't take the three points. We are all disappointed."

Viewed dispassionately, Neil was right to rationalise that, "It's not a problem at the minute." The last three words there being the operative ones, as that might not be the case if the same old failings persisted, or indeed if the other results hadn't come up quite so kindly for Hibs as they'd done over this particular weekend. What was worrying though was the way the momentum had undoubtedly faltered, after the fantastic run from Brondby away through to Dumbarton away (League Cup flop excepted.) No-one needed reminding how difficult it could be to get the green train rolling along the right tracks again after such a blip, with memories of Morton at home the previous season still in mind. That was the moment the League was effectively lost and conceded to the huns. You only had to look at the manner in which the latter had generally steamrollered their way to ultimate victory, demolishing opponents as they went, in much the same style as the jambos had done the season before. From a very early stage, both had looked like eventual champions, much as we might have wished otherwise. Hibs had been very good in parts already during the current campaign – but they were certainly not at that level – yet.

In a bid to rehydrate my body after its Famous Five Stand fry-up, I hastened along to the Four-in-Hand post-match, for a refreshing half-dozen or so pints of cider. Although the ostensible reason was to stage a sales 'n' signing session for 'Moonshine on Leith', my previous book. Flogging my Hibernian-related witterings around the local hostelries had generally been quite a fun experience and I'd met some interesting characters along the way. (Not to mention international ones. When punting my first Hibs book, 'Growing Up in Green' in the same venue, the first two buyers were German and third was Swedish. So hi to Markkus, Dieter and Kent if you happen to be reading this.) The most lucrative day of sales for that volume was unsurprisingly the glorious day Hibs beat Rangers 4-0, to such an extent that a mini-queue formed. I felt like J.K. Rowling for a moment. Although by the time Kano was calling last orders it was more a case of 'jakey rolling'... However, the guy at the front was thinking long and hard about what sort of dedication he wanted scrawled on the title page, along with my priceless signature. I offered up a few Hibs-related suggestions as the queue continued to lengthen and mutterings of "Hurry up, ya radge!" became increasingly audible. Then a light-bulb suddenly switched on in his brain.

"I've got it!" he said, beaming ecstatically, as inspiration had clearly struck like a bolt from the green. "Can you just write 'FUCK THE HUNS' on it?"

"With the greatest of pleasure," I replied, proceeding to do that very thing.

It certainly trumped the ordeal of doing signings for my first book, 'Carspotting: The Real Adventures of Irvine Welsh', which was published by Black & White. They had organised a signing session in Waterstone's at Ocean Terminal and my hangover that morning felt terminal into the bargain. I really wasn't looking forward to what was up ahead. Put it down to imminent stage-fright. Matters weren't improved when I entered the shopping centre to find enormous blown-up posters plastered all over the windows, most of which featured Irvine, myself and sundry other shady characters in scenes of drunken degradation and chemical imbalance from about thirty years before. Unfortunately though, it appeared that I was still clearly identifiable, even after all that time. Two teenage girls had glanced at the window and then glanced quickly at me, as I was also gawping in some horror at the images thereon. Mind you, these had been accessed from original photographs which I'd furnished the publishers with in the first place, so I really only had myself to blame.

"THAT'S YOU! YOUSE ARE THE GUY IN THE WINDAE THERE!" yelled one of them in an accusatory sort of tone.

"WHIT ARE YOUSE DAEIN' IN THE WINDAE, PAL?" demanded her pal suspiciously, looking me up and down critically.

"...Not me. My twin brother..." I lied wearily, feeling suddenly even more hungover, if such a thing was possible.

Soon I was sitting inside the shop, behind a long table piled high with books, grimly awaiting thousands of my fans to come streaming through the doors at any moment. Within half-an-hour, there must have been about a dozen of them there already. Unfortunately, I recognised two right away.

"Oh for fuck's sake," I muttered under my breath.

"Is there a problem?" asked the lovely young lady from Waterstone's staff, who had apparently drawn the short straw and had been tasked with looking after me for the duration.

She'd been most attentive from the start, offering me a choice of tea, coffee or bottled water.

"No thanks – I've brought my own," I'd said, producing my customised plastic container somewhat shakily. Of course, it was full of a mixture of vodka and lemonade, but I saw no reason to enlighten her of that fact. Now she was concernedly inquiring if there was some sort of a problem. I took a dirty great slurp out of the bottle to steady my nerves.

"Well...there might be. You see these two women about halfway down the queue there – quite tall, one blonde, the other brunette?"

"Uh-huh?"

"They're both in my book," I admitted. "But they don't know that – yet."

"Oh...that'll be a nice surprise for them then!" she exclaimed brightly.

"Oh no it won't."

As they drew closer, I was frantically trying to recall just how cruelly I'd slagged them off or taken the piss in print. I'd changed their names, naturally, but there was absolutely no doubt at all that they'd *instantly* recognise their unflattering depictions therein. Soon they were up close and personal, looking even fiercer than I'd remembered, from all those years ago.

"Is there anyone you wrote about that we know?" I heard myself being asked.

Oh sweet creeping Jesus.

"Well, there's some...er, *composite* characters as it were...*loosely* based on real people from way back," I babbled unconvincingly, "and I *do* stress only *very* loosely based on..."

So they duly bought a copy each and departed, by which point my anxiety levels were soaring through the roof. I gulped the voddy down like a man dying of thirst in the desert. There was still half-an-hour of signing time to go and there was every chance they'd adjourn to the nearest pub and start idly flicking through the pages. If they came across the chapter featuring themselves then that was me well fucked, I thought resignedly. I could visualise them storming back into Waterstone's and proceeding to kicked seven shades of shite out of me whilst my adoring public looked on in mute horror. Maybe make for some great publicity for sure – visions of 'HUNGOVER AUTHOR BEATEN TO DEATH IN BOOKSHOP' type tabloid headlines the following morning, but that was of little consolation. As it transpired though, the rest of the session passed off uneventfully and I've managed to avoid them ever since. So compared to that, selling and signing Hibs books in the high spots of Leith was a pleasurable breeze, believe me.

One player more pleased than most to have come through the United game unscathed was Jordon Forster, making his first start for the Hibees since the tail-end of season 2014 / 15. Of course in the intervening period he'd had his seaside sabbatical with the Plymouth brethren as well as having to contend with all his various physical ailments.

"Having come on last week when Lewis was sent off I felt I'd be starting against United," said the big defender, "but it was obviously the manager's call. I just trained hard through the week, doing the same things I do every week but, perhaps, with a few extra per cent thinking I'd be playing. I'd signed my new contract knowing there were good defenders here, guys who had played a lot together last year, so it was going to be tough to get a game. I was under no illusions I'd be playing every week."

It was good to see Jordon back to where he really belonged and he seemed realistic regarding his prospects about making a more permanent breakthrough in the first team, while not shirking an opinion on recent travails.

"I think you can look at outside factors in the draw with Queens," he reasoned. "Lewis being sent off, the artificial pitch, the horrible weather and it would be fair to say a point was not the worst in the world. But we should have beaten United. I thought we completely dominated in the first half but we let them back in the game. We should be beating teams 3-0 and putting nails in coffins, especially at home. We can't hide the fact that we should have won the game, so it's depressing for everyone."

There was disappointment also on the Wednesday night, in the much-hyped Champions League for the ladies' clash at Easter Road, the girls in green and white going down 6-0 to Bayern Munich. But there was no disgrace in that, against full-time professional opponents. Manager Chris Roberts praised a valiant effort from his team, pointing out that their adversaries were the female equivalent of Barcelona, a team of World and European Cup winners and Olympic gold medallists. The lower tier of the West Stand was healthily filled out, with both sides receiving a good backing; there hadn't been that many Germans at Easter Road since the Bayern big boys' team played Raith Rovers there a couple of decades ago in European competition.

Over at the PBS, Robbie Neilson was boasting about his team of assembled international 'stars'. The glum-faced Gorgie gaffer mumbled monosyllabically that, "We have a Moroccan internationalist, a Cameroonian internationalist, a Scottish internationalist, we have Zanatta and Godinho away with the Canada Under-20s and Perry

Kitchen in the American squad." Meanwhile, the American squad were in the kitchen. Have you see the size of these guys? Christian Nade looked positively anorexic in comparison. But I don't know why Robbie thinks this is so admirable – after all, Hearts have always been a team with strong, proud Lithuanian roots and surely that was in danger of being compromised?

Vlad the Mad must be birling in his grave. (Not that he's actually dead yet, but the Chechen bodyguards dug the grave anyway, just in case he couldn't keep up the protection payments.) When he fled the PBS without a bolt to his name and leaving behind a trail of debts that would have made even Craig Whyte blush, Vlad said that he'd be quite happy to go back to driving a taxi if that's what it took to survive. Christ, can you imagine getting into the back of that cab after a night on the piss and falling asleep? You wake up a day later in a Kaunas back-street with 'Ten Million Euros' flashing up on the meter and masked thugs from Chechnya holding guns to your head, persuading you to cough up sharpish. I must admit though that the Lithuanian loony (or Russian radge – no-one ever seemed entirely sure which) was great entertainment value when he was steering the maroon submarine into ever choppier waters. Anyone who could regularly get away with calling the Blazers 'a bunch of monkeys' while going ape is OK with me, although clearly out of his tree.

In a week when Celtic unveiled a thirteen year-old, Karamoko Dembele, in their Development Squad, Neil Lennon displayed that he too was not shy of giving precocious talent a chance, as Yrik Galantes took the field for the Hibs' wee team. Mind you, in comparison he was a positively ancient fifteen.

"We want him to develop with the rest of them," said Neil. "I'm not saying he's an outstanding talent, but he's got something because the guys think he's good enough to make an impact. I worry about going younger and younger (as Adam Johnson said to the judge). I think eighteen is the cut-off point in terms of playing for the first team, unless they're really exceptional. Dembele may be – but it's far too early to judge."

There was maybe some justification for the Hibs' gaffer's approach to emerging youth, as he'd been in the Celtic hot-seat when Dizzy Izzy had hightailed it to the bright lights of London with the cry of "Feruz a grand old team to play for" still ringing in his lugs, at the tender age of sixteen. Neil had been of the strong opinion that young Islam had been ill-advised, which was certainly borne out by subsequent events. Yo-yo-ing around various lonely soccer outposts on loan-deals after failing to cut the mustard at Stamford Bridge and developing a reputation for being 'difficult', Izzy had wound up at Easter Road under Stubbsy. "Izzy here to stay, though?" was the question on everyone's lips. Er, no. He eventually disappeared altogether in Turkey after doing an over-night runner from a training camp while with his latest short-lived Kazakh employers.

So Lennon's reticence in pushing youngsters too far too soon was understandable, although I find myself getting irritated when managers and pundits make excuses for the foibles of 'young' players often in their early twenties, or insinuating that they are not ready to step up to the plate at such a callow age. Peter Cormack and Jimmy O'Rourke were already playing for the Hibs *first* team aged sixteen, don't forget! (The latter making his debut against Utrecht in the Fairs Cup and later celebrating its tenth anniversary in the most spectacular style, scoring the winning goal against Celtic in the 1972 League Cup final.) But they don't make 'em like Peter and Jimmy any more, more's the pity. File under 'really exceptional', as referenced by Lennon.

Whatever, Neil didn't see fit to throw any emerging whizz-kids into the fray against St. Mirren, for the Irn Bru Cup-tie on October 8th. Conversely, he opted for pretty much a full first team, Alex Harris being the sole non-regular amongst them. His selection was certainly worthwhile, as he put his side one up eight minutes before the interval, but a stunning free-kick from Stevie Mallan brought the Buddies right back into it, four minutes later. Nothing wrong with his strike, but plenty wrong with the award in the first place, which looked highly questionable.

However, this was grim fare throughout, with plenty 'amateur' defending in the manager's view, as well as the usual haphazard and wasteful finishing at the other end. Keatings and Forster were both guilty of missing cast-iron chances, but Dylan McGeouch was unlucky to see a rocket shot crash off the post. It looked like petering out in a 1-1 stalemate with extra-time to follow, until the second dodgy decision gave the Saints a scarcely merited victory near the end. Substitute Clarkson had been fortunate enough to view a deflected effort rolling towards the net with Lawrence Shankland right behind it, seemingly just to make sure. That was enough for the linesman to flag for offside, before being over-ruled by the whistler, who adjudged the player had not in fact touched the ball.

To be honest, I really wasn't too bothered with the outcome of this, a Mickey Mouse competition which the fans have little appetite for. Only just over 4,000 turned up, which speaks volumes really. More so than ever before, Hibs need to one hundred per cent concentrate on the League (and the Big Cup too, of course, when that rolls around again.) But to me it seems ridiculous to risk injuries to valuable players in tournaments like this which just serve to clutter up the fixture list unnecessarily. If they'd got through this tie, Hibs may have had another three games ahead of them and with the nonsensical introduction of teams from Wales and Northern Ireland there was no telling where they might have ended up! (I wonder how Alloa Athletic felt about trying to balance their books, being obliged to make a marathon trip to the back-end of Wales, to participate in a match which drew less than 600 spectators?) Of the other ties played the same day, two attracted similar attendances and Dunfermline failed to hit the 2,000 mark against Queen's Park.

Still, there was no hiding from the fact that this was another deeply disappointing performance from Hibs. The status of the tournament may be inconsequential, but that doesn't let the players off the hook in any way. The gaffer was certainly far from happy, saying, "We're losing to St. Mirren at home and that shouldn't be happening. I think some of them are hiding at the minute. It's definitely a psychological thing, it's not a physical thing. In the main I am not getting what I want from the players so that's something I need to address. It's senior players as well with no thought about what they're doing. Maybe I need to look at myself and ask what I'm doing wrong but we train them as well as we can."

Subconsciously sounding like a circus ringmaster there, maybe Neil needs to let up a bit on the overly shouty aggressive approach to matters. While some players like Jason Cummings had been honest enough to admit that they *needed* to be yelled at from time to time, it's debatable whether that is really effective overall. Every manager has his own style of course, but we shouldn't overlook the fact that Hibs' two best managers since bouncing back from the lower division last time, Tony Mowbray and Alan Stubbs, were hardly renowned ranters and ravers.

Hibs were without the services of Super John McGinn for the latest let-down, as he was away on Scotland duty – which turned out to be a super waste of time as he didn't even get a look-in against Lithuania. Didn't even get as far as the bench! Manager Gordon Strachan's face was starting to resemble that of foul-mouthed failed hun chef Gordon Ramsay (pre Botox) and it was little wonder the deep lines and furrows were becoming ever more pronounced with every set-back on the international front. There can be few surer ways of accelerating the ageing process than to take up a job managing the national side.

However, he claimed optimistically that the showing in the second half was, "The best we have played in a long time," which seemed to indicate that his brain was ageing similarly, right into the early onset dementia time-zone, if he really believed that to be the case. Not that it would be much of an accolade anyway, even if it was true, given Scotland's form of late. They lost a goal at home to a country ranked 117th in the world and but for a last-gasp equaliser from James McArthur could already have waved goodbye to any hopes of making the World Cup finals in 2018. John McGinn would almost certainly have performed better than most of the disjointed individuals in blue did that night, had he been given the chance.

However, the Hibs man did make an appearance for his country four days later, as he came on in the seventy-sixth minute to replace former Hibee Steven Fletcher. By that time it was far too late as Scotland crashed to a woeful 3-0 defeat away to Slovakia. Still, John made an impression almost immediately, taking control of the ball in the middle of the park and finding Leigh Griffiths with a slick pass to set up a half-chance. Leigh had also come on as a substitute, some twelve minutes earlier along with Ikechi Anya and had looked more effective in the time allotted to him than his team-mates all put together had done, in the preceding hour. Those three players might well have made a significant difference if they'd been on from the start, which reflected very poorly on Strachan's team selection. He continued to make optimistic noises about possible qualification, but few were listening. The chances of reaching the final stages of the World Cup were already as good as dead in the water.

Closer to home, Lewis Allan's loan-deal at Livingston was cut short, largely due to his lack of opportunity in getting a regular game. Their first choice players had been in good enough form to keep him out and he'd only made four appearances as a substitute since August. So he'd look to be back in with the Development Squad almost immediately, as would Liam Fontaine hopefully, the latter in a bid to regain full fitness after two months on the sidelines with a calf injury.

Meanwhile, club captain David Gray was still beating himself up over his part in the loss to St. Mirren, lamenting that, "I should have done better. I gave the ball away in an area we should not have been playing in at that time." He did point out that they hadn't been playing too badly overall before that – the irritating habit of losing goals from set-pieces notwithstanding – but conceded that the game against the Buddies had been the lowest dip so far, in terms of general performance. Hibs had now lost three times at home already and for the third time in four games they had gone ahead, only to find themselves unable to maintain the advantage. A vast improvement would be required, away to a buoyant Raith Rovers on the middle Saturday of the month.

Over at the PBS, there was singing and dancing in the streets, as the jambos finally got the go-ahead from the Council to start construction of their long-awaited new stand. One stipulation was that it had to be 'disaster proof'. The old one certainly wasn't, as shown by the calamity witnessed by its inhabitants on January 1st, 1973. But this latest scare was apparently because of the potential hazard posed by chemical leakage from the old bond through the adjoining wall next door. Luckily Craig Levein found one of Christian Nade's old Hearts tops in the dressing-room and spent a long tiring night atop stepladders with Anne Budge, sealing up the danger area with that, whereupon a safety certificate was duly granted. The surveyors spent a considerable amount of time explaining the regulations to Craig, but became concerned when they realised that he was even less animated than usual. Later they found out their mistake – they'd been addressing one of the waxwork dummies from the newly-opened jambos' museum instead.

On Wednesday 12th, Hibernian Ladies made the trip to Germany for the second leg of their Champions League Last-32 tie. Obviously, they never stood a hope of overcoming Bayern Munich's 6-0 lead from the first encounter, further compounded by losing a quick goal again, within six minutes. But there was consolation at least, in the shape of a terrific twenty-five yard strike from Abi Harrison just before half-time to peg the home team's advantage back to 3-1 on the night. Bayern scored only once in a second half largely dominated by the Hibettes and manager Chris Roberts declared himself proud of their never-say-die spirit over the double-header. So the Hibernian and Beatles connections continued to coalesce – McCartney, Lennon and now Harrison... But where were the Starrs of the future?

Down in East Lothian, there were alarming reports that the 'killer clown' craze which had been generating hysteria in the media had now spread to Scotland. Police were later seen leaving Garry O'Connor's house with a pair of size sixteen shoes, an outsize bow-tie, a fully loaded water-pistol and a fake red nose sealed in an evidence bag. Asked to confirm his name in court, Gaz claimed that he couldn't remember, but he was pretty sure it wasn't Johnston. He wasn't going to fall for *that* one again. "The whole thing was just a circus," he bitterly remarked to reporters afterwards.

Two days after Bob Dylan was awarded the Nobel Prize for Literature, I found myself glumly staring out of the window, 'The Freewheelin' Bob Dylan' blasting through the speakers in tribute. 'Dreich' seemed an almost inadequate word to describe the prevailing conditions outside. "...and a hard rain's a-gonna fall," croaked Bob rather unnecessarily, omitting to add "in Kirkcaldy as well," but I'd already sussed out you don't need a weatherman to know which way the wind blows over in the Kingdom of Fife. However, by the time our contingent had vacated The Duchess suitably refreshed at 2.45, the hypnotic splattered mist was slowly lifting (as Dylan might well have said if he'd been there, which – rather surprisingly – wasn't the case.)

The first half was pretty grim fare, with neither side establishing any sort of rhythm and notable only for the major controversial issue of the day, eight minutes before the break. Naturally I was in the pie queue at the time and missed it. But there was general bemusement from my companions when I returned to my seat and also from Neil Lennon afterwards, who declared himself, "Gobsmacked. Absolutely gobsmacked." I then learned that Marvin Bartley had been sent off for the second time this season, a surprising turn of events to say the least, as Big Marv had never fallen into the 'dirty player' category. His last red card was of course rescinded and the Hibs' gaffer emphasised that he was even more confident that this would be dealt with in a similar manner, once it had been officially appealed. Confusion was understandable, as referee Stephen Finnie (who had a shocker throughout) had initially blown for a free-kick to be awarded *to* Hibs and on then producing the card gave the impression that is was going to be shown to the Raith player for committing the foul. But to the consternation of all, he then flashed it at Marv instead. His alleged offence? Retaliation apparently, although Neil adjudged it as no more than "a little kick out."

Luckily, Hibs improved considerably from the restart and you could have been forgiven for thinking that it was the home side who had been reduced to ten men, as they were continually forced onto the back foot. It was all Hibs for long spells, but – as against Ayr United – the ball was often pinging back and forth across the park, rather than more directly towards goal. However, numerous players came within a whisker of getting a touch on it, which would in all likelihood have been enough to secure three points. Raith had very few clear-cut chances, their occasional forays up the park being ably dealt with by Hanlon and McGregor. I thought Daz in particular had an excellent game, mopping up anything and anybody that came his way. For his part, Paul Hanlon came the closest of any to scoring, with a header off the crossbar. Grant Holt had a good game too and was far more forthcoming than even his gaffer, regarding the dreadful performance from the officials.

"He's booked me for an elbow. I've flicked the boy in the eye with my finger. I asked if he was alright and he said he was fine. One of their boys makes four fouls in the first half, he's taken Fraser Fyvie out twice – and Marvin – and he hasn't booked him. Where's the commonsense? Then you go into the box and someone has two arms around you and the linesman tells you he can't see it. The ref says "no holding" and then that happens. I don't get it. I've got a linesman telling me he couldn't see me getting pulled over in the box. That's his job – to get an angle to see what's going on. Twice he missed it. And then there's a handball."

The handball was certainly the most clear-cut of three valid looking penalty claims and there was another laughable incident when Martin Boyle (on for Keatings) was shoulder-charged over the touchline while racing towards the goal. The Raith defender made no attempt to play the ball whatsoever. Perhaps he was one of the five that Finnie had already booked, but he escaped scot-free for a challenge that would have done credit to Tam 'Jaws' Forsyth in his heyday. It was amusing watching Lennon racing after the referee as the whistle blew at half-time and he understandably sought him out at the conclusion of the 0-0 stalemate too, but Finnie and his two partners in crime had already fled the scene and left Stark's Park. So the Hibs' gaffer made a call to the SFA's head of refereeing, to seek an explanation.

"The sending-off sends your plans out of the window," he pointed out. "We looked in the ascendancy and then having a man sent off changes it. But I don't want to take anything away from my team – they were absolutely brilliant, our goalkeeper had nothing to do. Holt was outstanding, used all his experience and I thought their back four struggled against him."

One pleasing aspect for Hibs was that Queen of the South's completely unexpected capitulation at home to Morton had propelled them to the top of the League, albeit on goal difference only. But rather ominously, Falkirk were now only a single point behind them after victory over Dunfermline and Dundee United another two points adrift of that. It looked as if both sides who had extremely poor starts had put that behind them and were starting to hit their stride. It was the second time that other results had generally turned out kindly for the Hibees, but there was no doubt they were going to have to return to winning ways as soon as possible, if they wished to hang onto this slenderest of leads.

On the same day, Hibs Ladies turned in a stunning performance in their Scottish Cup semi-final, on the back of their brave but ultimately fruitless showing against Bayern Munich. They demolished Hearts 5-0 at Ainslie Park, to set up a final against Glasgow City at the start of November. Hearts manager Grant Scott held his hand up, saying, "When you look at the changes Hibs made at half-time, they had four international players coming off the bench. We don't have an international player in our squad, so that tells you all that you need to know. It's a different level."

The following week, John McGinn declared his readiness to play two games within two days – if Scotland manager Gordon Strachan opted to select him for the international squad to face England at Wembley. That game was scheduled for November 11th and John was eager to aid Hibs in their vital home League game against Falkirk the day after, come what may.

"I'll have to wait until the squad is announced and see if I'm involved. It's not so far from London to Edinburgh," he said optimistically. "So I'm happy to get a flight back and play for Hibs as the Falkirk game is a massive one for us, but we'd have to see if that would be possible."

Of course, Hibs were obliged to do without Super's services in the recent Irn Bru Cup-tie, but for some inexplicable reason the Scotland gaffer didn't even deem him worthy of a place on the bench against the Liths, despite him being voted 'Man of the Match' in his international debut. That may only have been a friendly, but John had done enough to prove his worth in the brief time allotted to him against Slovakia.

Iron Rod was later spotted wearing his underpants on his head while dancing a jig of joy down Albion Road, which seemed a tad excessive way of celebrating a 0-0 draw in Kirkcaldy. However, the sight of the trusty biscuit tin wedged firmly under his armpit gave the game away, as Hibs announced a £200,000 profit for the eleven months up until the end of June. That certainly compared favourably with a loss four times that for the previous period and a similar deficit for the one preceding that. That was in no small part due to the excellent runs in both main cup competitions and with the big spike in season ticket acquisitions added to the £1.1 million generated by the share issue, it was all looking quite rosy on the financial front.

Ahead of the next impending trip over the Forth Bridge – to Dunfermline – came the worrying news that Farid El-Alagui was still in possession of his lucky pound coin. He'd been using it a hell of a lot more since swapping Easter Road for East End Park that was for sure, kissing it after every goal he scored. With his recent bizarre 'hat-trick' (one of the goals was of the 'own' variety) the shiny round object was starting to develop love bites. Farid revealed to the Press that he'd found it on the pitch at Falkirk five years ago and it had never been out of his sight since. No wonder Peter Houston's in a permanent bad mood, as it was he who'd accidentally dropped it in the first place. He'd worn out the knees on countless pairs of breeks crawling around the park under cover of darkness looking for it. Finder's keepers, or, more accurately, *Farid's* keepers then? Apparently so. He'd obviously had a very frustrating time through near permanent injury when at Hibs, but spoke fondly of his tenure there.

"It was tremendous for the fans that the team won the Scottish Cup. I was on the open top bus the next day and while it was a fantastic experience to see what it meant to them, I felt like a passenger."

Well, Iron Rod did charge him £1.60 for a single fare from the City Chambers to Leith Links, before flinging him off en route for putting his feet up on the seats. Farid's plea that his ruptured Achilles tendon was playing up again failed to placate the Chairman. However, he eventually got his money back after complaining to the Omnibusman that the journey from the High Street to Leith Walk took about four times as long as usual. Like most Hibbies, I was quite happy to see Farid doing well in Fife, whilst secretly hoping that he would at least temporarily misplace his lucky coin before October 22nd.

The day before that, Hibs received the news that Marvin Bartley's red card against Raith had been rightly rescinded, which was doubtless good news. But that still didn't excuse the fact that – yet again – they'd been forced to play a large chunk of an important League game minus a man. Three points had been dropped against Ayr United (from a point when Hibs were on top) and two lost against Raith; we certainly can't attribute *all* of that to competing with reduced numbers, but it clearly had a significant impact on both games. However, as usual, the culprit in this case (referee Finnie) wasn't asked to account for his actions and escaped scot-free.

Over at Parkhead, Brendan Rodgers had apparently become trapped in a time machine which had promptly whisked him back to Lisbon, 1967. Speaking about Kolo Toure's horrendous blunders which cost his team dearly in the Champions League game against Borussia Moenchengladbach, Brendan praised his player's overall outlook.

"This is a guy who, at thirty-five years of age, could have travelled anywhere in the world to play. Instead, he wanted to play for a top European club in the best possible competition he could, so he came here to Celtic."

A top European club?? In your dreams, pal. When he made this assertion, Celtic were lying bottom of their group, with only one point from three games and had already conceded *twelve* goals. This peculiar malaise of erroneously imagining that the Old Firm were somehow of the same European standard as they were 45 – 50 years ago seemed to affect formerly rational people as soon as they parked their arses in the hot-seat at either Parkhead or Ibrox. Warby was the same when he started out – when he wasn't taking offence right, left and centre where none was intended, or confidently proclaiming how enthusiastically English clubs would embrace the notion of the Old Firm playing in the Premiership. The only field in which Rangers hadn't manifestly deteriorated was in that of extraordinary levels of mass hooliganism, at least judging by their fans' behaviour the last time they crossed the border for a competitive game. Was it any wonder they shelved the European Cup-Winners Cup altogether, after the wholesale destruction of Manchester city centre in the noughties? Still, it showed the huns hadn't lost their touch there – comparing favourably as it did with the rioting and mass sacking of Birmingham (1979) – which occurred during and after a 'friendly' (!), the bluenosed blitzkrieg in Barcelona (1972) and a nightmare in Newcastle (1969).

Brendan wasn't the only sporting figure to put his foot in his mouth however, on the same day as top Scottish stunt cyclist Danny MacAskill did even better. He'd come in for some stinging criticism from feminists who had taken exception to his filming inside the grounds of the Playboy Mansion in Beverly Hills, surrounded by scantily-clad lovelies. Seeking to placate irate viewers who had watched footage of him soaring two-wheeled over a swimming pool full of bikini-wearing babes, Danny claimed that the whole thing had been "an honest mistake on my part." Emphasising that the terrain suitable for performing stunts was the most important factor location-wise, he could hardly have chosen his words worse, in an attempt at mitigation. With a straight face, Danny Boy explained that, "It turned out there were decent bits to ride." Oo-er, missus!

Up for a more positive piece of publicity was former Hibee George McCluskey, who was promoting his autobiography, the rather unfortunately titled 'Playing for the Hoops'. However, he hadn't forgotten his time at Easter Road, particularly *that* tackle by Graeme Souness which saw the latter red-carded on his debut game for Rangers. As the Hibs man was carried off the field in agony on a stretcher, he had the presence of mind to inform Sooey that he was a coward as that big Village People moustache appeared beside him. Later, the arrogant one did try to apologise, but apparently "an old boy on the ground-staff armed with a broom chased him away." He revealed that he revelled in the nickname bestowed upon him by Hibbies and was chuffed when a Supporters Club presented him with a T-shirt emblazoned with the legend 'BEASTIE'. George soon took to wearing it while warming up, but his manager was less than enthusiastic.

"Alex Miller didn't like me wearing it. "Shall I tell the fans that?" I said. He had to win them round so he relented."

The player wasn't shy about speaking his mind and was equally forthright when, as a teenager, he met two of the Rolling Stones totally by chance at a pizza restaurant in France. (As you do.) Many people might have found themselves somewhat tongue-tied under the circumstances, but not the bold Beastie. He promptly told Ronnie Wood that he preferred his work with The Faces and kept harping on about the merits of him getting back together professionally with Rod

Stewart. The fact that the other Rolling Stone present just happened to be Mick Jagger didn't faze him in the least.

"Listen, George," the guitarist finally said, "I've just joined the best rock 'n' roll band in the world and you want me to get back with Rod?? I love what you're saying, but it's not going to happen!"

So to East End Park to take on the Pars and the main talking point from the off was the non-appearance of Jason Cummings. The previous season Alan Stubbs had confined him to the bench in one particular game, only to see him almost instantly score when finally given his head in the second half. But here, Lennon didn't see the necessity of putting him on at all, despite his team trailing by a single goal into the second period. He opted for Grant Holt to partner James Keatings up front, after both had impressed on the previous weekend's trip to Fife and that decision was vindicated as big Grant eventually put the Hibees ahead with a penalty and also scooped 'Man of the Match' award. However, the second main talking point once the murmurings over Jase's no-show had diminished somewhat was another inexplicable decision from a referee, who chose to award a spot-kick to the home side halfway through the first period. An 'incident' which no-one except the man in black saw, apparently, as there was no sign of protest from Dunfermline players or fans. Darren McGregor said later that when he'd queried it the clueless Muir replied that someone had pushed someone else, but he couldn't identify which Hibs player had shoved which equally mysteriously unidentifiable Pars player! You really do despair at the standard of officialdom, as week after week these black-clad buffoons continue to make blunders which they're never called to account for. Assistant gaffer Garry Parker said diplomatically, "At half-time we did think it might be another of those days. We didn't think it was a penalty but you have to get on with it." Hibs duly did that after Higginbotham netted, with Keatings striking a free-kick off the bar, prior to a Shinnie cross flashing across the goalmouth just agonisingly out of reach for either James or Grant Holt to get a toe to it. Fraser Fyvie was next up to have a pop with a fine free-kick of his own which goalkeeper Sean Murdoch did well to keep out and by the time Hibs hit the woodwork again – through Paul Hanlon this time – you could empathise with Parker's 'another one of these days' assessment.

But ten minutes after the restart the visitors finally got the reward that their play had merited, although for once this time luck was on their side. Another Keatings effort took a wicked deflection off Nat Wedderburn and there was no way Murdoch could readjust his positioning in time to deal with that. Hibs had their tails up now and doubled their tally on the sixty-sixth minute with a penalty conversion, which, in contrast to the first half award, was indisputable. Pars defender Ashcroft clumsily bundled Andrew Shinnie over and Holt made no mistake from the spot. By this time Martin Boyle had come on for Keatings and with Hibs now seemingly in control the manager deemed it unnecessary to propel his top scorer into the fray, preferring to give Brian Graham a chance instead. That proved to be a shrewd move, as the substitute put the game beyond any doubt with a goal one minute into time added on.

"In the second half we showed character and the potential we have," said Darren McGregor. "I would say that was our best forty-five minutes of the season. We scored three, didn't concede and we didn't allow them to create much, so I thought it was good."

"We deserved that and from then on we controlled the game," said Garry Parker with reference to the deflected equaliser. "We deserved to win in the end. The manager had a right go at them at half-time and rightly so, but they are good lads and they went out there and showed what they are all about. We just want to keep winning games and try to climb away at the top. That is our main objective as we keep striving to get promoted."

It was another day when results elsewhere generally conspired to aid the Hibees' challenge once again. Raith had a fine away win at Falkirk to keep both sides tied on the 17 point mark and Queen of the South's second surprise defeat in a week left them just one point ahead of that. Dundee United moved just ahead of them on goal difference to claim second spot after a less than convincing home victory over Dumbarton, which left Hibs now out clear in front by three points. Daylight between us and the rest of the pack at last! We could hope that finally our team would find enough to at least maintain that healthy gap and seek to widen it gradually over the forthcoming weeks and months.

It was fitting that Dunfermline were the opponents at this particular time of year, as the following Thursday saw the 25th anniversary of a famous result over the same side roll around. Incredibly, it was a quarter of a century since Hibs had lifted the Skol Cup, as the League Cup was rebranded that season, with a fine 2-0 win over the men from Fife. They'd done it the hard way too, reaching the final by dint of four consecutive victories in the competition away from home, beating Stirling Albion (at MacDiarmid Park), Kilmarnock, Ayr United and then Rangers, the latter in an absolutely towering semi-final performance at Hampden, with Keith Wright scoring the solitary goal. So it was back to that almighty public convenience jokingly referred to as an international soccer stadium to face the Pars in the final on October 27th. That was how I chose to describe the venue in my booklet entitled 'Storm The Gates of Hampden', which I knocked out through the fanzine network in the heady aftermath and reading back through parts of it twenty-five years later I was struck by how some things never change regarding viewing cup finals, when you have a personal stake in them. For a start, this had been the first time in my Hibs supporting career that my team were taking part at the ultimate stage of a knock-out competition as *favourites*. Yet – naturally – we were all still shitting ourselves.

The title of my wee publication had been inspired by the utter fuck-up by the authorities, who had in their infinite wisdom decreed that, as the game didn't involve either of the Old Firm, there would be no need to make it an all-ticket affair. I arrived just before 2 p.m., with four pals and, although kick-off was still over an hour away, we decided due to the size of the crowds already building up, to enter the stadium there and then. This was easier said than done, as none of the turnstile operators appeared to have any change. By 2.30, storming the gates of Hampden was your only option if you still remained outside and didn't fancy trying to blag your way into the Dunfermline end – the section behind the goal on the old west terracing. The Hibs sections were already full up as over 30,000 Hibbies were occupying the space and no-one knew how many would manage to get in the 'wrong' end in the half-hour preceding kick-off. In addition, 'around 4 – 5,000 were locked out' according to media estimates at the time, but it was probably considerably more, as the authorities tried to play down their colossal ineptitude which had led to such a potentially dangerous situation developing. This was only a couple of years after the Hillsborough Disaster too.

We were blissfully unaware of this, on tenterhooks as Hibs looked unsure and jittery from the beginning, but their opponents were in an even worse state. They'd endured a spectacularly bad run of results in the League, but they were still a Premier Division outfit and had reached the final by sheer dogged determination. Hibs should still have been coasting at the interval and their superiority was there for all to see, with Keith Wright and Gareth Evans coming closest to breaking the deadlock, but it was still all square as the teams trooped off up the tunnel at the break.

However, the second half was barely under way when Mickey Weir played a neat one-two with the man they called KEITHKEITHKEITH and he was homing in on goal when a wild attempt at a tackle brought him crashing to the ground. Up stepped Tommy McIntyre to take the resulting penalty and he seemed unruffled by the spectacle of Pars keeper Andy Rhodes dancing around dementedly on his line in an attempt at putting him off. The centre-half stuck it away coolly and the pressure was relieved – slightly.

Our opponents were galvanised into some sort of counter-attacking strategy by that and there were a few nervous moments as they pressed down on the Hibs goal. In retrospect, they never really looked like equalising, but one lucky break would have been enough to see them draw level. However, the clock was already ticking down when Mickey Weir – having an excellent game – cleverly slipped the ball behind the Pars defence to pick out the lurking Keith Wright. The latter moved forward confidently and then side-footed the ball calmly beyond the reach of Rhodes. Virtually the whole ground erupted in a frenzy – but it wasn't quite over yet. A tremendous thirty-yard free-kick from Brian Hamilton – who also had a superb game – came thundering back off the post, even as we leapt up to celebrate a third goal, so we had to make do with just the two. Then the final whistle blew and scenes of unrestrained joy broke out all over the Hampden terracing.

I still couldn't believe it. I felt numb. It had been nineteen long years since I'd witnessed a cup final victory in the same competition and only the far-off sight of the ecstatic green and white clad figures lifting the trophy convinced me that it was indeed for real. But as the players came running triumphantly past our vantage point the spectacle of our mad goalie John 'Budgie' Burridge wearing the daftest most elongated top hat you'd see in a long time had me doubting the veracity of my eyesight yet again. The Hibernian heroes that day were:- Burridge, Miller, Mitchell, Hunter, McIntyre, Macleod, Weir, Hamilton, Wright, Evans and McGinlay, with Orr and Beaumont on the bench.

The return bus journey was initially a peculiarly subdued affair, as if a fair number of the passengers had not quite taken on board what had just occurred – until we reached the Maybury roundabout. We were greeted by hundreds milling around the stationary open top bus, as yet unoccupied by the Hampden heroes who were still on their way and from then on the atmosphere just grew and grew into one of an all pervasive ecstasy. The crowds lining the streets all the way back into town, with particularly big clusters at Corstorphine, Roseburn and Haymarket were an incredible sight. Opposite Ryrie's we were almost side-swiped by a bouncing double-decker full of Hibbies which came careering down Dalry Road, the driver having obviously taken a detour right through Gorgie for the enlightenment of the jambo populace. This was just a foretaste of the scenes of Hibbie hysteria along the entire length of Princes Street, especially at the east end where the Duke of Wellington was already festooned in green and white scarves and flags. I was instantly transported back to 1972, when myself and fresh-faced youthful mates had gathered there after emerging from the Waverley Station, to await the triumphal homecoming of Turnbull's Tornadoes to the old North British Hotel after that famous win over Celtic.

We piled off the bus at Pilrig and straight into Robbie's, until the green grapevine announced the imminent approach of Miller's magicians. With glasses clutched lovingly to their breasts, everyone surged out into the street again, as a huge 'LEITH HIBS' banner was unravelled right across Leith Walk. Then the open top bus crawled into view and a mighty roar went up as Gordon 'Geebsy' Hunter brandished the sparkling silverware aloft from the centre spot on the top deck. A quick dash up Iona Street followed, to repeat the experience as the bus came back up Easter Road, after being routed along Duke Street on reaching the foot of the Walk. My agile mate got rather carried away and shinned acrobatically up a lamp-post, to exclaim at the top of his voice "BUDGIE! HEY BUDGIE! BUDGIE BUDGIE BUDGIE!" It was possible he'd got rather stuck for words but no matter, as the big keeper leant forward from the top deck, giving the masses a clenched fist salute while jutting his chin out in ridiculously exaggerated fashion. I swear his jawbone just about brushed off the tenement wall behind me.

Everyone then poured back to the stadium where someone had thoughtfully left the gates open and we pushed through to our usual spot halfway along the main terracing to exchange hugs and salutations with other pals who'd had the same idea. Then the seldom heard chant of "THERE'S ONLY ONE ALEX MILLER!" rolled around the stadium in a great wave, as the manager emerged onto the pitch with his players. In fairness, it didn't last *that* long however and Lexo declined to join his charges as they ran over to salute the crowd. Then, after bawling out a selection of classic Hibernian anthems, we all dispersed to our own favoured hostelries to continue the party long into the night. Little did I know then that sixteen years would elapse before we'd do it all over again...

On the exact date of the anniversary, the St. Patrick's branch of the HSC staged a victory celebration of that auspicious occasion at the Hibs Club on Sunnyside. The St. Pat's crew had done an admirable job regarding organisation and managed to get eight of that cup-winning outfit to attend, as well as manager Alex Miller (the no-shows being Graham Mitchell, Pat McGinlay and – somewhat inevitably – Budgie.) I received an invite from Stuart McLeod of St. Pat's – cheers again, Stuart! – and enjoyed a great night of reminisces and laughs in the packed-to-the-gunnels Famous Five Suite. The event was anchored by Luke Shanley, the man on the telly, who opened up proceedings by remarking, "Well, this makes a nice change from my day job – hanging around outside Ibrox asking stupid fucking questions about Joey Barton." Luke was excellent, very funny and obviously knew his subject matter down to a 'T'. Asking about Budgie's non-appearance and if he was as mad as was generally perceived, club captain Murdo Macleod said, "No, he was worse than that," and explained that after he'd emailed out invites, he eventually got a reply of sorts from the eccentric goalkeeper of yesteryear. Apparently, Murdo received a picture of Budgie posing on a beach in Dubai (where he now lives) wearing a manic expression on his face and little else.

"That was it!" said Murdo. "So I had no idea if he was coming or not."

We were then treated to edited highlights of the titanic semi-final against Rangers and footage from the final itself.

"So, did you dive then, Mickey?" enquired the anchorman, with reference to the penalty award.

"Absolutely not!" protested Mr Weir, lamenting how he was still stuck in a room on his own at Hampden two hours after the final whistle, as he'd been selected for the random dope test. But he was so dehydrated and knackered he couldn't have passed the parcel, let alone passed water.

"I thought they'd have just left without me!" he said of his team-mates, revealing that he was very chuffed that they hadn't done so, despite the huge delay. Meanwhile, officials back in Edinburgh were in something of a panic, as the open topped bus sat forlornly at the Maybury, awaiting the heroes' return. Where the hell are they, was the question on everyone's lips. Are they celebrating somewhere en route?

The years certainly seemed to have been relatively kind to most of those present, Mickey himself and Willie Miller in particular looking remarkably similar to the way they were a quarter of a century ago. Other squad players who didn't actually feature in the final were also there and Joe Tortolano had everyone in fits with a tale about his brief career as a promoter of sunbeds. ("I got them free for a year," explained Joe.) Mark McGraw and unused sub on the day, Dave Beaumont, also put in an appearance.

Pies and Bovril were duly dispensed at half-time – I've often been guilty of mixing my drinks, but that's the first time it's been a combination of Belhaven Best and beef tea.) The evening wound up with a question and answer session and then club legend Pat Stanton dispensed richly-deserved awards to the Class of '91. A wonderful night, but one tinged with a lot of poignancy too – never far from the surface was the realisation that this really *was* the team that came back from the dead, soaring to such heights only a year after the despicable Wallace Mercer attempted to kill off Hibernian F.C. for good.

Fast forward back up twenty-five years, to find James Keatings sidelined for a minimum of six weeks after injury incurred against the Pars. James had clashed in a fifty-fifty challenge with Dunfermline defender Jason Talbot and instantly felt his left knee 'explode'. Right away, he feared he'd done in his anterior cruciate ligament, a situation which had kept him out for a whopping eight months when he was a teenager with Celtic. It wasn't as bad as that, mercifully – although quite bad enough – but James declared himself feeling 'lucky' in view of what had transpired before.

The last League game of the month saw Hibs face up to the team who were struggling more than most, but the Saints had still gone marching on after their visit to Easter Road in the Irn Bru Cup.

"They came here and beat us last time so we want to change that tomorrow," vowed Fraser Fyvie. "It's a top versus bottom game, but I don't think St. Mirren are a club who should be in that position. I'm sure their fortunes will turn, but not tomorrow."

Well, Fraser's opinions were certainly validated, at least in the opening stages. It was hard to reconcile this apparently lively go-ahead bunch as the same lot who were currently propping up the Championship and they might well have scored right at the start, catching the Hibees on the hop somewhat. In these early stages they created more chances than many other outfits had managed over an entire ninety minutes at Easter Road, with Morgan, Mallan and Hardie all having opportunities in front of Marciano's goal. However, Neil Lennon's men had by far and away the best defensive record up to this point of any of the main Championship contenders and, by the time Martin Boyle opened the scoring on the eighth minute, it looked as if the Saints had already shot their bolt. What a lovely goal it was too, as a fantastic through-ball from Andrew Shinnie fell for Martin who produced a superb dinked finish to outwit the generally impressive Langfield in goal. Selected from the start for once, the player seemed determined to prove that he was far more than just a 'super sub', which was borne out by a top-drawer 'Man of the Match' performance overall. He might well have doubled his tally too, not long after, but the Saints' goalie did well to block that powerful effort. His fellow front-man Grant Holt was on target on the thirty-fourth minute mark though, with another low strike and even at that early juncture it looked unlikely that the visitors would be able to recover.

There was no doubt that going in two goals to the good at half-time was a major relief, given how often solitary goal margins had been nullified in the recent past and as the second period progressed, Hibs proceeded to up the tempo. This was an extremely assured display overall, although as usual there was a slight sense of frustration that it could not have been more significant in terms of the score-sheet. A gilt-edged chance to put it beyond any doubt came with the award of a stonewall penalty, but although Holt struck the ball firmly enough, Jamie Langfield did well to get down and snuff out the spectacle of a third. The floodgates might have opened up in that event, but as it was we had to make do with a two-nil victory, enough to maintain a three point gap at the top of the table over Dundee United who had a narrow 1-0 victory over Falkirk at Tannadice.

No Jason Cummings – again – although he was on the bench, but Neil preferred to go with Bartley, Graham and Harris when the time for fresh legs came. A definite sense of there being more to this situation than meets the eye was clearly evident amongst the supporters, but a quick glance at the match stats seemed to vindicate the manager's tactics. He'd resisted putting Jason on the previous week even as his team were trailing in the second half and it was his two recent acquisitions who ultimately sealed the victory, with Holt successfully notching a penalty on that occasion and Brian Graham scoring almost immediately on entering the fray at the end. Now, on this day, he'd once more started with Grant which had paid off again and Boyle was absolutely on fire throughout. Was Jase becoming surplus to requirements? It was looking increasingly like it and only time would tell, but the manager was all for focusing on Martin's endeavours for the moment.

"We see him more as a central player than as a winger," said Lennon. "And he has goals in him. Technically he is good and he has pace which is always a problem for defenders. Physically he is not the biggest and there were times when, early on in the season, he was getting knocked off the ball far too easily for our liking. He has taken that on board and we saw a very good all-round performance from him, not just his pace and his trickery but also in taking the ball in and being a good link-up player as well. I'm absolutely delighted with the contribution he made."

There was a nice touch during the half-time interval, as most of the Class of '91 League Cup winners were paraded on the pitch, receiving a standing ovation from the crowd. The man with the microphone then took his life in his hands, by innocently enquiring of Alex Miller what he thought of Budgie. Presumably he hadn't read the account in 'Budgie: The Autobiography of Goalkeeping Legend John Burridge' (co-authored by Colin Leslie) of how he once came to physical blows with his manager. The assault was only halted when Murdo Macleod smashed him (Budgie) over the head with 'a big telephone'. It was to be expected that someone with the goalkeeper's borderline mad personality was never going to see eye to eye with Lexo, who he described as *"the biggest pessimist I've ever seen."*

So, as the anniversary celebrations drew to a close, I think it would be fitting to end this chapter with a personal anecdote, preceded by some choice Budgie quotes, with possibly the finest opening line of any footballer's life story. We all have tenacious former 'Hibs Monthly / Mass Histeria' fanzine editor and Scotsman sports correspondent Colin to thank, by prizing these gems out of the man himself.

Prior to being sectioned under the Mental Health Act, with his playing days now behind him: *They say that when you go mad, the men in white coats come and take you away. That's not true. It's the men in green boiler suits.*

On being carted off by the aforementioned green boiler-suited men: *After I'd been overpowered in my bedroom, injected in the bum with a sedative and dumped in the Priory, my first thought when I came to was to hatch an escape plan.*

On an England goalkeeping legend: *Peter Shilton? I wouldn't let him keep my pigeons.*

On being on the receiving end of a downbeat Lexo team-talk before a game: *For God's sake boss, it's St. fucking Mirren not St. Peter we're dealing with! I've played about 700 top league games and you're trying to make me scared of St. sodding Mirren!*

To the opposition forwards, lining up in the Hampden tunnel before the 1991 League Cup semi-final: *Hey Hateley! I'm going to break your back if you come into my six-yard box, you big fairy! And I don't know what you're laughing at, McCoist. You were a failure at Sunderland and you couldn't cut it, son! You had to come back to Scotland and beg for a game!*

To the entire Rangers team: *The whole lot of you are fucking rubbish. You play in a chewing-gum league. If you want to play in a big league, come down south and prove yourselves there!*

*Colin's book was first published in hardback in 2011, by John Blake Publishing.

My only personal encounter with him occurred on the return rail journey from a 1-1 draw with Motherwell at Fir Park during 1991 / 92 season (our goal being scored by KeithKeithKeith.) Word had spread that Budgie was aboard, travelling on his own, so as a fully non-paid up roving correspondent for Hibs Monthly, I hastened along to the carriage in question. (At this time I was developing an unsavoury reputation for ruthlessly ambushing unsuspecting Hibs players past and present in the most unlikely of locations – which always happened purely by chance – and then badgering them into doing something for the fanzine. Surprisingly perhaps, they usually did.) Budgie was no different in this respect, graciously passing me his home phone number when I asked if he'd be prepared to participate in a full interview, with only the salutary warning, "Just dinna ca' us during 'Coronation Street'!" I duly forwarded it to Colin in the editor's chair, who luckily took heed of this when he eventually made the call. It was only later we found out the reason why – as part of his in-house training regime, his wife would spontaneously fling oranges at him when he was on the sofa engrossed in the goings-on in Weatherfield, to test his reflexes for saving unexpected shots. If that alone doesn't qualify the man for legendary status, I don't know what does...

5.

NOVEMBER: TIME FOR ZEROS

'FANS WANTED FOR SECTARIAN SINGING' announced The Evening News headline on the first day of the month, reporting that the police were seeking to identify the guilty jambo hun-wannabes who had made the rail journey from Inverness to Edinburgh a hellish one for everyone else. Well, that can't be too hard, chaps! You'll know them by their noise and there's a fair chance they'll be too incapacitated by being up to their knees in Fenian blood to run away very quickly, when they see you brave boys in blue coming.

"This sort of behaviour won't be tolerated," said a British Transport Police spokesman rather implausibly – after all, it had already been tolerated for about three hours. The Evening News could have worded their heading in a lot clearer fashion too. When their hun readership saw it they thought it signified there was a career opportunity beckoning, inviting contestants to take part in the popular television show, 'Britain's Got Bigotry'.

Across town, Hibs' head of marketing and commercial operations, Greig Mailer, declared himself well pleased with the initial sales of the 'Time For Heroes' DVD, which had been flying off the shelves in the Hibs shop since its release four days earlier. I was too mean to buy it – just as well, because when I caught a bit of it at a mate's house I realised I'd seen it before. On May 21st, actually. Aye, it's a bloody repeat! Mailer said, "We got good feedback from the players themselves, who are after all the stars of the movie." Listen pal, if I'm forking out all that dough I'm expecting to see some *real* actors take the lead parts, not a bunch of amateurs. I would have gone with – Jimmy Logan to play Conrad Logan, Ewan McGregor as Darren McGregor, Paul Newman as Paul Hanlon, Liam Neeson as Liam Fontaine, David Niven as David Gray, Ronald Fraser as Fraser Fyvie, Bob Dylan as Dylan McGeouch, John Sessions as John McGinn, Juliet Stevenson as Lewis Stevenson, Anthony Hopkins as Anthony Stokes and Jason Connery as Jason Cummings. Una Stubbs as manager(ess), naturally. Then I *might* have been prepared to cough up £25. But only if it was showing at the Fountain Park 'Extreme Screen' with free popcorn thrown in. Oh, and a choc ice at the interval.

As Hibs entered the penultimate month of the year sitting atop the Championship table, one very pleasing and rather overlooked aspect could be gleaned by taking a glance at the 'Goals Against' column. 'Six' was the magic number there, indicating a defence considerably more miserly than those of any of their main adversaries. Indeed, no other team throughout all four divisions could match it, which was of great satisfaction to the Hibs' captain.

"As defenders we pride ourselves on clean sheets, so it has been good," remarked Sir Dave. "We've lost a few goals from set-pieces which we want to tighten up on, but overall we have been solid. If we can provide a solid base we have so many creative players going forward and we'll give ourselves a good chance."

David could certainly give himself a well-deserved pat on the back and dispense the dumps too in the direction of Fontaine, McGregor and Hanlon. They'd all been very impressive of late, to such an extent that although plaudits were down to the man between the sticks too, he frequently hadn't had too much to do, thanks to the mopping-up abilities of those just in front of him.

David was already looking ahead to the following weekend and another run-in with the only team to have secured a League victory over Hibs so far. Destination – Ayr. Operation – Revenge!

"We want to put things right after that result," avowed his Gray Eminence. "We were very disappointed with that, but we knew it would be a hard game."

Even harder when you're unjustly reduced to ten men for a big chunk of it, obviously.

"It's a tough place to go," acknowledged David. "We know, having drawn there pre-season and we'll be expecting another hard game."

Going into this one on the back of two consecutive victories should certainly act as a confidence booster and Hibs would again be bolstered by the fact that two of their main challengers would be in contention with each-other, as Dundee United would take the long road to Dumfries.

"There are a lot of teams who can take points off each-other in the League, so it's about getting consistency," he went on. "The League looks like it might go down to the wire but from our point of view we're at the top just now and we just have to focus on staying there."

The second day of the month brought with it the alarming news that apparently the playing of Proclaimers' songs in the comfort of your own home was now an offence which could lead to a custodial sentence. That was the unhappy fate of a Gorgie-based Hibbie, who had been tapping his toes to the strains of 'Sunshine on Leith' in the wake of the 2-2 Scottish Cup draw with Hearts last season. This naturally incited a mob of jambos who had been passing by to tan all his living-room windows in with a barrage of bricks and other missiles – yet *he* got sent down for eighteen months! Admittedly, there was the small matter of him chasing the scumbos down the street with a machete immediately afterwards, but it was probably his innocent explanation which riled up the sheriff when he appeared in court. His solicitor recounted that his client had gone into his kitchen "to make some toast and cheese and was using the implement to cut the cheese. He tells me that his brother had pinned a Hibs flag to the window and was shouting at rival supporters and to add fuel to this behaviour he was playing 'Sunshine on Leith'. This had the desired effect and bricks were thrown and the windows were completely put in. My client came rushing through and ran into the street and had the knife, which he dropped instantly when asked to do so by the police." However, the only part Sheriff Crowe took issue with was the reference to 'a knife'; in his view it was "verging on a machete – a lethal weapon."

Well, it's an easy mistake to make. Only the other day I was using a samurai sword to butter my toast when I became aware of a ladder appearing outside and a strange figure visible through the glass. I instantly raced outside and cleanly decapitated the potential burglar with a single swipe of the butter-spreader which I'd momentarily forgotten was still in my hand. Of course, by the time I'd realised it was only the window-cleaner it was too late, but at least I could empathise with the Gorgie vandalism victim. And nowhere in the reportage was there any mention of the jambos receiving any sentence for their brick-hurling actions. Just as well he was only playing The Proclaimers and not Nick Lowe's 'I Love the Sound of Breaking Glass'. Then they'd probably have tanned in his bedroom, bathroom and kitchen windows too.

By the end of the week, Super John McGinn had, as expected, been named in Gordon Strachan's squad for the Armistice Day showdown against England at Wembley. John had been around the international scene since he was but a slip of a lad, as he used to attend Hampden regularly courtesy of his grandfather Jack, then heid honcho of the SFA. He was always keen to store up pearls of wisdom imparted to him from the Scotland squad back then, while getting his picture taken with them – not a straightforward matter in those pre-selfie times. To this day he remained committed to absorbing as much as he could, especially from former Hibees Scott Brown and Steven Fletcher.

"If I can do half as well as he's done in his career, I'll be doing well," he said, referring to Broony. "You just try and take wee tips from these guys. I call myself 'The Sponge' because I try to soak up wee bits and bobs from everyone when I'm away."

Despite the fact that Scott B's abrupt about-turn regarding his international retirement might prove a hindrance to the current Hibs' man making a breakthrough, he was full of praise for his Celtic counterpart.

"The midfield has obviously been strengthened (by Broony's return) so I didn't know if I was going to miss out. All the midfielders will have been thinking the same, but if he's going to help the team and country then I'm all for him coming back. He's a top player. He helped me massively when I went away with the national team before and he's been the best player in the country this season. I'm looking forward to seeing him."

John's club manager was obviously pleased to see him becoming established within the Scotland set-up, but was, understandably, more focused on his on-going contribution to the Hibernian cause. However, the midfielder had already indicated his willingness to turn out for Hibs the day after the England game, should the need arise.

"It depends on how much I play, if at all, on Friday. I'll probably come back up for the Falkirk game and see how the manager feels about me playing. As far as I'm aware, we're flying back up after the game, so I'm more than happy to play for Hibs on Saturday."

He was also looking back somewhat ruefully to his previous outing against the Auld Enemy, at Under-19 level. They'd lost 3-0 and then coach Ricky Sbragia had given them the full-on Fergie-esque hairdryer treatment afterwards. Changed days though, as a fair number of that side had failed to make a real breakthrough at the higher level, whereas John now looked to be well on-track, which had hardly been the case then.

"At that point, I was never really a pick for Scotland at that level. I was always floating in and out but I think that can help you because it makes you hungry. You just want to prove people wrong and over time people start believing in you and realise you can play. I'm obviously delighted to make my way up to the full squad but I know I need to keep performing if I'm to stay there, because there are top-class players sitting at home and itching to get involved. I don't like to take it for granted."

John's eyes were now turned towards the next immediate challenge, with a visit to Somerset Park, Ayr. Their manager Ian McCall observed that, "I've watched a couple of Hibs games and in the match against Dundee United for example, it seemed they got to the stage to where they were struggling to get that second goal to kill it off."

Hibs had an even more trying time of it at home to McCall's team of course, which he felt they didn't get enough credit for. He did acknowledge though that in light of his lot's poor start to the campaign, it was something that few would have foreseen.

"It does sound pretty ridiculous, not the fact that Hibs had only lost one game, but it was us that beat them. Even after the sending-off we still had to score two goals to win and we actually had another good chance to add a third."

Happily though, on the 411th anniversary of Guy Fawkes's original firework display being cancelled due to Government interference, it was a case of 'remember remember the fifth of November' for the Hibees. There never looked like being a repeat of their earlier fixture against the Honest Men here, as Martin Boyle once again turned in a top-notch performance, with a double to his name. He'd already caused the home defence all sorts of problems before latching onto a Lewis Stevenson pass and beating keeper Fleming with a low shot right into the corner. His pace had propelled him past the Ayr backline on numerous occasions and he looked the man most likely to score, right from the off. Martin had started off partnering Grant Holt up front again, declaring, "It's brilliant! The manager's put me in a new role and I've adapted well. So it's been great and hopefully I can continue scoring goals." Well, he did that alright, adding another in the second half and on this form it seemed like Jason Cummings could be warming the bench for a good while yet.

His next successful strike arrived twenty minutes after the break and although a single goal lead had often proved a tenuous one, there never looked any danger here of Hibs taking their foot off the gas. This was a great team effort all round – "the best of the season," said Lennon – with every man playing his part and the midfield providing quality service for the strikers up front. None more so than Fraser Fyvie and Super Sponge McGinn, who inter-acted superbly before the latter set up Martin to rifle the ball between Fleming's legs for number two.

"He's not just quick, he's clever," said Neil. "He's a good foil for Holty and he's playing that well he's keeping Jason out of the team at the minute, which speaks volumes for his performances."

Hibs continued to dominate, saving the very best for last, with an absolute sizzler of a free-kick by McGinn from thirty yards smashing into the back of the net, before the goalkeeper even had time to react. Jason did get a few minutes at the end as he came on to replace Andrew

Shinnie, but by that time the visitors were already home and dry, having secured their biggest away win of the campaign so far.

"You can't really ask for much more in terms of tempo and the quality of football we played," said Neil, sounding like a satisfied man for once. "We thoroughly deserved to be a goal ahead (at the interval) and we finished the game emphatically as well. We had some great play and some great goals. To win as well as that is a difficult thing to do, so I am absolutely thrilled." As to his internationalist's sensational strike, he went on, "It'll give John a huge shot in the arm. He's got that in his game though and it'll obviously give him a huge boost ahead of the game on Friday. It's a testament to his talent playing at this level that he's in the Scotland squad, so obviously Gordon (Strachan) and his staff think very highly of him, as we do."

For the opposition, Ayr gaffer Ian McCall was glumly pragmatic.

"It was a disappointing day for us, with a great crowd in the ground and a great atmosphere, but Hibs deserved to win. They played very well."

Back-to-back clean sheets for the first time in nearly two months – time for zeros in the 'Goals Against' category again, perhaps?

Elsewhere, Dundee United recorded a thumping 4-1 away victory at Queen of the South, whose early promise looked to be already fading fast. The former table-toppers had now slid into the bottom half of the League and there was no doubt that the visitors to Palmerston Park had now emerged as Hibs' main challengers, at least for the time being. But the three point cushion remained and another three points now separated second and third, with Raith Rovers sitting six points behind Hibs on the twenty-one point mark.

The following day saw another trophy being bagged, as Hibernian Ladies wound up their season by lifting the Scottish Cup, after a hard-fought victory over Glasgow City at Hamilton's Superseal Stadium. The

Hibettes went in leading 1-0 at half-time through a goal by Lisa Robertson, but got pegged back in the second half when an unfortunate defensive mix-up allowed their rivals from the west to equalise with twenty minutes left to play. That was tough on the girls in green and white, who should have been further ahead at the interval as Lucy Graham and Lizzie Arnot had both come close – taking a leaf out of the boys' book there, it seemed.

A goal-less half-hour of extra-time followed, before a penalty shoot-out was required and right away it looked like possible curtains for Hibs, as goal-hero Robertson blasted the first kick over the bar. But now it was the turn of Jenna Fife in goal to display some heroics of her own, with a save to deny Glasgow City their fourth conversion in a row. Kerr then missed a seventh kick and a 6-5 victory margin it was to the team from the east.

Highest plaudits to the girls, for defeating a team who were nigh-on invincible in the League and for overcoming their disappointment in Europe so swiftly. That trophy would now join the League Cup in the cabinet, which they secured by beating the same outfit in the final of that competition back in June. Said their delighted gaffer, Chris Roberts, "I thought the goal we lost was unfortunate, it was a slip but I felt we still could have dealt with it better. It wasn't a case of holding on. We were gutted we didn't win it in 90 minutes, gutted we didn't win it in 120, but we got there in the end. We've brought another Scottish Cup back to the club, so I think it shows great progress of the club as it's not often Hibs have been described as a team that wins trophies."

Too true, but Iron Rod blanched when he saw the hike in insurance premiums now that there were so many priceless trophies jostling for space on the sideboard. (Most folk had forgotten that the 1991 Skol Cup was still there too, as the Blazers at the time didn't want it back. It was only rediscovered when Jason noticed the inscription thereon after he'd filled it to the brim with warm water to wash his hair out of, one morning.) A lackey was quickly summoned to give it a polish and – SHAZAM! – all was revealed. Rod resisted the temptation to wheech it along to Cash Convertors under cover of darkness, but ultimately it was Edinburgh Council who were the beneficiaries. The dazzling glow from all that silverware was so bright when the curtains were left open that they could safely dispense with street-lighting in Albion Road, Albion Terrace and Albion Place altogether.

Wearing shades to protect their eyes from the glare, the attendees at the Monday AGM dutifully trooped in, to hear generally positive contributions from all the relevant movers and shakers at Easter Road. Neil Lennon, just back from watching a couple of matches in the Republic of Ireland to weigh up the talent, spoke of potential recruits coming on board during the January transfer window. He also denied that he'd be seeking to offload anyone, reiterating that he harboured no regrets about turning down Peterborough's seven-figure offer for Jason in the summer.

"It was important that we keep him because without his contribution we probably wouldn't be sitting on top of the League."

He seemed to refute that there was anything to read into his current absence from the team other than a dip in form, which had allowed Martin Boyle to seize his chance and step up.

"As a young player you get peaks and troughs. It's not nice sitting on the outside looking in, but hopefully that will reinvigorate him."

Head of Academy coaching, Eddie May, was also happy to report that there were several bright prospects coming through the ranks too.

With the international showdown against England fast approaching, the man who gave John McGinn the chance to flourish at Easter Road declared his pleasure at seeing his former young charge doing so well.

"It would be fantastic for John if he could play a part on Friday," said Alan Stubbs. "It would probably be the biggest game of his career so far if he did, considering the rivalry between the teams. When we brought him in, we thought he could push and do well and that's proved the case. I was just part of John's development, I don't take any credit for that. The credit is for John himself. I think he'll just keep on getting better."

Stubbsy's spiel was somewhat overshadowed however, by the three big midweek headlines, which were (in order of global importance) as follows: 1. Dundee United drew level with Hibs on points after beating Dunfermline 1-0 (but with an extra game played and still lagging behind on goal difference). 2. Jason got himself sent off as he turned out for the Development Squad's 4-1 defeat by Kilmarnock. 3. America's answer to Vladimir Romanov somehow managed to get himself elected President of the whole goddam shootin' match. The similarities with the former Tynecastle dictator were uncanny – big mad hair, a history of dodgy business practices and a talent for insulting people. One calls the SFA 'monkeys', the other calls Mexicans 'rapists'. "I'm gonna build a wall and Mexico's gonna pay for it!" trumpeted Trump. "I'm gonna build a stand and Edinburgh Council's gonna pay for it!" ranted Romanov. Vlad was always "going to make Hearts great again," and The Donald kept insisting he was going to do likewise to the USA. Although you might be forgiven for asking just when exactly was it great the first time around? During slavery? Prohibition? Segregation? The war in Vietnam?

Never mind all that though, the question closer to home was – will Jason make Neil's nerves grate again? You'd have thought so, in his actions for the wee team, a game which his gaffer actually attended. However, as a shrewd fellow once pointed out, people who live in glass houses shouldn't throw stones, a maxim clearly taken on board by Neil.

"We've all done it. We've all lost our temper at an official," he said, possibly reminiscing about his own trips from dug-out to banishment in the stand. "Whether it warranted a red card or not is debatable."

But the positive news at least from the player's standpoint was that his manager declared his contribution up until the sending-off as, "Outstanding. I was really pleased with him. While he must be disappointed at not playing, he is not showing that on the pitch and I was really pleased with how he set about this match."

He also added that Jason would be in contention to play against Falkirk.

One man who wouldn't however was 'Rocky' Marciano, after his country made him an offer he couldn't refuse. Frustratingly though, he picked up a knee injury while training with the Israeli squad, so he would not now feature in their fixture in Albania anyway. Maybe just as well, as he might then have more than just a knackered knee to worry about – authorities had uncovered a plot by Islamic State to launch a terrorist attack. FIFA had strongly advised Israeli fans against travelling to the Balkans, saying that at this rate they'd be more welcome in the Palestine end at Parkhead.

There was no place either for John McGinn in Strachan's team to face the English, which was probably just as well. Apart from the selfish Hibernian considerations, it would have in all likelihood been a dispiriting experience for any emerging player. Granted, Scotland played fairly well for lengthy spells and didn't deserve to lose by three goals, but the last ten minutes were painful to watch, as England resorted to taking the piss. Chris Sutton was refreshingly candid in the ITV studio afterwards, when many still seemed reluctant to point the finger at the manager. The former Celtic striker observed that it was Strachan's poor selections and tactics in the two games preceding that one which had ultimately scuppered any chance of a berth at the World Cup Finals.

So to a visit from Falkirk, Ross Laidlaw back between the sticks in Marciano's absence and Paul Hanlon waxing lyrical about current hot-shot Martin Boyle.

"He has been great. This is the first time that he's had a proper run in the first team for a number of weeks. He's never let being a sub get him down. He's a lovely character to have around the place and that's the sort of guy you want in your team. His pace really frightens a back four. No matter how fast defenders are, he is lightning. His confidence is sky high right now."

In the event, Martin's scintillating form wasn't quite up to recent standards, with the quicksilver player often failing to latch on effectively enough to numerous balls being punted his way by team-mates. However, Falkirk were well-aware by now of the danger he might pose and their defence was always alert for any passes directed his way. It was a typically dour, niggly performance from the visitors – if ever there was a team playing in the image of their glum chip-on-the-shoulder gaffer, it was the Bairns. There was certainly nothing to suggest from the off that this one would be significantly different to many other tussles with the same lot of late. A vastly superior attack-minded Hibs struggled to break down an outfit who'd just had 'HERE TO PARK THE BUS' stitched beneath the club crests on their shirts. Happily, McGinn's pointless sojourn with the Scotland squad didn't seem to have affected him adversely, as he was back to shooting from distance with confidence. His efforts were bolstered by sterling service from Fyvie and Shinnie and also aided by an industriously mobile Grant Holt up front. But the Hibees should still have been able to take advantage of their numerical superiority, after Taiwo received his marching orders on the twenty-fifth minute. The former Easter Road man had gone in very hard on McGinn, but it was no worse than many other challenges which had gone before. Referee Beaton was shamefully weak, in failing to clamp down on the overtly physical stuff and time-wasting from Falkirk throughout. Time and again, Houston's hammer-throwers got away with this behaviour and the officials' reluctance in dealing with it appropriately only serves to encourage it.

One rather strange aspect of Hibs' generally tip-top defending which must have had Lennon tearing his hair out was their inexplicable laxity when facing up to set-pieces. There was some sense of inevitability therefore, when the visitors forced a solitary corner after a break forward thirteen minutes from the end. Baird sprang onto that decisively and no blame could be attached to Ross Laidlaw, who had virtually nothing to do up until this point, but the ball was still in the back of the net. There was a sense of bemusement that a team who had dominated to the extent that Hibs had done could somehow find themselves a goal down and now in danger of dropping all three valuable points. Credit then to Paul Hanlon who levelled matters six minutes later with a header and then aided his team-mates in a mighty push to ultimately seize the day. Super John McG was denied twice in this closing spell as a wickedly taken corner almost sneaked in of its own volition and then again when a firmly struck shot was pushed just wide of the post. Bairns' keeper Danny Rogers demonstrated yet again why he is the stand-by sticks-man for the Republic of Ireland, with an excellent performance overall. A frustrating afternoon for Hibs and their supporters, but a point was secured where three might well have been lost – and they were still top of the League.

"Falkirk defended manfully," acknowledged the Hibs gaffer afterwards. "But you expect that. My players know teams are going to come here and make it as difficult as possible for us, especially if they go down to ten men. We lacked a cutting edge, a creativity, that spark. Their goalkeeper made a couple of good saves but we did not make enough clear-cut chances to get excited about. We had twenty shots and only five on target; it shows our conversion rate could have been better. But we'd scored pretty heavily in our last three games so I can't pinpoint that as a problem."

As for our man between the posts, it was probably more frustrating for him than anyone else. He accepted that, if available, Ofir would be the first choice – "He was signed to be the No. 1, he's an international goalkeeper and he's been doing well enough to be called up by Israel again," – but naturally wanted the chance to prove himself. However, the bus-parking Bairns had put the mockers on that, to a large extent.

"I didn't have a save to make and yet lost a goal which was very frustrating for me. You want to be able to pull off a couple of saves to show what you can do. Sometimes you get a quiet game, sometimes you are busy, but there's nothing you can do about that as a goalkeeper."

Afterwards, I received an annoying text from a Falkirk acquaintance – from its tone you could have been forgiven for thinking that Hibs had just cheated them out of a well-deserved victory. What is it with grown men (and sometimes women) who think it is the height of wit to zap you dodgily spelt unpunctuated messages on the occasion of your team failing to win? In my previous book, I alluded to the blizzard of texts I received in the wake of the disastrous Scottish Cup final of 2012. But in fact, only one solitary communication had beeped in right on the final whistle, the remainder came later. Paradoxically, that made me even *more* irritated – so now those jambo fuckers are actually feeling *sorry* for me, are they?? My temper wasn't improved when I studied the contents of the one sent at 16.45, although it certainly wasn't that time where the sender lived, as the jambo in question was then resident in Boston (Massachusetts, that is – not the Lincolnshire version.) Knowing that I resided uncomfortably close to Pink Bus Shelter territory in Edinburgh, he sneered 'wont b settin foot ootside yr hoose 4 the 4seeable future, LOL.'

Well, I had to wait eleven months to get my revenge, but it was quite sweet when the unexpected opportunity presented itself. As I sat in front of the telly watching the scenes of carnage following the bombing of the Boston Marathon, I was gripped by a malicious sense of joy, which was rather inappropriate, considering the deaths and injuries. But what sealed it was the report that one of the bombers was still on the loose and as a result the entire city was in an indefinite state of 'lockdown' – no-one was allowed to move around unauthorised. Further footage showed heavily-armed SWAT teams scouring the streets with machine guns at the ready as military helicopters buzzed menacingly overhead like big angry wasps. Grabbing my phone gleefully, I tapped out the following in a frenzy, before zapping it across the Big Pond to the eastern seaboard of the USA – 'who won't be setting foot outside their fucking hoose 4 the 4seeable future NOW, eh?? LOL. P.S. 7-0 n 6-2 still trumps 5-1. GGTTH.' Never had the chance afforded by the killing and maiming of innocent people cheered me up quite so much.

Also looking decidedly cheery as he was photographed by the Press up Gorgie way was former Hearts Chairman, 'Gorgeous' George Foulkes, wearing a pink shirt overlaid by a V-necked maroon jumper. Where did he buy this combination ensemble – the club shop? It looked like the sort of 'two-in-one' article of clothing you'd sell to jambos who had difficulty in remembering which bit went on next when getting dressed of a morning – after the string vest had been carefully tucked into the grey jogging bottoms, of course. The reason for the Gorgeous One's appearance in the city's western badlands was to toot his trumpet about the building of the new stand, with work due to start any day. Dode admitted though that, "The timescale has been a bit too long." Seeing as he was boasting to a Press Conference back in 2007 that the new build was imminent *then*, that smacked slightly of understatement. And even that was *ten* years after they'd finished running up the original part of the redesigned PBS. However, the

Council knocked back that proposal anyway, probably on account of the fact that Vlad the Mad was calling them a bunch of marmosets, while raving and drooling that a *thirty* thousand seater was the very least of the requirements, as he shortly expected Hearts to be crowned Champions of Europe. When Gorgeous finally realised that Romanov was off his trolley it was too late, as by that time he'd been tasked with extricating Hearts from the Pieman Deal. This came about as a result of Vlad's equally insane predecessor Chris Robinson agreeing to flog Tynie to Cala Homes and move the jambos Locke, stock and barrel to Murrayfield – whether to the rugby stadium or the ice rink was never actually clear. So Dode had to do the dirty and then appease the relevant parties over broken promises, but claimed, "They didn't make it too difficult for us to get out of the deal. I think that they realised that Hearts is an institution in Edinburgh." Well, so is the Royal Edinburgh Hospital, which is where The Pieman and Mad Vlad should have been carted off to in straitjackets years ago. Still, the future was looking bright now – especially if you happened to be in the pink paint manufacturing business.

Across town, Liam Fontaine was speaking at the Radio Forth event being hosted at the Usher Hall to salute the Hibees' Big Cup triumph and reiterated how much he was enjoying his stint at Easter Road. The big man was one of the many whose contract was due to expire in the summer, but declared himself relaxed enough about the situation.

"I've been in the game long enough not to let it affect me. When the time is right to speak about it, we'll take it from there. I love the city, the group of lads we've got, so it's a good place to be. I believe this club has still got a lot of potential, so of course I want to be part of it."

There was no doubt that the issue of new contracts could be a thorny one, given the uncertainty regarding Hibs' likely status the following season. It was only to be hoped that within a few months the picture might be a good deal clearer, as a consequence of them establishing an unassailable lead at the top of the Championship table.

One man who seemed to regret not still being part of it all was the departed Dominique Malonga, who'd been frozen out of the set-up at Pro Vicelli in Italy. Dom made the decision to move when he felt that the circumstances were right to do so, but it hadn't worked out for the best.

"I knew if I left it would feel like unfinished business for me, because my main goal when I arrived was to go up with Hibs. I really regret that I didn't do that. I loved everybody at Hibs – it was a true family." He paused, before adding, "You never know – maybe one day I will come back," which possibly could be construed as a mild threat, by those Hibbies who didn't exactly go a bundle on his often overly languid style of play. But certainly no-one who witnessed his absolutely sensational solo goal against Aberdeen in the League Cup-tie the previous September was likely to forget it in a hurry. It was right up there with Martin Boyle's blistering first-time thirty-yard rocket against Livingston for goal of that season, or indeed any other one you'd care to mention. So poor old Dom wasn't enjoying life on the Riviera for the time being, but the Scottish Cup final result had cheered him up no end – "even though I wasn't there, I had a lot of emotion," – and promised that he'd be back in Edinburgh someday, to take in a game at Easter Road at the very least. Also, to see his hairsprayed 'sibling' too of course, who he still kept in touch with.

"Jason's my guy, my little bro'!" he declared.

Which possibly might come as something of a shock to the respective Malonga and Cummings' sets of parents...

On Friday the 18th it was announced that the Hibernian Community Foundation would be awarded £9,500 to deliver its preventative alcohol education project to schools. The initiative would commence throughout twenty selected seats of learning in Leith and north Edinburgh, to warn pupils about the dangers of alcohol misuse. They could surely save money by just parking them up outside The Spey Lounge at chucking-out time, which would surely put the majority off the bevvy for life. The previous weekend a mass brawl which had erupted inside the premises spilled out into the street, with numerous people being seriously injured. Unfortunately, the polis said they were too busy trawling through footage from Hampden on May 21st looking for people who might have damaged an advertising hoarding to bother with Some Crime on Leith. 'My jaw was broken, my jaw was broken, sorrow, sorrow...''

Charles Bennett, the HCF's Chief Executive, explained that they planned to scare the youngsters off the demon drink by showing them three short films, as a form of 'aversion therapy'. The first, entitled 'Drive My Car' featured Russell Latapy and Dwight Yorke belting back the rum as they careered through the city streets in the latter's Mercedes, while celebrating Hibs winning the Scottish Cup in 2001, a trifle prematurely (aye, the one where they lost 3-0 to Celtic.) The second, 'Leigh Lady Leigh' starred 'Leigh Griffiths & His Love Children', in which the striker leads the karaoke lunchtime sing-along in The Roseburn, with a cute choir consisting of his eight kids sired by ten different girlfriends. The third – and by far the scariest – is simply billed as 'Derek Riordan's Greatest Hits'. Edited down from its original seventeen-hour long running time, it comprises CCTV clips from some of Deeks' top evenings out on the town, where bouncers are insulted, heads are butted, butts are headed and feet and fists fly merrily with wild abandon.

"If that doesn't put them off the sauce for good then nothing will," said Mr Bennett, who had remained teetotal ever since he'd woken up one morning at the top of a lamp-post in Dirleton with his trousers missing, following a night out with Garry O'Connor.

The following day, a team who earlier on had looked like serious contenders in the Championship paid a visit to Easter Road. But unfortunately for Queen of the South, their form of late had taken an abrupt downturn and they were smarting after four defeats on the trot. Happily, they were smarting even more at the conclusion of this one, having by then upped that to five in a row. Hibs proceeded to completely dominate from the start, causing the manager to exclaim that he'd just witnessed, "One of the best performances I have seen against any opposition as a manager at any club." No small praise, from a man who had overseen Celtic's victory over Barcelona in the Champions League. While that assessment may seem a trifle over the top it was refreshing to hear from a gaffer who had in the past seemed rather hard to please. "The players did everything I wanted them to do. We looked powerful, intense, hungry and the quality of the football and the chances we created was superb. That was the benchmark for them but they are getting better as the season progresses."

Yet again, he opted to switch things around a little and yet again his decision paid off. Very early on too, as Brian Graham – selected to partner Martin Boyle up front in place of Grant Holt – fired home the opener after only seven minutes had elapsed. Such was the home team's dominance it was surprising that we had to wait until three minutes before half-time before the tally was doubled, courtesy of a McGinn strike which was diverted into the goal by the legs of Queens' defender Chris Higgins. But, as usual, they'd passed up some good chances, been unlucky too when a Boyle effort cracked off a post and had the highly competent Lee Robinson in the opposition goal to contend with. Queens also hit the post with a free-kick and Dykes missed a sitter from close in after getting round Marciano, but that really was about their quota for the day.

There were fun and games at half-time as Jason – left languishing on the bench again – took time out from a warm-up around the track to pause for autograph signing and posing for the camera lens with youngsters at the front of the Famous Five Stand. He was clearly enjoying himself so much that he was still thus engaged when the teams emerged from the tunnel for the second segment, possibly intentionally irritating his manager to some degree. Jase doesn't like to be left out of the limelight, but Lennon allotted him a fair chunk of time to make his mark halfway through, by which time Hibs were 3-0 up thanks to Sir David Gray getting on the end of a McGinn corner. That came just after a pitch invasion, as a bushy-tailed Reynard appeared on the park near the away end, before attacking down the wing in a burst of pace that would have done Martin Boyle proud. Looking alarmed by the noise, the creature veered off left to disappear up the side of the West Stand. Surely an opportunity for the stadium DJ to blast out The Sweet's 1970s classic 'Fox On The Run' over the tannoy? Never mind Gorgie Farm, over the years the hallowed Easter Road turf has played host to more wildlife than a raft of David Attenborough documentaries. We've seen a Budgie flapping around between the posts, a Bear in defence (Yogi), a trio of Frogs (Sauzee, Boozy and Zitelli), a racehorse on the wing (Nijinsky, aka Arthur Duncan), a mouse in midfield (Mickey, aka Alex Edwards), not to mention 'The Wildebeest' himself, Willie Jamieson and now there's a Crane pecking about somewhere in the background too. Neil would go on to say later that Darren McGregor was 'an animal' – but he meant it in a good way. And only last year a flock of sheep got disoriented and were bleating loudly in distress long before Jase and Dom consigned them to the abattoir of League Cup oblivion.

The Hibees saved the best for last however, as a powerful angled finish from Boyle slammed past Robinson on the sixty-fifth minute and from then on they really were on easy street. Martin's lightning speed as usual caused plenty problems for the Queens' defence, but it would probably be unfair to single any one player out for special praise. Over a highly satisfactory afternoon's work, every man played his part; a first-rate genuine team performance overall.

Daz McGregor referred later to Fraser Fyvie's suggestion that the consistency shown by him and Paul Hanlon had been such that the international manager could do worse than considering pitching them into the Scotland set-up.

"If Gordon Strachan wants an old carthorse then I'm willing to oblige. But I'm happy to be here, happy to be playing and anything else is obviously a massive bonus."

Back to establishing a three point lead over Dundee United (who eked out a goal-less draw away to Morton) and now a pivotal game against the Tangerines coming up at the start of December – "A big test for us," observed the gaffer. "We're going into it knowing I couldn't have asked for a better performance than we put in against Queens. I don't think that there would be many teams in the country, bar the top ones, who could have lived with us."

In fairness, their opponents were maybe suffering from something of an identity crisis. Not long ago Alex Harris had featured in their ranks, but one glance at their line-up could have had you imagining you were in fact reading out a Hibs team sheet from the 1970s instead. Marshall, Brownlie and Higgins, just for starters...

A couple of days later, the Hibees of that era (and those of the following decade) cropped up in conversation, as I ran into former Hibs director from the Kenny Waugh administration, Alan Young, in Leigh Griffiths' favoured west Edinburgh watering-hole. It was Alan who had provided the anecdote concerning the late Hibs chairman and Sean Connery for my last book, but over a few pints in The Roseburn, we found ourselves conversing about a mutual acquaintance, who had also furnished me with some good tales in the past. To wit, one James O'Rourke. As I mentioned in the previous chapter, no ex-player was safe from my attentions back in the fanzine days. I'd originally got to know Jimmy when he ran The Corstorphine Inn during the early 1980s, where he'd be obliged to shove Irvine Welsh unceremoniously out the door on many a drunken occasion. By the time I was involved with the 'zines, I'd often bump into him in The Diggers, Tynecastle Arms or Roseburn, as he was then employed in a Gorgie bookmakers. (Despite their pink-tinged locations, the three aforementioned hostelries have always had a hardcore of Hibs supporting regulars.) Jimmy would gleefully recount some often dodgy stories about adventures with his Turnbull's Tornadoes' team-mates, which I would attempt to commit to memory, before writing them up later on. But inevitably, next time I encountered Jimmy he'd be looking mildly pensive.

"Eh…I didn't tell you that tale about… (use your own lurid imaginations to fill in the gaps there)… did I?" he'd say worriedly.

I'd sigh, knowing what was coming next.

"Yeah. You did actually, Jimmy."

"Well don't print that, for God's sake! More than my life's worth!"

"I won't mention my source though."

"Doesny matter! They'll soon guess where it came from!"

So, reluctantly, I'd usually acquiesce. Which was a shame, because there was one cracker, concerning a fat Moped-riding Nigerian prostitute when Hibs toured that part of Africa in the late 1960s. (In an utterly bizarre episode, their visit coincided with the country's descent into civil war and paranoid officials from the breakaway state of Biafra suspected that the Hibs team were either mercenaries or British paratroopers in disguise, there to fight them on behalf of the Government! What, with those hippy hairstyles and sideboards??)

Anyway, the Nigerian hooker story never saw the light of day to my knowledge – at least not from my pen – but on another occasion I'd written a piece which I thought I'd better run past Jimmy first. This time I was as certain as I could be that there were no incriminating details therein, which could cause him any problems, but my heart sank when he started tutting and shaking his head, on perusing the very first paragraph.

"No, no, this won't do at all. You *really* can't print that bit!"

"Why on earth not?" I groaned wearily.

"Cos you say right at the start – 'The other day I met former Hibs favourite Jimmy O'Rourke in The Tynecastle Arms at eleven o'clock in the morning,' that's why not."

"So what?"

"Well, I'm meant to be working in the bloody bookies then, aren't I – not supping pints with you!"

Fair point, I had to concede.

So Jimmy's secrets remain safe with me – apart from that one obviously – and the one about the time he got out of his head with Walter Smith at a Crosby, Stills & Nash concert. *What...??*

With a free weekend looming before the televised clash with Dundee United, Neil Lennon was quick to issue a reassurance that his charges wouldn't be treating it as a holiday.

"They are going to work hard," he declared. "I don't see the need to give them extra time off. And, in any case, some players do not like having too much time off. We'll have a normal week, probably give them the weekend off and then begin to prepare for United."

It would also give the manager time to reassess John McGinn's situation, as the midfielder was definitely going to need time out once he'd had surgery on his injured ankle. Keats was already out for a minimum of six weeks and John was looking at potentially a longer period on the sidelines. It was uncertain as yet when the operation would take place, but you'd imagine that the Super One would like to get it over and done with as soon as possible.

For Hibs fans who hadn't yet been put off by the prospect of a trip to Dundee in *December* for an *evening* kick-off on a *Friday* when the match was live on the telly anyway, there came a further consideration for those aiming to let the train take the strain. The ridiculous revelation had just been made public, that rail journeys between Edinburgh and Dundee (and Perth) now took *longer* than they had done during the reign of Queen Victoria! Almost unbelievably, steam-powered trains in 1895 could make the trip to Tayside in fifty-seven minutes, as opposed to the sixty-four minutes required today. Likewise, a journey to the hometown of St. Johnstone now also took seven minutes longer than it did at the arse-end of the 19th Century. Maybe they didn't have to contend with the wrong kind of snow (or leaves) on the track back then of course. What a fucking joke. Scotrail? Clot-rail, more like. Opposition MPs were up in arms when the news broke and demanded an explanation in Parliament from Transport Minister Humza Yousaf. Unfortuately though, he wasn't there – his train had been derailed due to a freak tsunami and plague of toads in Tomintoul.

Meanwhile, Brian Graham was at the wind-up with Jason over their respective goal tallies – Brian's strike against QoS was his fourth for Hibs, but he already had six under his belt for Ross County before moving to Edinburgh. (His journey took sixteen hours, as his train was re-routed via Carlisle after the wrong kind of sheep were found to be blocking the line near Aberdeen.) Being an arithmetically sound guy, Big Bri soon worked out that four plus six usually equalled ten, but Jase apparently wasn't having it. According to him, he was still top scorer with eight.

"He says the six I got for Ross County don't count," explained Brian. "But to have scored ten before the end of November isn't bad. I always set myself a wee target but I never reveal it. If you hit it, it is brilliant, but sometimes you don't."

Hope this merry banter between the striking rivals wasn't the cause of the keeker that Brian was rather colourfully sporting, down East Mains way? Absolutely not, insisted the player. No, that was the result of Paul Hanlon sticking the heid on him. Accidentally, presumably...

Jason finally got a belated reward for his industrious efforts once thrown on against Queens – he'd clearly been desperate to get a goal then, but finally hit the target on the Tuesday night, as the Development Squad ran out 3-0 victors over the Pars at the Oriam. Oli Shaw got the other two, which was enough to keep the wee Hibees at the top of their League as well. Jase's fellow sub from Saturday, Marvin Bartley, played most of the game too and Alex Harris featured for the full ninety minutes.

The following evening, Celtic predictably flopped again in Europe, losing 2-0 to Barcelona at home and causing flags to be flown at half-mast throughout the east end of Glasgow. Not only there, but also in the flat directly above mine, annoyingly enough. The Celtic supporting ex-car thief had an irritating habit of displaying his Celtic banner in the front window, every time the Bhoys played in Europe; judging by the majority of their performances it didn't seem to occur to him that it was, if anything, a bad omen. After reading about the experiences of the Gorgie Hibbie outlined at the start of this chapter, I was always expecting jambo or hun passers-by to lob a brick in its direction, quite possibly breaking my window instead, if their aim was poor.

Returning from The Diggers after half-a-dozen pints, I then noticed that his wife had pinned his Celtic top out on the back green washing-line, where it had frozen solid. On an impulse, I sneaked out and replaced it with my pristine 1970s Hibs 'Stanton' top, taking up position behind the curtains the following morning to await the results. I heard the footsteps come click-clacking down the stair and exiting through the rear door, whereupon the air was suddenly rent asunder with a loud, unearthly shriek, as his missus beheld this remarkable transformation. I peeped out, to see her standing there, also frozen to the spot in much the same manner as his Celtic shirt had been, twelve hours previously. She was goggling wildly at its superior replacement, as if she simply couldn't believe her eyes.

"Jimmy, Jimmy!" she started yelling.

Funny time to break into an Undertones song I thought, but the aforementioned bleary-eyed Jimmy came traipsing down the stairs post-haste, to ascertain the cause of her distress. He looked like he couldn't believe his eyes either, probably initially putting the sight that greeted him down to his over-indulgence in certain substances. For since retiring from the car-stealing business, he'd seen the light, turned over a new leaf so to speak and reformed himself as a cannabis dealer and wasn't averse to sampling his own wares. However, it was only a matter of time before the finger of suspicion was being pointed unwaveringly in my direction.

"It wisnae me, a big Bhoy did it and ran away," I would later lie half-heartedly.

As the week drew to a close, nominations for fans' representatives on the Board were starting to trickle in. The first fans to be voted in as non-executive directors, Amit Moudgil and Frank Dougan, had served their two-year stints and would be able to stand again, if they wished. One possible candidate had emerged, which would seem to be an overwhelmingly popular choice, as no less an absolute Hibernian legend than Pat Stanton had his name put forward.

"I have always felt it was important that the club and supporters felt connected and that the voice of the ordinary supporters was heard," said Pat. "I can assure fans that, if elected, I would ensure that this happens and that I would serve the club and supporters with the same passion as I did as a player and manager. Like every other supporter, I want to see Hibs back at the top of Scottish football again."

Leeann Dempster, whilst stressing that the club must not be seen to influence the voting process, said, "Clearly, to have a club legend like Pat be prepared to serve in this way recognises the value that he, and others, put on the process of supporters electing directors to represent them on the Board."

However, Pat would later withdraw his name, for reasons unclear, but he maybe figured he'd endured enough Hibernian-related hassle in an official capacity over the years anyway.

As Hibs sat idle over the last weekend of November, the Scottish Cup diddy round got under way, with their next home opponents in the Championship receiving an almighty fright. Dumbarton escaped with a 0-0 draw away to Bonnyrigg Rose, before an excellent crowd of 1,552 and must have been very relieved at living to fight another day.

Twenty-four hours later, Celtic easily swept Aberdeen aside by three goals to nil to lift the first major trophy of the season, as the League Cup was secured. At least the authorities had now seen enough sense to get the tournament over and done with long before Christmas, rather than letting it drag on into springtime and act as a distraction to other important fixtures, as had been the case with Hibs in the previous campaign.

Neil Lennon's concerns would now focus on the biggest game of the season so far, knowing well in advance that he'd have to face Dundee United missing some key players. Fraser Fyvie now looked a doubt too, as McGinn would finally get a break until his ankle problem was resolved and Keats would seem to be some way off a return just yet, at least going by the original prognosis. Dylan McGeouch would probably be utilised, but it was doubtful if his hamstring woes had fully cleared up either. So there was plenty for the gaffer to mull over, but with a pool of players more extensive and varied than anyone else in the Championship had at their disposal, it could have been worse. Thankfully too, Hibs were going into the last month of the year playing the best football they had all season and certainly had nothing to fear.

6.

DECEMBER: ONCE IN ROYAL SIR DAVID'S CITY

'NO STYLE NO BOTTLE NEILSON OUT'. Yes, the pissed off pilots who flew that punctuation-free banner from the aircraft that swooped over the PBS last season finally got their way, as rantin' rovin' Robbie prepared to depart for pastures new. From the architectural splendour of Edinburgh to the barren discount warehouse strewn landscape of Milton Keynes, a sort of English version of Livingston without the excitement and glamour. From a team that's lying second from the top in Scotland to a team that's lying in sixty-fifth place in England and one of only three sides south of the border who'd yet to win a home game this season. Even Rotherham had managed that, albeit only once. Neilson's move seemed to make as about much sense as Stubbsy's shift to the foot of the Championship, although Robbie was aiming even lower. A whole division lower, no less. (Stubbsy's record as being the manager with the shortest ever tenure in the Rotherham hot-seat had already been beaten, as Kenny Jackett's jacket was on an even shooglier peg and became detached permanently not long after he'd hung it up, on arrival. Cheerio, cheerio...) Anyway, it was clear that Annie Budge was in heavenly pursuit of a big name to replace the glum-faced one, as jambo Igor Rossi gave the game away at the end of the match against Rangers, by revealing a T-shirt which stated 'I BELONG TO JESUS'.

"Christ Almighty!" said Craig Levein, on hearing the news.

"That's the very felly," confirmed Annie.

Igor wasn't the only Rossi in the news, as Fausto of that ilk, an Italian midfielder, was apparently storing LSD on behalf of the drug-dealing Hibs manager. That was the initial impression given by The Evening News headline anyway – 'LENNON KEEPS TABS ON FORMER JUVENTUS MIDFIELDER'. Latterly seen keeping company with Dominique Malonga while on loan at Pro Vicelli, the player was now a free agent and under observation by Neil. However, several clubs from America's MLS were reputedly keeping an eye on him too.

Hibs got down to business at Tannadice in the table-toppers' tussle, with McGeouch in the midfield as expected and Marvin Bartley on from the start too. Neil's selection limitations due to the injured parties were evident with the appearance of Martin, Crane and Eardley on the bench ("Martin Crane you say? Was that not the old guy in 'Frasier'?" – Hibs TV critic.) Neither of the young 'uns featured, but Eardley replaced Fontaine right at the end, by which time Jason had also made a second half appearance. Bolstered by an excellent crowd of nearly 11,000, given the adverse circumstances outlined in the last chapter, there was a minute's silence for the victims of the Brazilian team plane crash in Colombia and then we were under way.

Hibs' profligacy in front of goal had been apparent in earlier matches (which luckily for them hadn't proved fatal due to their overall superiority), but that was always likely to have consequences against the Arabs. They'd been on a very impressive run of ten unbeaten games and Hibs were unable to capitalise on chances even after Blair Spittal was forced to vacate the park for a lengthy period in the first half. That was down to an accidental clash which resulted in a colourfully bloodied nose (with another one yet to follow), although if Grant Holt had got his way the claret would have been liberally splattered all over the pitch and the stands as well. That incident may have escalated after the traditional clichéd 'spot of handbags', but unfortunately the mountainous Hibs striker is known to carry a brick in his. It took half his team-mates to drag him away from inflicting some serious damage on his opponents. However, that was all still to come and Hibs were perhaps fortunate to go in still all square at the interval. They were no doubt missing Fyvie and McGinn in particular; even when not fully fit the Super One had been an indispensable cog in the green machine of late. When Spittal finally did re-emerge with several stitches holding his hooter together, he latched onto a loose ball in the Hibs' goalmouth and only a timely lunging intervention from the ever-reliable McGregor saved the day there.

The second half was only eight minutes old when the visitors were served up a seemingly gilt-edged opportunity, courtesy of a penalty award. It was certainly justified, which was more than could be said for a bit of argy-bargy between Boyle and Holt over the right to take it. Unfortunately, Martin won out there and proceeded to hit a poor effort which was never going to trouble the excellent Cammy Bell in the Arab goal. He saved it easily and twenty minutes later the tables were turned when Fontaine desperately tried to prevent substitute Simon Murray from homing in on goal. He crashed into the United man and there was no doubt about that award either. However, the difference between the kicks lay in their execution and the impressive Tony Andreu was clinical in his delivery, sending Marciano the wrong way to put his team in front. Jason and Brian Graham were thrown into the fray to try and salvage something, as Shinnie also pushed up to aid the forwards, but the home team had the initiative and weren't going to surrender it easily. It was always going to be a tight encounter and the Hibs defence looked solid enough to foil any attempt at United increasing their lead, but they failed to rattle their opponents too much at the other end. The men in tangerine held firm and it was undoubtedly a disappointing conclusion to the biggest game of the campaign yet. There was some measure of consolation though in the fact that the Hibees retained top spot in the Championship, albeit only on goal difference, for the time being.

Neil Lennon said afterwards, "I didn't think we were at our best in the first half. But in the second we were in the ascendancy and the game hinged on two penalties. If we had scored then we were well on top in the game and we had a few chances after that. I don't think we deserved to lose the game, so it's a sore one."

His opposite number, Ray McKinnon, was understandably in a buoyant mood.

"We're delighted to be up there joint top of the League now, but nothing is won in December," he declared. "I said before the game I didn't think this was a defining game because there's so far to go still. But tonight we're delighted. Cammy saved their penalty and we scored our penalty, that's what it came down to in the end. It was a good hard-fought win against an excellent team."

It would certainly be a concern to Hibs how much United had improved since the start of the season, as McKinnon bedded in as manager and embarked on strengthening his team throughout. Even as initial contenders such as Queen of the South had fallen away, the Arabs had gathered momentum and now had a stability about them that was lacking in most Championship sides. Falkirk were now lying six points behind in third place and given their bloody-minded tenacity and ability to sneak up the table almost unnoticed as they'd done during the last campaign, Neil wouldn't be counting them out either. In light of the play-off let-down over the last two seasons, no Hibs fan was looking forward to a similar scenario unfolding again and the fervent hope was that Hibs would find it within themselves to pull away significantly from the rest of the pack, come the New Year.

As for Holty, if he truly fancied himself as 'Rocky' – and I don't mean our goalie – he could do worse than look to the example set by former Hibee Eoin Doyle. After throwing his current team, Preston North End, a lifeline by scoring in their away fixture to Sheffield Wednesday, he then apparently saw red twice over. Firstly, when the mist of that hue descended in his brain and then again when the referee flashed a similarly coloured card in his direction immediately afterwards. This was as a result of Eoin deciding to have a square-go with his own team-mate, Jermaine Beckford, on the field of play, which also led to the latter's dismissal. Preston went on to lose 2-1 and to say manager Simon Grayson was displeased would have been something of an understatement.

"You expect it in the playground between four or five-year olds, not from two professionals who've been in the game a long time," he raged. "For something like that to happen is embarrassing. It's a joke. It's a disgrace."

I liked the look of Doyle after Fenlon had brought him to Easter Road in 2011 and he scored some valuable goals – one in the 4-0 demolition of Dunfermline that season and most notably in the crazy topsy-turvy Scottish Cup semi-final against Falkirk in 2013, when Hibs finally nicked it 4-3 after extra time. But he faded out of the picture, before moving on later the same year.

At the PBS, the jambos were unveiling the successor to Robbie Neilson, who at first glance appeared to be...Robbie Neilson. *Eh??* Oh no, hang on, that's the new assistant bloke instead, clearly chosen for his resemblance to Robbie, one Austin McPhee. Sounds like the sort of thing you'd pick up off Arthur Daley's used car lot in 'Minder'.

"Hello squire, I'm looking for a quality second-hand motor?"

"Luvly jubbly, guv, got this cracking little 1970s Austin McPhee 'ere, fully road-taxed with MOT..."

No, the new top dog in the Gorgie kennel was Ian Cathro. *Who?* No, I'd never heard of him either. There was a rather weird photo of him on the back page of The Scotsman, wearing a strangely inhuman expression on his little hobbit face, looking for all the world like Merry or Pippin from 'The Lord of the Rings'.

"He may only be thirty, but we are convinced that he has all the tools required," head factotum at the PBS, Annie Budge, was quoted as saying. A rather harsh way to refer to your playing staff there, Annie, but hey! It's your baby after all. And judging by Cathro's appearance it can't have been that long ago since he was taking baby steps himself. He'd better watch he's not caught by the truancy officer anywhere near Tynie High between 9 a.m. and 3.45 p.m. – he looks that young he'll probably get done for skiving school. The banner headline in The Scotsman read – 'CATHRO VOWS TO BRING 'ENERGY AND EXCITEMENT' TO TYNECASTLE'.

"Energy and excitement?? At Tynecastle?" gasped Craig Levein in horror at the Press Conference. "Over my dead body."

Stepping adroitly over Craig's corpse, Cathro declared, "We're going to want to use the ball. We want to get as close to the opponents' goal as we possibly can." Well, at least he's picking up the rudiments of the game quickly. Talk about stating the bleeding obvious.

"He's widely regarded as one of the brightest young coaches in the game," enthused Annie B, before a gaggle of dumbstruck journos.

Aye, he fair sounds it too, given the wisdom of these remarks.

"It could be an enjoyable ride," concluded Cathro, smiling lewdly at his new employer, causing Annie to drop her eyes and blush the pinkest shade of pink you'd seen since the PBS last had a fresh coat of paint.

Meanwhile in faraway Buckinghamshire, Robbie was still trying to justify his move south. He claimed that he'd spoken to Alex Smith, who had in turn sought the opinions of Sir Alex Ferguson on his behalf. Fergie had then advised that moving to the Dons was "one hundred per cent the right thing to do." Well, he would say that wouldn't he, he used to manage them with a fair degree of success, after all. Yes, whereas Sir Alex had been referring to Dons of the sheepish variety five hundred miles away on the north-east coast of Scotland, Robbie had unfortunately assumed he'd meant the lot faffing about near the foot of the third tier in England. Oops! Still, it was too late now and Robbie would just have to look at the positives – for example, compared to Edinburgh buying a house was going to work out a whole lot cheaper. Mainly because no-one in their right mind would want to live in Milton fucking Keynes...

"He's one of the most exciting young managers in the country!" blathered the MKD chairman.

Well, maybe so, but sadly he's also one of the dullest in the towns and the cities.

On the continent, the biggest Blatter merchant of them all was incontinent with rage, as the Court United in Normalising Transparency in Sport (CUNTS for short) threw his appeal against his ban back in his big fat face.

"You're taking the piss!" stormed Sepp, as the yellow stream trickled out of the bottom of his trouser legs.

But the court held firm, upholding the banning of the former big cheese of world football, as well as that of his sleazy sidekick, Michel Platini.

Both had been prohibited from any involvement in the sport until 2021, by which time old Sepptugenerian would be an even older Octogenerian, but you wouldn't put it past the geriatric old fraudster to try and wangle his way back into the FIFA fiefdom even then. Naturally, Blatter went on bellyaching that he was innocent of any wrongdoing, that the verdict was 'incomprehensible' and that Miss Switzerland 1976 was a right goer, so she was, phwoarr! He also added that as he was now skint, would it be OK if he passed the hat round for some hopefully generous donations? As for his old chum Michel, well he was doing very nicely for himself, thank you very much. He'd received so many 'little gifts' from Sepp in the past that he'd recently opened a highly lucrative stationery outlet in central Paris and was doing a roaring trade selling shed-loads of recycled brown envelopes.

Back in Edinburgh, the shocking news then came through that the new Hearts gaffer had apparently died suddenly. Slumped in front of the telly, I watched in some puzzlement as the funeral cortege slowly passed from one end of Cuba to the other, as weeping mourners filled the streets. I knew he'd been around a bit before pitching up at the PBS, but I didn't realise that he'd made such an impression on the island nation. His short time at Tynecastle had clearly taken its toll, as he'd aged sixty years practically overnight and grown a big macho beard before turning up his toes. I'd hardly have believed it, if I hadn't heard with my own ears the newsreader with the lisp announcing that Cathro, the father of the nation, former comrade-in-arms of Che Guevera and hero of the revolution had passed away that very morning.

Meanwhile, the second top side in the Lothians area secured what was justifiably being described as their greatest result ever, as Bonnyrigg Rose defeated Dumbarton 1-0 away from home in the Big Cup replay, to set up a mouth-watering derby against Hibs in the next round. Annie Budge quickly ordered yet another repainting of the PBS, in an attempt at impressing the neighbours, should the big teams decide to stage the showdown there.

Neil Lennon was still keeping a beady eye out for potential new recruits with Enzo Reale the latest to cross his radar. The twenty-five year-old Frenchman had come up through the academy at Lyon and moved to Lorient for a cool million quid in 2012. He was currently a free agent, after leaving League Two side Clermont in the close season. Kris Commons was still in the frame too; apparently frozen out of Brendan Rodgers' plans at Parkhead, he was a player the Hibs gaffer knew well. Neil had signed him for Celtic from Derby County six years previously and the attacking midfielder had made an immediate impression back then.

As to the intriguing upcoming Scottish Cup-tie, the Hibs manager was broadly in agreement with the notion of the PBS as a possible venue.

"I've no issue with it and it probably suits both teams. Financially for Bonnyrigg, it would be very good. And we are used to the environment at Tynecastle, I don't know much about the pitch at New Dundas Park. I'd be in favour of that, no problem."

By the end of the first week of the last month, that grand old lady of shimmering allure finally pitched up at the Hibs Supporters Club again, after trailing her seductive ribbons of green and white glory around numerous schools, pubs and clubs. Yes, the Scottish Cup was in the bag, as we go marching on...to a celebratory evening courtesy of St. Patrick's HSC.

"Ladies and gentlemen, will you be upstanding please and give a warm welcome to – Danny Handling and Martin Boyle!" announced the chairman, whereupon everyone arose clapping loudly, awaiting with expectation the appearance of the Hibernian hot-shots. On cue, the doors to the Famous Five Suite swung open to reveal...a random bloke coming back from the toilet. That only served to increase the volume of applause, which he modestly acknowledged. Why can't the crowd at Easter Road accord *me* similar respect when I return to my seat from the pish-hoose, I rather jealously ruminated.

"OK, I think we'll try that again," sighed the MC and happily this time Danny and Martin did materialise, going on to pose for pictures with the fans and the silvery old dame herself.

Endless re-runs of the final flickered before my eyes on the various screens – as they weren't running in tandem I soon lost count of the score, although I missed almost as many goals as I normally do on aforementioned match-day 'comfort breaks' anyway. Then after a few cut-price pints served up by the extremely pretty barmaid, I was back and forth to the lavvy as usual and had completely lost the plot by the time Hibs went into an apparently unassailable 16-4 lead. I'd always been too feart to watch it back again ever since May 21st, just in case one of these days Rangers actually won, proving irrefutably that I'd just been imagining it after all. Hibs winning the *Scottish Cup??* Aye, pull the other one. However, by the time the night was drawing to a close, Sir David Gray's stunner in injury time had been played so many times over with the commentary cranked up to maximum volume that even I became convinced it was a beautiful reality after all.

As I sat lost in reverie on the last number one bus heading west, a diminutive jambo acquaintance got on somewhere on London Road.

"Where you been the night then?" he demanded, in that nosily aggressive manner that scarf-twirlers often adopt.

"Watching Hibs lifting the Scottish Cup," I stated truthfully.

"Fuck off – that was six months ago, ya senile drunken Hibbie cunt," he observed pleasantly, before thankfully getting off again at the West End. Ah, these little things that are sent to try us...

Much like mischief-making muppets in the media, who already were trying to stoke up the hoary old chestnut about Hibs' capacity for lasting the pace, on the back of one solitary defeat. It could surely only be a matter of time before the 'Hibsed it' phrase crept back into their lexicon, having been curiously absent since May 21st.

"An attack of the Hibee-jeebies amongst a certain section of the support," Andrew Smith asserted in The Scotsman, before Liam Fontaine quite rightly shot him down in flames.

"I don't agree at all; it's not that it's not happening, we are doing well," retorted the big man. "We are putting points on the board. It's one game. I don't see why you are trying to make a big thing of it. It's very early. There is so much more game time to play."

He emphasised the strength of the squad overall and reckoned James Keatings was well on his way to making a return.

"Keats is on his way back from injury now, I saw him today in training and he's looking sharp. We have a lot of options and a lot of strength to our team."

Credit to the same newspaper for its coverage elsewhere though, of a famous former Hibee's return visit to Easter Road to launch his memoirs, 'Hibs Through and Through: The Eric Stevenson Story'. A quintet of Turnbull's Tornadoes comprising John Brownlie, Pat Stanton, John Blackley, Jimmy O'Rourke and Alex Cropley joined some of the flying winger's 1960s compatriots in an event redolent of high nostalgia. Eric could have been a Tornado himself had things worked out slightly differently, but he wasn't harbouring any regrets.

"I enjoyed the social side of football," he admitted. "Maybe I enjoyed it too much, because there were times when I'd go missing. Eddie (Turnbull) weeded out the slackers and I was one of them."

The booze culture was firmly embedded throughout football back then and Eric was happy to be in the thick of it. In fact he couldn't recall any fellow players who *didn't* drink – apart from Peter Cormack.

"Some were good trainers though and I wasn't. When I quit playing my head was away because my first marriage had fallen apart, but the high life had caught up with me as well."

He was pretty much a fixture in the side when I first started watching Hibs, but moved to Ayr United late in 1971 on the same day that E.T. signed Alex Edwards from Dunfermline. Making his debut as a teenager, he later turned down Manchester United's overtures, preferring to remain with his beloved Hibees. This was despite seeing many of his friends and contemporaries take the high road south or abroad for greater fame and financial reward, Joe Baker and the two Peters (Cormack and Marinello) amongst them, but, "I was playing for Hibs and thought I'd be there forever," he wistfully recounted.

Although never earning a full international cap, he did play for the Scottish League against Northern Ireland in 1970 and was well-aware that he could have done better in that arena. Recalling a trip to Hampden to cheer on his team-mate Neil Martin playing against Italy, he was on the receiving end of an earful from the fearsome Jock Wallace, then still managing Berwick Rangers.

"Stevie, you need a kick up the fucking arse," the ex-jungle fighter informed him tersely. "You could be playing in this game tonight – the potential you have is incredible. But you have too much nonsense in your head and are aye out socialising."

This was arguably a bit rich, as Eric and Hibs goalie Willie Wilson had been kind enough to give the future Glasgow Rangers firebrand a lift through to the match, but he found himself in meek agreement.

"I said, 'I know, Jock, I'll have to get a grip.' But a minute later I was asking, 'Shall we stop at Whitburn for a couple of pints?'"

Eric was also involved in the mental Nigerian mercenary mix-up as outlined in the previous chapter, with rather more prominence than he might have wished. Him and Colin Stein were named personally by a spokesman for the Biafran seccessionists in an address to the United Nations Security Council in New York, as two of the chief suspects!

"That was pretty scary," admitted Eric, with some degree of understatement. "But the games were great fun. I was playing keepy-uppy before the first one which got the crowd excited so I proceeded to show off the whole time. The locals jumped up and down and shouted things I couldn't understand. Honest, it was just like playing in front of the Tynecastle enclosure!"

Recently in recovery from a serious cancer operation, he hadn't been well enough to attend Hampden on May 21st, but was happy to own up to dancing around his living-room with his wife on the final whistle, crying tears of joy.

"I was born a Hibbie and I'll be one to my dying day. I'm just glad that day was delayed long enough for me to see them win the trophy."

So Dumbarton dragged their Scottish Cup-shellshocked carcasses along to Easter Road on December 10th, although you wouldn't have thought that this was a team who'd just been turned over by Bonnyrigg Rose. Certainly not within the first half hour or so anyway. It was hard to avoid the conclusion that Hibs were still struggling to find their rhythm without the midfield fulcrum of Fyvie and McGinn; it was equally hard to discern any recognisable game-plan and they looked a bit nervy and hesitant from the start. The Sons deserve some credit for at least having a spirited go in the opening period and Hibs had Paul Hanlon in particular to thank for mopping up occasional through-balls which might have led to more clear-cut chances. As it was though, their opponents didn't have too many of those, with Darren McGregor also turning in a stalwart performance at the back. Hibs had been handicapped by the loss of first choice players further forward, but you felt that as long as the defensive duo kept up their excellent work there was little danger of major breakthroughs by their adversaries pushing up. For me, Hanlon was the top player on the day, shading it over official Man of the Match Andrew Shinnie and notching the solitary first half goal, almost on the stroke of half-time. He'd had a good chance from a Shinnie corner denied by goalkeeper Martin before that too, which would have given Hibs the minimum cushion you generally feel is required to relieve the jitters a bit.

"We started off a bit sluggish, a bit flat," admitted Neil Lennon. "We had to come to terms with the way Dumbarton set up, but once we sorted that out we were fine. We finished the first half very strong."

Hibs were also bolstered by the return of Jason Cummings to partner Brian Graham up front and although perhaps not back to peak form after his lay-off, there were flashes of his irrepressible self of old. He also laid on the corner which led to the opening goal.

The second half commenced in much the same manner as the first, but within fifteen minutes Hibs had regained the initiative and never looked in any danger of capitulating. Stand-in keeper Ross Laidlaw had a quiet afternoon from then on. In contrast, Alan Martin at the other end was kept pretty busy and it seemed only a matter of time before the home team increased the lead. This they finally did on the seventy-fifth minute, as Brian Graham found the net with a firmly struck shot which was helped on its way by the leg of a defender. But it would probably have gone in anyway and was no less than Hibs deserved for their tenacious efforts since the quietish opening spell. Dylan McGeouch replaced Marvin Bartley just before that and was soon in the thick of it, trying to create more chances for the forwards. It wouldn't be Jason's day that way though and he revealed later that he wasn't feeling one hundred per cent fit, having been sent home suffering from a heavy cold a day or two earlier.

"I did feel a bit rusty – you need a few games in a row to get the feel back. I had a couple of chances that probably would have gone in at the start of the season that just aren't going in now."

Still, there was no doubting his eagerness and sense of relief at being back in the limelight.

"I was delighted to be back amongst it. I was missing it. I didn't realise how much I actually missed it and took it for granted. Now that I'm back in I just want to stay in because it's a good team to be playing in."

"I would have liked to have won more comfortably," admitted Neil Lennon afterwards. "But it's three points and another clean sheet, so I'll take that. We didn't flow as well as we can but once the game opened up we looked a bit better."

"You can't always win playing the best football," acknowledged Paul Hanlon. "It's about winning ugly sometimes and it can lead you to a championship, that's what we're going for."

The result left things very much the same at the top of the League – Dundee United's 1-0 away win at Ayr United ensured it was still neck and neck, with only Hibs' superior goal difference of seven keeping them out in front. Falkirk were held to a 0-0 draw at home by Queen of the South and Raith lost to St. Mirren, leaving them now eight points and eleven points off the pace respectively. Morton were sitting just above Rovers courtesy of a goal difference of plus one, despite losing to the Pars.

The same weekend, the Weedjie polis finally attained their magic target number of arrests for the events at Hampden in the summer.

Appropriately enough under the circumstances, the total now stood at '114'. But they still weren't satisfied and proceeded to issue another raft of out-of-focus blurred shots of suspected pitch invaders. As one of them bore more than a passing resemblance to Darren McGregor and another to Paul Hanlon, perhaps it wasn't that surprising that they were on the turf after all. Mind you, yet another rapscallion looked awfully like Mark McGhee... Particularly in light of the football authorities having decided to take no further action ages ago, was it not about time the polis gave it a rest too and found something better to do with their time? Long overdue, in my opinion. They failed to do their job properly on the day and seemed to think that continuing to make a song and dance about it seven months down the line was somehow going to redress the balance and sucker the public into regarding them as models of tenacious efficiency. Bit too late for that, methinks.

Meanwhile, the statisticians had been hard at work and identified one clear area where there was room for improvement where capitalising on opportunities was concerned – namely, those arising from corner kicks. The Falkirk game a month previously had only been the most extreme example of Hibs' failings here, where eighteen corners were gained in contrast to only one for the visitors. Baird had got on the end of that one and turned it into the home net, which wasn't dissimilar to the situation at home against the Arabs. There, they had three times as many as the visitors (nine, as opposed to three), converting from none of them whilst United ensured that one of theirs at least would pay major dividends. Last season we'd been somewhat spoilt in that department with regards to delivery, as Liam Henderson was usually bang on from the corner flag and of course we were now missing McGinn's expertise in the same area. But the dearth of chances actually converted couldn't surely be solely down to the odd occasionally ineffective cross-ball. They had three times as many corners as Queen of the South on their last visit to Palmerston Park too, yet failed to score there and that statistical balance had been pretty constant throughout the rest of the Championship games played so far. Only *once* had the opposition garnered more corners and that had been in the very first game of the campaign, away to Falkirk at the start of August. Time for Neil to up the ante with intensive training in this discipline at East Mains, as well as brainwashing them with repeated viewings of Hendo's heroics from the corner flag at Hampden back in May and Stokesy and Sir David's subsequent spot-on reactions.

However, the gaffer was still busy identifying potential recruits, in anticipation of the transfer window opening up in the New Year. Enzo Reale had had a run-out with the Development Squad but it didn't look as if Neil would be pursuing him any further. It wisnae Reale, in other words. Neil then turned his gaze towards Aaron Kovar from MLS side Seattle Sounders, a winger who was apparently useful on either flank. Eighteen year-old Oli Shaw, fresh from scoring a hat-trick against Partick Thistle in the Development League game, looked to be edging ever closer to the manager's first team plans too.

"Oli did very well yesterday," said Neil, of his performance in a game which propelled the Wee Hibs three points clear at the top. "He is coming on really nicely. I wouldn't say he's that far away. I have seen a big improvement in the last four to six weeks."

By the end of the week, such was the extent of the casualty list that the manager was toying with the idea of bringing someone in on an emergency loan deal, out-with the transfer window. Dylan McGeouch was injured again, which left Neil pretty much bereft of his first choices in the midfield area, even as the absent John McGinn was voted Ladbrokes Championship Player of the Month for November. But it was goalkeeping back-up he was firstly focusing on, with the acquisition of Cowdenbeath's nineteen year-old Jamie Sneddon on trial, along with the even younger Maciej Dabrowski from Lech Poznan.

"He has really impressed us," said the gaffer of the latter. "He looks a good goalkeeper and has bags of personality as well."

Jim Duffy's much rejuvenated Morton were the upcoming opponents and perhaps Hibs were secretly hoping for a return of Storm Desmond, who had successfully wiped out the corresponding fixture the year before. Brian Graham could look forward to revisiting the home of his first employers, alongside Ross Laidlaw, who had been in the same Raith Rovers team when they'd thumped Morton 5-0 at Stark's Park half a decade ago. Ross had stayed put in Kirkcaldy, whilst the much-travelled forward took a somewhat circuitous route to Easter Road, with pit-stops at Dundee United, St. Johnstone and Ross County along the way.

On the very morning of the match against the men from Greenock, came the announcement that after months of rumours Kris Commons would indeed be joining Hibs – up until January 15th anyway. He'd had a fraught relationship with previous Parkhead gaffer Ronny Deila, but was of course well-known to Neil Lennon, who rated him highly.

"Kris is an experienced, technically gifted player, so him coming in at this time is of benefit to the side as the games start coming in over the festive period. With us missing a lot of our regular midfield players, it is good to bring in someone with a lot to offer, even on a short-term basis."

The thirty-three old midfielder – veteran of over two hundred appearances spread over five years in the hoops – observed that, "It has come about very quickly, but I think it make sense on both parts. I can try to get some football under my belt and give Hibs a helping hand as well. As much as I am trying to help Hibs, the club are trying to help me out a lot, so I'm grateful to them for giving me the opportunity. I'm also thoroughly looking forward to hopefully helping them on their way."

Certainly, if he made even a fraction of the impact enjoyed by the Celtic loanees of the previous term, we'd all be very happy indeed.

However, any fanfare for the Commons man was always likely to be muted, as Hibs toiled unconvincingly throughout a generally grim first half. Neil threw his newest recruit on from the start, which possibly smacked slightly of desperation, given how long it had been since he'd played a full competitive game. It would therefore be unfair to judge him on this showing and no doubt he'd improve over the coming matches. But there were precious few notable performances from any of the visitors during the opening period and they could count themselves fairly fortunate not to be trailing to a far more effervescent Morton side. Jim Duffy's men had a good chance as early as the fifth minute with a shot which flew just over the bar and again some ten minutes later when a powerfully struck angled effort ended up on the wrong side of the post, although Ross Laidlaw looked to have that one covered. He was to be called on a mere sixty seconds after that, but was well positioned in the centre of the goal as this time the ball was fired directly at him. Hibs were afforded a lucky opportunity when a mix-up in the Morton defence left goalkeeper Gaston briefly stranded as the ball fell kindly for Brian Graham, but he made a total hash of it. His subsequent shot was screwed well wide of the target. Commons' only real contribution was a slick cross to pick out Lewis Stevenson, but his finish was of the same calibre as his team-mate Graham's, unfortunately.

Hibs did improve after the break thankfully and Commons became more involved, dropping back into a more defensive position to gather the ball from deeper areas, before unleashing passes to his now more animated colleagues. The ineffectual Graham made way for Grant Holt on the sixty-fifth minute and he too looked lively, but the sad truth was that Hibs still looked very unlikely to actually score. They were arguably in the ascendancy at this stage as the home side started to run out of gas somewhat, seldom creating chances to equal those they'd engineered in the first half. That all changed though with only eleven minutes left to play, as a sudden surge forward saw two shots crash off the Hibs' crossbar in quick succession, before Oliver sealed it with a finish from close in. The visitors were really up against it now. Neil must have been sending up a silent prayer of thanks that he'd seen fit to introduce Jason to the fray just before that set-back. Within a couple of minutes Hibs had been awarded a free-kick and – surprisingly perhaps, with Commons available – the long absent Cummings curled an absolute beauty into the corner of Gaston's net. Just as well, because you couldn't have seen Hibs on this form managing to conjure up an equaliser in open play. It ended 1-1 and, as had frequently happened the previous season, they'd failed to take advantage of their main Championship rivals slipping up earlier on. (Raith Rovers also held Dundee United to a draw in their 3 p.m. kick-off.) It might have been two points dropped in the League race here, but given the overall standard of play on display, it felt more like a point gained.

"We didn't pass the ball as well as we can, but I thought we had the better of the second half and were in the ascendancy when they scored," said the manager. "We had chances to win it, but on our first half display we have to do better than we have done in the last two or three games. We can play better than that, no question. Defensively we were good but in the final two-thirds we have to do a little bit better."

A *lot* better, I would say, but Neil was right to praise his defenders, as again Hanlon and McGregor looked a very comfortable double-act for the most part. Indeed, a crunching Daz tackle possibly saved the day right at the death, after a mistake by Marvin Bartley gave Morton an opening to maybe nick it.

Mickey Weir was fairly unequivocal in his Monday newspaper column, citing apparent lack of intensity, commitment and desire – "It looked as if we were just going through the motions." He emphasised what an undoubted loss McGinn was, but concluded more hopefully that Commons would prove to be an asset, as would a re-energised Jason. Lennon admitted that he'd regretted not starting with the latter and you'd imagine the goalscorer would now be back in his plans for the immediate future.

Stevie 'Side' Burns in his weekly 'Fanzone' piece for The Scotsman was possibly even more scathing. He pointed out however that one advantage of the 5.15 p.m. live screening was that it afforded him the option of switching over to 'Pointless Celebrities' on BBC One, after ten minutes. There he had been enthralled to learn some previously unknown facts about Fatima Whitbread, which certainly trumped watching Hibs on Alba.

Meanwhile, the sidelined James Keatings was speaking highly of his old Parkhead compadre, having been a youth player there when Commons was an integral part of the picture. Keats compared him to Scott Brown, in the way that he always took time out to speak to and encourage the young hopefuls and assist in their training sessions.

"It's a great signing for us," he enthused. "Personally, seeing him coming in is a big boost. He is a top quality signing who is going to help the team. Hopefully he has a successful period and enjoys it – and then hopefully he wants to stay."

Well, time would tell with regard to that, but Kris had stressed that he'd never really felt surplus to requirements at Celtic and hadn't received any indication to that effect from Brendan Rodgers. Injury had put paid to his inclusion in the new manager's plans since his arrival and he was still intent on reasserting himself in the Hoops' first team.

'In a drear-nighted December / Too happy, happy Tree / Thy branches ne'er remember / Their green felicity' as the other Keats wrote two

centuries ago, which seemed appropriate as his modern day near-namesake would hopefully be poetry in motion for Hibs again soon. He looked in fair old fettle as he was photographed in front of the happy, happy Xmas tree in his green and white Santa hat. Next to him was a puzzled looking wee laddie clutching a big parcel, clearly thinking, Christ, that Mr Claus sure looks a whole lot younger when you see him in the flesh, as he eyed up James's beard and headgear. The occasion was the first team squad's annual visit to the Sick Children's Hospital to dispense some prezzies and read out rude jokes concealed inside Jason's special X-rated Christmas crackers. With the current crocked level of the team would it not have been more appropriate for those lazy bloody bairns to have been visiting them? A passing surgeon took one look at their peely-wally pusses and was thinking about keeping them all in for tests, when he was distracted by a loud noise. He whirled round to see Jason had pulled another cracker, but few would have blamed him – she was the best-looking nurse on the ward by a country mile.

Just to show that they were getting in the Christmas spirit too, those fuckwits at FIFA then fined the home nations varying sums for the crime of displaying poppy symbols on their shirts during the Armistice Day World Cup qualifiers. The governing body bans political symbols and had made it clear that they considered the poppy to be one, whilst the associations in question claimed it was no such thing. You can bet a certain former Hibee and current Celtic player was regretting his decision to return to the international fold quite so hastily, after his premature 'retirement'. FIFA instantly slapped an extra 50,000 Swiss francs fine on Scott personally, when they saw he was brazenly displaying the name of a former one-eyed Scottish Labour Prime Minister on his back. They were then informed than in an attempt at concealing his emblem of wartime remembrance from their prying eyes, he'd had it cunningly tattooed on his penis instead.

"That sounds like a load of poppycock," said Toby LeRone, the Swiss chairman of FIFA's disciplinary committee. "You wouldn't catch me with that stamped on *my* cuckoo clock."

It was little wonder really that the Swiss were getting all stroppy about the poppy and symbols pertaining to world wars, seeing as they'd been too cowardly to take part in either the first one, or its even bloodier sequel.

World football's body was also in a state of flux, as they were obliged to advertise for nominations to fill the vacant European positions on the Fifa Council. Heid bummer Gianni 'The Fanny' Infantino was puzzled when he kept receiving applications from dyslexic office drones in Methil; it transpired they'd mistakenly mis-read the 'a' in Fifa as an 'e'. The openings had arisen as a result of two of the current incumbents standing down and a third being bombed out for his part in the 2006 World Cup bribery scandal. First to chuck his astrakhan hat in the ring was Russia's deputy Prime Minister, Vitaly Mutko, on the understanding that he'd complete an eligibility test. Presumably to ascertain if he was vitally crooked into the bargain.

(Question 1. Have you ever been convicted of a criminal offence? 2. Do you have a history of telling porkie pies? 3. Are you continually in state of denial? 4. Do you have deep pockets? (i.e. roomy enough to accommodate cash-stuffed brown envelopes.) 5. Which prog-rock band did Rick Wakeman used to play keyboards for?

If you answered 'Yes' to all of them you were a shoo-in. As Mr Mutko was Russian Minister of Sport throughout the entire state-sponsored Olympic doping disgrace – later saying, "It wis nowt tae dae wi me," when the shit hit the fan – he was already a prime candidate for one of the vacancies anyway.

On the Tuesday before Christmas, Keats turned out for the Development Squad and lasted just over an hour in their thumping 4-1 win over Dundee at the Oriam. That kept the wee team at the top of their League too, aided again by a blistering performance from Oli Shaw, who notched his second hat-trick in a row. (He had some way to go though, to emulate Jimmy O'Rourke's feat from forty-four years ago – in the run up to Xmas 1972 he managed *six* hat-tricks, in just under three months for the first team!)

It was announced on the same day that, as expected, the PBS would be the venue for the Scottish Cup-tie against Bonnyrigg Rose. Doubtless the best option, although the main stand was likely to be out of commission due to the redevelopment work.

"Bonnyrigg is expected to be a ghost town on the day!" trilled the Press.

"No change there then," remarked the publisher of this tome, a native of the hometown of the mighty Rose.

Hibs were now looking ahead to their Christmas Eve fixture, where they were likely to be up against Rudi Skacel, Kevin McHattie and Jason Thomson, while Gary Locke stocked his two smoking barrels in the dug-out. Er, hang on, I thought the jambos were no longer in the same division as us?? No they weren't, but unfortunately the jambos in disguise were, masquerading as Raith Rovers for the foreseeable future.

"It's going to be a tough game," predicted Darren McGregor. "Gary Locke will want to win at Easter Road and there's a few jambos who'll want to celebrate their Christmas by beating us. They had a good result against Dundee United last weekend, they've an experienced manager with experienced players who will enjoy coming here, so it's up to us to make it as uncomfortable as possible for them."

Daz's stellar contribution to the backline meant that his team – with nine shut-outs to their credit and only nine goals conceded – could boast the most miserly defence of any professional outfit in the whole of Britain.

"People keep telling us that but we don't go into games thinking about it," he claimed. "We try to be organised, to do our job and I think we have done that quite well over the past couple of months. We pride ourselves on keeping clean sheets."

Over at the headquarters of Police Scotland (a.k.a. 'Scot Squad'), it appeared that some joker had surreptitiously changed all the office calendars to 'April' when no-one was looking and drawn a big red circle around the first day of that month. It could be the only explanation surely, as – shifting their focus from Hampden on May 21st for a moment – they tried to show that they were unbiased, by homing in on a jambo miscreant instead. The blurred CCTV image released was of such lamentable quality it wasn't even clear if the vague blob was of human form at all – as it purported to be of a scarf-twirler, it may well not have been of course. The picture was in black and white and it could just as easily have featured a panda – or a zebra. Luckily, Scot Squad had a vital clue in the hunt for the culprit, suspected of misbehaviour at a Hearts v Celtic game *six months ago.*

"He is described as being between twenty-five and thirty-five and was wearing a maroon top," the eagle-eyed public were informed.

Christ, that fair narrows it down a bit, eh? Good luck with that, then...

"Jingle bells, Kirkcaldy smells, Rovers make us heave, Oh what fun it is to draw with Raith on Christmas Eve..."

Going into the Xmas period with a song in our hearts, any sense of 'fun' turned out to be only fleeting and largely confined to the last couple of minutes – after Martin Boyle's equaliser. For this was yet another encounter during which Hibs chucked everything bar the kitchen sink at their opponents in the first half, producing some lovely touches, creating numerous chances, yet finding themselves a goal down four minutes into the second half. Sometimes it's just plain baffling. For before the interval, Hibs were in the ascendancy to roughly the same degree as they'd been just over a month previously against Queen of the South, which resulted in a 4-0 victory. But they just could not put the ball in the net. The man who mainly made them tick here was Dylan McGeouch, back in the fold again after his ankle injury and he must have felt frustrated watching a trio of his lay-offs go to waste. Holt mis-read his intentions and failed to pick up a neat pass, Jason hit another straight at Cuthbert in the Raith goal and Andrew Shinnie made a hash of a third. The latter was often guilty of over-elaborate play when a simpler more direct approach might have paid dividends and Cummings didn't have a whole lot of clear-cut chances over the piece. Plus points were a big improvement in Kris Commons from the previous week and a very assured performance from young Scott Martin alongside him, on from the start. 0-0 at half-time was frustrating, but it still seemed only a matter of time before the roof caved in on the Fifers.

The second half had barely got under way, when a cross from Rovers' Chris Johnston picked out the giant Jean-Yves M'voto, who rose unopposed to head past Laidlaw and open the visitors' account. Hibs sent on a restored James Keatings to replace Commons and he was quick to make his presence felt, taking a string of corner kicks which caused some anxiety in the Raith defence. However, by this stage they'd got so many men behind the ball they were inadvertently helping to keep Hibs at bay, as the ball ricocheted hither and thither, pinging off various bodies. Under such circumstances of course there was always the chance that the ball would take a deflection off someone and find its way into the net via that method, but it wasn't to be. That little shite Skacel was finally subbed before he was sent off, to a richly-deserved cacophony of booing from the home support. He came perilously close to putting Dylan McGeouch out of action again with a wild lunge on the half-time whistle which earned him a yellow card and he should have been shown a red for his predictable '5-1' gesture when leaving the park. If there's one Czech that deserves to be bounced from one end of Leith to the other before being cancelled altogether, it's him. Plenty players receive bookings for over-indulgent goal celebrations (Jason up on the fence against the jambos last season springs to mind), so referee Aitken was extremely lax in not further censuring Skacel for his antics. I'd already left my seat and had no sooner turned my back on the pitch to exit, when a roar of relief went up as Boyle (on to replace Jason fifteen minutes earlier) apparently fired in a low shot to beat Cuthbert and at least salvage a point.

"We could have won two games with the amount of chances and possession we had," sighed Lennon. "We had twenty-one attempts at goal – it was like the Alamo at the end. And that sums it up really. It's not as if we're not playing well. The first half we were excellent but, when you are on top, you have to take your chances. I've got to look at the performance. Did we play well? Yes. Did we create chances? Yes. Plenty. But we need to score when we are on top because if we had scored early on we would probably have won the game comfortably."

For the second week in a row, the gaining of a measly point initially seemed like a bonus, before harsh reality kicked in. Hibs had simply dropped far too many of those lately, with only one win so far throughout the last month of the year, allowing Dundee United to open up a two point lead at the top. They defeated St. Mirren 2-1 and were the form team in the Championship for now, adding extra significance to their next visit to Easter Road, scheduled for January 6th.

So we'd been bumped off the top of the League, even as Storm Babs gleefully ripped across the country causing disruption already exacerbated by the rail strikes. Throw in the terrorist attack in Berlin, cluster bombs in Yemen, the siege of Aleppo, the fatal plane crash in

Russia, the plane hijack in Libya, Donald Trump threatening to start a nuclear arms race, the Chilean earthquake, a typhoon in the Philippines, suicide bombings in Turkey and Iraq, the deaths of Rick Parfitt and George Michael, the Queen's runny nose and Santa eating all the pies – merry Christmas, everybody! (Or "Hah! Bumbag!" as the estimable Ebenezeer Scrooge would no doubt have remarked instead.)

Still, Charles Dickens' classic curmudgeonly character was probably enjoying his Christmas more than Ian Cathro, who was talking turkey after rising Lazarus-like from the dead and then instantly regretting it. Since taking over at Tynie, he'd managed to amass one point out of a possible nine and even that was highly fortunate, as Partick Thistle had absolutely ran rings around the jambos in the previous week's draw. Now he'd just masterminded the tricky act of snatching defeat from the jaws of victory, as a two-goal lead at Dens somehow transmogrified into a 3-2 win for Dundee. D'oh! Killie were next on the bill and Cathro confidently told the Press that he "expects Hearts supporters to raise the roof tomorrow night." Christ, the building work on the new stand must be progressing at a lightning rate, if they're at that stage already. Wonder if Annie B had OK'd payment of the minimum wage for the scaffold-erecting scarf-twirlers to go to work? But confusingly, he was later quoted as saying, "On the basis we start the game the way I intend for us to start the game, the roof will come off." Well, make your bloody mind up. Is it going on or is it coming off? It can't be both. Just get it sorted before the green and white army march in to smell the Roses on January 21st...

"Jingle bells, Houston swells, His big heid's in the way, Oh what fun it is to beat the Bairns on Hogmanay..."

(Well, you could hardly expect me to write 'f*** the Bairns' in these sensitive times could you, guys 'n' gals?) But Whitney's heid was fit for bursting long before the start of the last game of 2016, the purple vein in his big baldy bonce throbbing to a dangerous level as his team could only draw with Dunfermline in midweek. In time-honoured petulant diva fashion he blew a gasket over a penalty 'that never was', one of his lot getting red-carded (nothing unusual there) and then stating bluntly that the referee had gifted the game to the Pars. He certainly wasn't for serenading the man in black with a rendition of "I Will Always Love You", put it that way. If ever there was a man who fails to learn from his past behaviour, that man is undoubtedly Houston. He needs The Bodyguard alright, to protect him from himself. Forever flying off the handle, issuing wild accusations and placing his foot firmly in his ever-flapping mouth. Should make for an interesting conversation when he's next up before the Blazers, after accusing an official of blatant cheating.

Foregoing the dubious pleasures of a visit to Falkirk on the last day of 2016, I was relying on radio updates to keep me abreast of developments in this one, although they were few and far between, due to the blanket Old Firm derby coverage. I was however pleased to hear that Hibs had taken the lead in the fifteenth minute. I was less pleased to then hear the same announcer admit that he had in fact been talking pish, it was actually 1-0 to the home team, not the visitors. Then he contradicted himself again, saying in true festive panto style, "Oh no it isn't," as apparently Hibs had almost immediately drawn level. Who the hell was this joker – Grant Stott? I was half-expecting him to add, "Look out, he's behind you," causing me to birl round and see Houston spring up from behind my sofa waving a sharply-honed meat cleaver in my face. Who knew what to believe? The situation wasn't helped by the fact that the day's fixtures kicked off in a staggered manner at fifteen minute or half-hourly intervals, so it was hard to work out what stage each game was at, in the brief snippets between the Weedjie war reportage from the siege of Ibrox.

When the smoke dissipated however, it appeared that Jason had indeed promptly cancelled out an opener by Craig Sibbald and the teams remained locked together for the rest of the first half. You're pretty much guaranteed an extremely close contest with the Bairns and this was no different in that respect to the numerous tight tussles we'd had of late. It was by no means a classic, my Hibernian acquaintances who had made the trip informed me later, the most pleasing aspect up to this point probably being the performance of young Scott Martin. Again, he seemed to have no difficulty in slotting in alongside his more established team-mates and never looked cowed in facing up to the likes of ex-Hibee Tom Taiwo, his far more experienced opposite number in midfield.

By all accounts, Hibs looked to be heading for their third draw in a row as the second half progressed, until the recent acquisition from whom a lot had been expected finally came good. Bairns defender Peter Grant brought down Martin Boyle (who'd come on to replace Cummings some ten minutes earlier) and the free-kick award was so obvious that even Houston didn't disagree with it. As Jason had already vacated the field, Kris Commons was clearly the man most likely to take it – which he did, to stunning effect. With only three minutes left, he blasted an unstoppable screamer into the net from just beyond the eighteen-yard line. The Falkirk gaffer wasn't at all happy with his defenders' actions, grumbling that Hippolyte's height might have made all the difference, if he'd chosen to line up in the wall and risk having his head torn clean off his shoulders. Kris Commons could certainly empathise with the tall striker's reticence there.

"For me, being in a wall myself, if anybody hits the ball towards my head, I'm ducking," he said. "So it takes a brave man to stand there when I hit it that hard to take one in the face. So I just went on instinct and hit it as hard as I could. With the wind behind me I just thought I'd hit it as hard as possible. I was aiming for heads and hoping they were going to move – and they did."

Neil Lennon had signed him knowing that, on form, he was capable of pulling something out of the top drawer which could decisively impact on a vital game and that was exactly what transpired here. Again, it had not been a vintage performance overall from an under-strength side, but this was a highly valuable result. Not least, because Dundee United unexpectedly lost to Dumbarton for the second time this season, meaning that Hibs jumped back up over them to head the table, this time by a clear point as well as a superior goal difference of plus eight. The rest of the pack now looked a long way behind, with Morton lying in third place after a last gasp equaliser at St. Mirren and although they had a game in hand over the table-toppers they were trailing the Hibees by eleven points.

There was good news too on the injury front, as Keatings made the bench (although he didn't feature) and McGinn and Marciano would also be in contention for the first game of the New Year, against the Arabs at Easter Road. Neil Lennon revealed that Fraser Fyvie and Danny Handling weren't far away from a possible return either.

"We've had some important players missing and we've had to work our way through it. Every win is precious and we have a big game on Friday. Being top of the table again could be very good psychologically."

Putting pen to paper as the old year drew its last breath was Jamaican winger Chris Humphrey, the former Motherwell player who'd just had his contract at Preston North End terminated by mutual agreement. The twenty-nine year-old was here until the end of the season at least and appeared enthusiastic about his move back north of the border.

"I am pleased to be signing with Hibs. The team are pushing hard for promotion this season and I'll hopefully be able to help us achieve that."

So 2016, the year which forever would be etched into the annals of Hibernian history as a result of the Hampden heroics in the summer, had ended on a pretty satisfactory note. We'd certainly have liked to be further ahead at the top of the table, but our closest challengers had just had an unforeseen wobble, which wouldn't do a lot for their confidence going into the table-topping clash the following Friday. Being Hibbies, we knew from bitter experience not to start counting our chickens, but at the halfway stage it was increasingly looking like a two-horse race for the Championship.

7.

JANUARY: TRAINSPOTTING WITH NEIL LENNON

One man familiar with Hibs' newest recruit was Grant Holt, who played with him during his spell at Shrewsbury Town. Grant managed to get on the scoresheet roughly once every two games when with the Shrews, leading to his eventual £400,000 move to Norwich City and he credited Chris was assisting in a good few of the goals.

"He will give us a good option with his pace on the wing, which is something we do not have at the moment. Kris Commons can play there as can Martin Boyle, but we don't have an out-and-out winger. We'll be looking for anyone who is brought into the club to help the team and push us on."

Chris could turn out to be the most popular Jamaican with a Hibs connection since reggae superstar Bob Marley used to catch the Whelehan Branch bus to away games in the late 1970s. (Allegedly, I should add.) Hibs Monthly fanzine were largely responsible for creating this myth I seem to recall and although I don't think I was guilty at the outset, I no doubt aided and abetted this preposterous tale growing arms and legs later on. If memory serves right, it was as a result of someone coming across a photo of Bob's son Ziggy wearing what vaguely a resembled a Hibs top that kick-started it in the first place. Anyway, let's hope that, unlike Bob, we're not left Waiting in Vain (for promotion) once again.

Back in the real world and Chris's old Shrews sidekick was admitting that the performance against the Bairns had been far from easy on the eye. But as he pointed out, "There have been games when we've played well and got nothing. Against Falkirk we played poorly and got a win – so which one do you want? We played better against Raith Rovers and got a 1-1 draw. We weren't happy with our performance at Falkirk, but that's the mark of champions."

Oh gawd, not the 'c' word please, Grant, not just yet anyway. Let's not jinx it this early in 2017.

"Our fans probably went away disappointed in terms of our performance, but they'd be singing and dancing into the New Year because we got the three points. All that mattered was the win. Had anyone said beforehand that we'd go there and come away with a 2-1 win, we'd have taken that."

Well, no arguments there. He also concurred with the oft-voiced assertion that other Championship sides tended to raise their game against Hibs, sometimes to an 'unbelievable' level. He'd watched plenty matches involving other outfits who were a million miles away in terms of performance and commitment from the standard they somehow attained when up against Hibs.

"Teams will try to frustrate and make it difficult for us but we have to keep answering the questions."

As to the Tangerine lot about to pose the next raft of questions at the end of the week, Holty was determined to make up for the disappointing outcome at Tannadice back on December 2nd.

"We'll be looking to perform this time because we feel we didn't do ourselves any credit – although we should probably still have won."

Meanwhile, Lennon was singing the praises of Scott Martin – rightly so – declaring him "one of the best players in the Development League all season." He'd been delighted with his performance against Raith initially, as that had been his first outing in a Championship game since the opening day fixture against Falkirk (although he did feature in the Irn-Bru Diddy Cup-tie at Turriff.) Scott got his chance against the Rovers after Marvin Bartley had been dropped in the wake of his indifferent showing against Morton the previous week and had seized on it eagerly. Now he'd impressed his gaffer further, in a bigger game at the Falkirk Stadium.

"The competition we have in midfield has made it very difficult for him to be in the squad," went on Neil. "But he's taken his chance and done really well. We are very pleased with his progress."

Over at Waverley Station, Scot Squad were forced to take time out from looking at photographs of the cup final pitch invasion for nine hours every day to deal with a far more pressing concern – apparently a scorpion had got loose on the London – Edinburgh train. Some daft bint had opened a piece-box and allowed it to escape, causing panicking passengers to flee in all directions. What on earth was she thinking of – having it for lunch?

"It was the wrong kind of scorpion," said a spokesman for East Coast Trains in a futile attempt at reassuring them. "It hadn't got a sting."

"Quite correct," confirmed Scot Squad. "There was no Sting present. We have ascertained that he is in fact a member of The Police. The rock band that is, not the Keystone Cops comedy outfit in the black and white checked hats. We will shortly be posting a series of images on our database and website in an attempt at identifying the source of the current problem."

True to their word, the following day the Press headlines screamed 'HAVE YOU SEEN THIS MAN?' accompanied by a blurred out-of-focus photograph of Michael Schenker, the original lead guitarist with The Scorpions. Scot Squad said that once they tracked him down they were confident that a pincer movement would lead to him being successfully apprehended.

So the first week of the year passed with a brief lull in the on-going celebrity death toll, as Hibs prepared to face down their main challengers. Chris Humphrey declared himself "fit and ready" to play if required, but was just happy to be part of a set-up where he felt wanted once again.

"It was a no-brainer," he said, explaining why he'd jumped at the chance to return north, despite plenty of English clubs being keen on what he had to offer. "When Hibs came in to say they were interested and you have a manager like that, you just think 'it would be fantastic to play under him.' Obviously I know Scotland very well, although Edinburgh is new to me. I visited a couple of times when I was at Motherwell but I've had a good look around since I've been here and it's a fantastic place."

Unsurprisingly, his abiding memory of his tenure with the Steelmen was partaking in the downright crazy and scarcely believable 6-6 draw with Hibs at Fir Park at the end of his first season there. The Hibees managed to throw away a four-goal lead on that surreal occasion, having led 6-2 at one stage and might even have gone home completely empty-handed as Motherwell also missed a penalty. But now he was looking forward to reacquainting himself with his old Shrewsbury striking partner and reminiscing about their last season playing together.

"Holty and I got thirty goals between us – he got twenty-eight and I got two. To be fair though, I think I got seven or eight assists! At Shrewsbury

I was very, very quick. I just want to try to bring some pace to the team and try and link up with the boys. I see Martin (Boyle) is very fast, as is Jason. It'll be nice to link up with them and Holty in the box – anything can happen. I'm just really excited. It's nice to have that excitement back in playing again."

His son and daughter would be in attendance at Easter Road, although the former was so young he didn't really understand why daddy wouldn't be playing for Preston any more. However, the shrewd purchase of a brand spanking new Hibs top for him soon had the desired placatory effect there.

In the event, the laddie must have been over the moon, as Chris had an absolutely sensational debut, on being handed a start by Neil Lennon. To throw on someone who hadn't kicked a ball in earnest for nigh on four months was undoubtedly a gamble, particularly in such a big game, but the manager's bold decision paid off in spades. The Jamaican dynamo didn't get a chance to buddy up with his old mucker Holty though, as Neil opted to go with Jason from the off, another brave call which was wholly vindicated. Indeed, you could have been forgiven for thinking that it was these two who were rekindling a double-act of their own, such was the ease with which they linked up with each-other. Humphrey looked like he'd been part of the set-up for ages and any lingering doubts about his pace perhaps being diminished by the passing years were firmly laid to rest. He teed up the first goal for his striking partner within six minutes and with Martin Boyle also in fantastic form the Arabs were almost immediately put to the sword. They simply had no answer to the terrific speed of Hibs' twin champion sprinters and their defence was cut to pieces time and again. Marvin Bartley returned to the middle of the park and he too turned in a tremendous performance, scrapping for (and usually winning) every ball, despite some rough stuff from the men in tangerine. The sponsors awarded him 'Man of the Match' which was some accolade, on an evening where every single player in green and white was worthy of plaudits. The United left-back, Paul Dixon, had a torrid time, fruitlessly trying to contain the electric Humphrey and it was no surprise when the latter ripped him up for arse-paper yet again, to set up Jason for a sublime second. We were just past the halfway mark of the first period and that only served to gee up the mercurial Jase even more, seemingly intent on notching a hat-trick before the interval. Well, he didn't quite manage that but it wasn't for the want of trying, although on a couple of occasions he might have aided his team better by passing, rather than choosing to go it alone. Still, few in the noisily buoyant crowd would have begrudged him the decision to do so.

Hibs eased up slightly in the opening period of the second half, but United created very few real chances and on the few occasions they looked on the point of a breakthrough, the reliable duo of Hanlon and McGregor were there to stop them. It must have been a dispiriting experience for our opponents – even if you got past those two, Ross Laidlaw was ever alert in goal, despite having little to do for long periods. Yet his concentration never wavered and he pulled off a superb instinctive save from Obedeyi, as well as blocking another couple of efforts confidently. Possibly the second loudest roar of the night from the sold-out home sections came with the introduction of Super John McGinn to the fray for the last ten minutes, before the loudest one then exceeded it, as he took possession from a corner kick. He then jinked past Scott Fraser and headed for the goal-line. Just when everyone was expecting a cross to flash over for the ever-lurking forwards he opted instead for a shot, drilling a wonderful effort from a very tight angle to beat the usually stalwart Cammy Bell in goal hands down.

On the final whistle, the players and manager ran over to acknowledge the fans' sterling backing, as The Proclaimers' 'I'm On My Way' reverberated around the stadium. Sitting on top of the world for sure; sitting on top of the League too.

"It gives us a boost and psychologically it gives the fans a lift but nothing more," said the manager, happy to play it down for the time being. On the debut by Humphrey for which he must take a lot of the credit, he added, "It has made me proud and surprised me. He is a good player, came in on Monday and stood out in training. He has not played in a while obviously. It was a bit of a gamble – sometimes it works and sometimes it doesn't. Thankfully he played well and started well and was aided by some other good performances – I thought Martin Boyle was outstanding. We looked like we might score every time we attacked, particularly in the first half. They showed their big game mentality because there was a lot of pressure or at least a lot of build-up."

All in all this was a wonderful display from Hibs, dispelling any remaining doubts about their tenacity and ability to last the course in yet another punishing Championship race. Some of the recent showings had not been top-notch, as Neil was forced to jiggle things around due to injury, but they had comprehensively beaten the team who looked like their only serious contenders for the League. Certainly, they all deserved a huge pat on the back after this encounter. The pundits on the following evening's 'Sportscene' were full of praise, particularly former Hibee Tam McManus, who got a bit carried away. Pointing to the fact that as usual it could and perhaps should have been more, he enthused, "Hibs could have won by three or four!"

"Er…they *did* win by three, Tam," interjected fellow panellist Steven Thompson.

"Well, they could have won by four or five then!" exclaimed McManus defiantly.

That day's fixtures saw both Morton and Falkirk win, to retain third and fourth places respectively, but for the first time this season Hibs were now clearly out ahead of the pack, four points ahead of United.

On leaving the stadium, I made my way along Albion Road and had just turned left onto Easter Road, when the number one bus obligingly drew up at the stop. This night just gets better and better, I thought, as sightings of said service at this time can be rarer than those of the Loch Ness Monster. I gratefully climbed aboard whereupon it quickly filled up with Hibbies, before moving off. Just as I was contentedly contemplating being back home in record time it stopped again, after travelling all of thirty yards. We could see a myriad flashing blue lights just up ahead.

"It'll be the polis escorting the United fans away," announced the voice of a Know-All from the back – there always seems to be one aboard when these kinds of situations develop. "We'll be on our way in a minute."

"I don't know how long we're going to be here, folks," said the driver at this point. "The whole road's blocked off."

"See?" remarked Know-All triumphantly, as if to say, "I told you so."

A confused hubbub ensued, whereupon most of the passengers opted to dismount again, when the driver opened the doors. As I was heading right across town I decided to stay put for the moment, to see what developed.

"No problems," said Know-All happily, also remaining in his seat. "It's only the polis – no ambulances or anything like that."

A Hibbie in front of me had been peering through the windscreen at the jumble of vehicles parked at odd angles up ahead and was growing increasingly hot under the collar.

"Oh aye?" he retorted, jabbing a finger towards the window on the Bothwell Street side. "What's that thing there then?"

"What thing?"

"That white thing with A – M – B – U – L –A – N – C – E written down the fucking side of it, that's what fucking thing," snapped his fellow passenger, before getting to his feet and making his way down the aisle.

As he got off, a policeman jumped aboard, to converse with the driver.

"That'll be us on our way now," beamed Know-All happily, quite unfazed.

"THAT'S AS FAR AS WE'RE GOING TONIGHT I'M AFRAID," shouted the driver. "The rest of you will have to get off now."

Just then, a roly-poly woman sitting on the inside of my seat suddenly opened her eyes and took her headphones off.

"Where are we?" she wailed distractedly. "WHAT'S HAPPENING?!"

"The road's blocked," I explained, grumpily reflecting that £1.60 was a bit steep for a journey of thirty yards.

I was trying to think of it as being 'ninety feet' instead, just to get my money's worth.

"WHY??" she howled, blasting my coupon with her hundred per cent proof rancid alcoholic breath.

She pushed rudely past me, staggered up the aisle and glared at the bearer of bad tidings.

"You're takin' the pish, pal!" she informed the driver, before tumbling clumsily out through the doors and collapsing in the street.

By the time I'd got off, she'd rolled over onto her back and was clawing impotently at the air with her chubby paws, like a giant malformed turtle trying to right itself. I delicately picked my way past her and chapped on the rear door of the ambulance.

"Yes?" demanded a harassed-looking medic, on opening up.

"Another customer for you," I offered, pointing at the quivering heap still spouting forth profanities from the gutter.

Ah well, it was a nice enough night for a walk anyway; a four-mile one as it turned out though, after I discovered I didn't have any more change. D'uh!

Meanwhile, those Premier League saps with the chilly willies were all away to sunnier climes for their January jollies. You've got to hand it to the authorities – the mildest winter in living memory is forecast, so they decide to have a three week break. Let's hope there's a deep freeze in February, that'll learn 'em! I'd stupidly put a fleece on under my jacket and sweated away about half my body weight before Jason got his second. By the time Super scored, I was a mere shadow of my former self. The nonsense of the shutdown was briefly discussed on 'Sportscene', with Tam McManus looking misty-eyed as he recalled his own winter break when still with Hibs. They did it in style back then – never mind, "We're all off to sunny Spain", the Hibees were bound for Scarborough Fair instead. Scarborough in Trinidad & Tobago, that is.

"Do much training there, did you?" enquired studio anchor David Currie, raising a quizzical eyebrow.

Tam remained non-committal on that, as well he might. When he returned he had a worse smoking habit than Russell Latapy, who had craftily orchestrated the whole hoopla, in order to visit his family for free.

By the start of the following week Jason was optimistically talking up his hopes of exceeding his goal tally of the previous season, despite his earlier barren spell and subsequent confinement to the bench. He was nearly halfway there anyway, so if he remained on form and Neil continued playing him from the start, there was no reason why not.

"Twelve goals is a decent return because I haven't started as many games as I would have liked. I will just keep plugging away, as every game I look to score as many as I can. I want to try to beat my record for last season. When you are not playing a lot of thoughts go through your head," he added.

Whoa, careful with that thinking stuff there, Jase, don't overdo it... He referred to the comeback by his close pal thus – "The Meatball came on and it turned into The John McGinn Show." Christ, just how many nicknames does any one player need? Not long ago the man in question was alluding to himself as 'Sponge'. Super Meatball Sponge, eh? Sounds like the sort of vile concoction you'd get out of 'Subway' at lunchtime.

Sir David Gray found himself in agreement with his manager, going along with his assessment of the year's first performance being the best of the campaign so far. He also acknowledged the contribution made by the newest recruit, saying, "I'm just glad Chris is in my team and that I'm not playing against him. Like Martin on the other flank he has real genuine pace which is hard to play against. I thought Chris was outstanding, he gave Dixon a real hard time but it could have been anyone. It was fantastic to see so many supporters there. When Easter Road is full like that, there's no better place to play football."

...But I would walk five hundred miles and I would walk five hundred more, just to be the man who walks a thousand miles to fall down at your door – especially if you had a few cans of beer in the fridge and a cup final DVD to view. But would you fly six thousand miles and fly six thousand more yourself, just to be the man who flew twelve thousand miles to see the cup upon the shelf? Well, an Australia-based Hibbie did just that, to join the approximately fifteen thousand folk who'd already had their picture taken with the silver lady. Unable to make it over for the final, he'd watched the game live in his local in Oz, but had at least completed the emotional pilgrimage to the Old Course at St. Andrews, where it was on display alongside golf's oldest trophy, The Claret Jug. On hand to help the old girl along towards the end of her marathon tour of hospitals, hospices, schools, church halls, pubs and social clubs were ex-Hibees, The Twa Kevins (Harper and Thomson.) We're getting that fatally attracted to the glittering bauble that the boys are just going to have to do their damndest to hang onto it for another year at least...

There was a belated accolade for one of the heroes of that afternoon last May, as goalkeeper Conrad Logan was in receipt of The Professional Sports Achievement Award at the Donegal Sports Star ceremony in Ireland. Indeed, if it hadn't been for Conrad's special brand of heroics in the semi-final, we might not have been back at the National Tip on May 21st at all.

"It means a lot," beamed the big man. "I really enjoyed my time with Hibs and I'll always be grateful to the club for giving me the opportunity to play after returning from injury. Personally, the last couple of months I spent there couldn't have worked out any better. Winning the Scottish Cup was special. It was a fantastic occasion for everyone involved, particularly the fans and it was amazing to be part of the side who won the competition for the first time in 114 years."

Then came sports news of a different kind from across the Big Pond – watersports that is, with the media alleging that the President-Elect Donald Chump had been partaking of such perverted pleasures with prostitutes. They're taking the piss surely, I thought. Well, either that or *he* is...

Likewise Dundee F.C., who seemed to have reluctantly shelved the idea of playing a 'home' Premiership fixture against Celtic in the USA, possibly in either Boston or Philadelphia. They'd actually had discussions with Celtic and the SPFL over this proposal; the lure being that they hoped to attract a bumper gate courtesy of the expatriate community and Irish diaspora on the east coast of America. Well it made a change from Celtic forever bawling and greeting that they wanted to play in England – how about *New* England, chaps – fancy that instead? Nah, thought not. But we really can't be encouraging this sort of thing. I mean, where will it all end? Stenhousemuir would be demanding to play their home games in Norway as a nod to their bonkers Scandinavian fan club (which is bigger than most of the attendances at Ochilview), Aberdeen would be ramming in an application for the Falkland Islands to capitalise on the extensive sheep population and the jambos would be wanting to play at Murrayfield – again. Cathro said he'd certainly be keen on that idea, as long as the SRU left those funny big extended posts behind – then his team might manage to score at home occasionally.

Also with scoring on his mind was Derek Riordan, who was sharing some unwelcome information about his sex life as well as opinions on Jason Cummings with the Evening News.

"I prefer to pull out to the left, whereas he's a bit more of a poacher," The Deekster was quoted as saying.

Well, at least the second part of that sentence contained positive news – but was it true? When Peterborough were after him at the start of the season he confessed he couldn't boil an egg, much less poach one. However, if anyone was wanting to shell out for him now, they were wasting their time.

"He's not for sale," stated Neil Lennon. "I want to keep him."

Meanwhile, Hibs were preparing themselves for a trip to the notoriously awkward venue of Dumbarton, by temporarily narrowing the playing surface on the training pitch at East Mains, to simulate the conditions they'd face at The Cheaper Insurance Direct Stadium over the weekend.

"This is a dangerous game for us," warned the manager. "I think it's the trickiest venue to go to in the Championship, particularly with the inclement weather at the minute."

They really should have dug out the wind machine down East Lothian way too, to add further authenticity. The howling gales which frequently tear through the wide open spaces and one-sided structure in the west are hardly conducive to good football either, as so many of Hibs' contemporaries had found out. Dundee United had gone there twice, only to emerge with zero points and Falkirk had left empty-handed as well.

There were further worries for the Arabs, when new Danish signing Thomas Mikkelson airily promised that he was all set to become 'the new Duncan Ferguson'. Ray McKinnon couldn't sleep for a week after he heard that, his dreams plagued by swarms of pigeons swooping through the hallways of Barlinnie.

At Easter Road, Neal Eardley's short deal came to an end, as he departed in the direction of Northampton Town. Brought on board as a potential stand-in for Sir David, he'd been largely surplus to requirements and had only featured twice as a substitute since late September.

By the weekend, I was halfway through my personal 'Dry January', which already felt like a whole lot longer than a mere fortnight. But by God, I was going to stick with this half-arsed annual fitness kick, even if it killed me. Death by boredom was surely looming on the horizon. So on Saturday I took a fourteen mile hike along the Water of Leith Walkway and back, timing my return for the full-time scores starting to trickle in on 'Sportscene'. I flipped on the box and...*what??* *Dumbarton's scored??* Whoa, steady on there – it's only *dumb* Barton who's managed that, as Jailbird Joey notched the solitary goal for Burnley on his comeback from an extended all-expenses paid holiday at the Ibrox Leisure Spa in Glasgow. Thank Christ for that. Happily, the news from The Cheaper Insurance Dire Wrecked Stadium was a whole lot better, with Hibs leading 1-0. As an extra bonus, Dundee United were losing 3-1 at home to Queen of the South, although the abysmal Arabs would ultimately claw it back to 3-3.

In the event, the Hibees did hold out for the single goal victory, although there were a few nervy moments, particularly in the second half. Fraser Fyvie made his return and lasted the full ninety minutes, as Fontaine deputised for Paul Hanlon who was absent with a pelvic strain. Like John McGinn (who came on in the seventieth minute), Paul had been playing through the pain barrier of late to aid his team-mates, but it looked like he'd only be out for a couple of weeks, hopefully. It was the ever-improving Kris Commons who made all the difference yet again, as he found himself well-positioned to intercept a poor attempted clearance by Darren Barr on the fourteenth minute. Looking increasingly sharp, the on-loan Celtic man struck a first-time effort past keeper Alan Martin and there were hopes that the Sons – like the Arabs the week before – might simply collapse after that as Hibs turned the screw, but it wasn't to be. It soon evolved into the standard grim slog on the narrow pitch with neither Humphrey or Boyle able to utilise their pace on the flanks which had so stymied United at Easter Road.

However, the back-line was in fine fettle again, seemingly untroubled by the change necessitated by Hanlon's absence and Ross Laidlaw continued to show that he was a cool customer when under any sort of pressure. Despite long periods of enforced idleness he's not one to let his guard down and he was quick to throw himself at the feet of Sons' striker Lewis Vaughan to smother an almost certain equaliser. He also saw one clip the bar and when our old nemesis Christian Nade suddenly rumbled into the middle, most Hibbies were resigned to the familiar fat curse striking again. Happily however, he was distracted by the sight of the pie-stand behind the goal and contrived to miss from all of two yards. So Hibs were living rather dangerously, although they improved once the double substitution saw Super and Holty come on for Humphrey and a largely ineffectual Cummings. Dumbarton had blown their best opportunities and never again came so close, as the game petered out with Jordon Forster replacing Commons for the last ten minutes. Hibs held on and although it was far from a classic, no-one had realistically expected it to be! We knew by now what it was like going to awkward venues like this and if it wasn't exactly easy on the eye, there was no doubt that the points garnered were the most important consideration.

"There's still a long way to go, but it's massive to go there and get the points," confirmed Ross Laidlaw. "Sometimes it isn't about the performance, it's just about getting the points, but we also kept another clean sheet which made it a good result away from home."

"I knew how difficult it was going to be," acknowledged Neil Lennon. "They'd beaten United and Falkirk, Steve Aitken had won Manager of the Month. It was important we got the first goal because if it had gone to Dumbarton they'd have camped in. They had a real good go at it, but these are the games you have to grind out."

So Hibs were now six points clear of Dundee United at the top of the table, with a vastly superior goal difference to boot.

The main post-match talking point was whether or not Kris Commons had indeed played his last game for Hibs, as his official loan period was now up, but that would be a matter for the backroom boys to thrash out with their Parkhead counterparts.

One man who wouldn't be sticking around any longer was Otso Virtanen, heading back to Finland to join a local club. It was probably best for all concerned – he'd only featured twice in the first team, once as a sub in the Scottish Cup quarter-final replay away to Inverness the previous season and against Brondby in the Europa qualifier. He'd looked very jittery in the former and lost a bad goal in the latter and clearly had no realistic chance of establishing himself between the sticks at Easter Road.

The League could now be put on hold for a fortnight or so, as attention switched to the upcoming Scottish Cup-tie against Bonnyrigg Rose, at the venue with a happy history for the Hibees lately.

"Our recent memories of Tynecastle are good," said Lewis Stevenson. "We've had some good performances and results there."

None more so than the League Cup semi win of a year ago or the scarcely believable comeback against the jambos in the Big Cup, roaring back to equalise from a two-goal deficit ten minutes before the end.

"Scottish Cup-ties before were the games we felt most pressure and a bit of that's gone since we won it," observed the only man to have done the double to gain both a League Cup and a Scottish Cup winners' medal with Hibs. He'd accompanied the cup on what had been a seemingly never-ending tour akin to that of Bob Dylan's, but which was now drawing to a close. Lewis had enjoyed the visits to primary schools on his home turf of Fife the most, marvelling at how the appearance of the Holy Grail would hold the attention and silence even the more boisterous classroom of youngsters. As to the DVD of the day itself, he wasn't one for looking back on past glories.

"I've honestly never watched it from start to finish. If I watch it I'd still be hyper-critical of myself – I hate watching myself on telly."

Meanwhile, our upcoming opponents were making fools of themselves with a photo-shoot in tribute to their most famous ex-player, posing for the camera while decked out in dicky-bows, white dinner jackets and Sean Connery face-masks. Hibs were neither shaken nor stirred by this display of male (James) Bonding. Agents 007, eh? It's Agents 007 Nil in green and white who are more synonymous with deadly shooting at Tynecastle, I'm afraid, chaps. O'Rourke, Gordon, Cropley and Duncan – they call them the unseen assassins, Miss Moneypenny...

This appeared in the Press at the same time as the revelation that the green green grass of home was getting right up Neil Lennon's nose – quite literally. His downstairs neighbour – a former Tennent's 'Lager Lovely' named Karen Thomson - had just been busted for running a cannabis factory from her spare room. Last time she'd gone away on holiday she'd asked Neil to water her plants and he'd innocently complied, unfortunately inhaling as he did so. He'd not been that stoned since the time huns were regularly throwing rocks at him in the street when he was still managing Celtic.

When he straightened up, the gaffer was quick to award a full-time professional contract to the laddie named after two former Hibees, Kane O'Connor. An Under-17 internationalist, he'd had a string of impressive performances for the Development Squad under his belt and looked to have a bright future. With a handle like that, how could he fail? If he turned out half as good as that Riordan O'Rourke he'd be doing OK...

With the Bonnyrigg tie now imminent, the gaffer could at least rest easy in the knowledge that he wouldn't be asked the yearly question posed to every Hibs manager since time immemorial, namely, "So when are you going to lay this jinx to rest then?"

"There was a psychological barrier we have got through and it just meant so much to everyone involved," was Neil's take on it. Obviously he hadn't been there at the time, but was well aware of the significance of the cup win. "Once you have the taste of that success then you want more. The players had the best day of their lives last year so why not aim for that again? Once you have a hold on something you don't want to let it go. You don't realise what you will miss until it's gone. The Hibs fans can bask in the glory of that day and I would like to do it again."

There was no danger he'd be underestimating our opponents either, especially in the wake of their shock victory in the previous round.

"There will be no stone left unturned from our side of the fence. We have had them watched and we have footage of them. We know they are a good team and probably could play in the League at some level. They have a good record in junior football."

Before the match I was treated to an early kick-off at the Easter Road hospitality courtesy of Irvine Welsh, in town for the World Premiere of 'T2 Trainspotting', which he'd alluded to as "the second most important cultural event in Edinburgh this weekend, after Hibs v Bonnyrigg." Ho hum, that'll be 'Dry January' kicked into touch then, I thought, popping guiltily into Middleton's for a sneaky wee half-pint on my way there at precisely 10.45 a.m. Welsh then proceeded to disgrace himself by ignoring the injunction against sweary words, when asked to give a spiel to the assembled diners and drinkers gathered in the hozzy suite.

"At least it puts to bed once and for all the 'they've no' won it since Buffalo Bill shagged Queen Victoria' shite or whatever the fucking jambos keep claiming," was his take on winning the big silvery beast, which stood there proudly gleaming within tantalising touching distance of Table One.

We were then joined by guests of honour Alan Stubbs and John Doolan, who turned out every bit the sort of smashing down-to-earth modest blokes you always imagined they'd be in person. Stubbsy took to the microphone (without resorting to effing and blinding – take note, Mr Welsh) and revealed that he couldn't have cared less about what transpired on the Hampden turf on the final whistle. But at the time he obviously had to pay lip service to the expectations of the outraged west of Scotland media when speaking about it. He'd felt quietly confident of securing the prize all along and felt that Rangers were running scared of Hibs despite their semi-final victory over Celtic, which was borne out by Warby's increasingly distracted behaviour as the clock ticked down towards May 21st. Interestingly, he'd also felt optimistic of ultimately overcoming the jambos in the earlier stages, even when they were 2-0 down in the first game with only ten minutes left! I personally congratulated him on that, saying that he was the first manager in a very long time to apparently understand the significance of putting one over on the maroon mob and having the savvy to instil in his players the belief that such a task was achievable, even at two behind.

Then came the rather surreal journey by coach across town to Tynecastle to face down the *other* Midlothian mob – it just felt odd travelling to an 'away' game (or was it a neutral one?) in the same city, with Easter Road as the starting point and then entering the stadium via the Wheatfield Stand. That was a first for me at least, as I'd been in the Gorgie Stand for the League Cup semi-final the previous season (same end as I'd stood in on January 1st, 1973) and it had been decades since I'd last squeezed through those shitty turnstiles on the Wheatfield Road side. There was no stand back then of course, just that sinister shed with the overflowing open pish-hooses at the back of the terracing. A quick trip to the lavvy revealed that not much had changed for the better there, at least...

There was never any danger that Hibs were going to approach this one with anything less than full concentration and commitment, despite their opponents' status. Everyone was well aware of their Championship scalp-taking in the previous round and Chris Humphrey was clear about Neil Lennon's outlook.

"The gaffer isn't going to take anyone lightly, no matter who they are. He prepares the same, looks at the opposition, comes up with a game plan and we go out and try and play to it."

Neil did make half-a-dozen changes from the side who'd defeated Dumbarton, the most surprising perhaps being Rocky's recall, as Ross Laidlaw had been doing a satisfactory enough job between the sticks. The Israeli must have been wishing he hadn't bothered, as he was soon crocked again after only twenty minutes, following an accidental collision with Liam Fontaine. So Ross took to the field after all, by which time his team were already two up with a third looming on the horizon.

Rose had given a decent account of themselves in the first ten minutes with a plucky opening spell, but keeper Andrews then made a howler in failing to collect a speculative effort from Shinnie. The Hibs man must have been surprised to see that one creep in at the corner of the net, but there was no mistaking the quality of the second goal, only three minutes later. A beautiful curler from Keatings would have eluded any goalkeeper and by the time Humphrey notched his debut goal for his new club Hibs were already on easy street. However, an undeserved penalty award just after the half-hour threw Bonnyrigg something of a lifeline and with the score 3-1 in Hibs' favour at the interval, they couldn't be counted out just yet. As we all know, a two goal cushion is generally the minimum you want where Hibs are concerned, to engender some sense of relaxation over the final outcome.

The second half was all of seven minutes old when Jason got the first of his brace courtesy of a Stevenson cross and Lewis himself made one of his rare forays onto the scoresheet shortly after that. A potential tanking looked on the cards now (shades of 1/1/73 again), but although the crowd were vociferous in their desire for seven, the fact that Rose scored from the spot put paid to any notion of the magic scoreline becoming a reality. Jase then got his second which was followed by another corker from Keatings and double figures were a distinct possibility with nearly fifteen minutes still remaining. Rose had tried their best and were far from disgraced, but were incapable of creating anything really after their bright opening and the huge gulf between the sides was now clearly apparent. You were left wondering just quite how shite Dumbarton must have been – *twice* – in the last round. If there's one thing in this world rarer than a Lewis Stevenson goal then that thing is surely one emanating from Jordon Forster, which transpired when the big defender got his head on the end of a Keatings free-kick. We had wanted seven and now had one more – with a seven goal margin. The fourth time I'd seen Hibs win 8-1 – they'd done it against Forfar and Ayr United in the seventies and Kilmarnock in the eighties and this one was every bit as convincing, if not more so.

That evening I was aghast to see myself and companion appear unwittingly on 'Sportscene', as the camera mercilessly zeroed in on the Wheatfield Stand at some point, during coverage of the highlights. Within half-an-hour my moby was swamped with texts from various lowlifes, all saying basically the same thing, i.e. 'who's that ugly fucker sitting next to Irvine Welsh?' Ho ho ho. Gratifyingly, he later confirmed he'd had a similar response, although in his case inquiring just who the ugly fucker sitting next to Sandy Macnair happened to be. But I'd never had much luck when featured on the telly in a Hibs context. At the League Cup Final of 2004 I was wearily making my way up the aisle towards the back of Hampden's East Stand with about fifteen minutes remaining, intending to view the rest of the grim spectacle from there before making a quick getaway. Unbeknownst to me, the TV cameras chose that very moment to zoom in for a rear close-up, as the commentator announced, "...and the dejected Hibernian supporters are already leaving the stadium *in droves*..." As I was wearing a daft green and white tammy knitted by someone's mad granny and had hair hanging halfway down my back at the time is was hard to deny my identity later, as every fucking scarf-twirling jambo I'd ever come across in my entire life appeared to have seen it and gleefully observed, "We could see you sneaking off..." John Logie Baird's wretched invention was becoming the bane of my bloody life. As Frank Zappa memorably sneered on 'Trouble Every Day' - *'Well you can cool it you can heat it / Cos baby I don't need it / Take your TV tube and eat it / And all that phony stuff on sports / And all the unconfirmed reports / You know I watch that rotten box until my head begins to hurt...''*

"I was very pleased with the way we approached the game," said a satisfied Neil Lennon after the Bonnyrigg blitzkrieg, "but we got a bit sloppy before half-time. So we had a few words and got the response we were looking for. We were excellent in the second half, I can't remember my goalkeeper having a save to make. The last time I was here my Celtic team got seven so we bettered that. Eight goals will give the players a lot of confidence and there were some like Jordon and John McGinn who needed the run out. Promotion is our priority and we can forget about the cup for a wee while now and concentrate on the League."

It turned out to be a weekend of hob-nobbing with Hibs managers past and present alright, as after exchanging pleasantries with Stubbsy on Saturday I then found myself rubbing shoulders with Neil Lennon in the

'T2 Trainspotting' Premiere queue on the Sunday. I blanched as we exchanged glances, the thought-bubble above his head clearly querying, "Is that the ugly fucker who was sitting next to Irvine Welsh at the match yesterday?" It was some bloody queue as well, snaking around that interminable red carpet at Fountain Park where I feared I was going colour-blind, until someone pointed out that the carpet wasn't the traditional red at all – it was an orange bastard instead, to fit in with the original 'Trainspotting' iconography. What a palaver to get into a cinema! Along a bit, along a bit more, round a corner, along another bit, past another security checkpoint... I cringed as a hundred photographers' flashbulbs temporarily blinded me again, waving vaguely at the cheering, screaming masses crammed behind the cordon, pathetically hoping they'd all mistake me for some top Hollywood thespian.

Once inside (screen number *seven* appropriately enough), I then accidentally trod on a top thespian's toes when trying to find my seat, squashing the wonderful Shirley Henderson's dainty tootsies, no less.

"Ouch!" she squeaked.

"Ouch!" Shirley Henderson just spoke to me! Wow!

"Sorry," I mumbled, trying to ignore Welsh smirking at me from the uber-luvvie seats in the adjacent block.

"That's OK," she replied graciously.

"That's OK," she says! Shirley Henderson and I are practically having an in-depth conversation! I wonder what she's doing later? This is what it's all about, the glitz and the glamour and a free bag of popcorn too...

The Hibs gaffer was at the after-show bash in 'The Caves' as well, along with David Gray, who I buttonholed after several quarts of free drink had cascaded down my parched throat. God knows, I like free drink as much as the next man – perhaps even slightly more so than the next man – but this was ridiculous. Every time your glass gave off even the merest *hint* of being only half full, a comely wench sprang into action with the bottle of vino to top you up. I was soon brushing famous actors aside to grab poor Sir David's hand which I proceeded to pump up and down vigorously as if my very existence depended on it. "Did you enjoy it?" he asked, as I babbled on incoherently about Hampden heroics last May. It only occurred to me later that he most likely meant did I enjoy the *film*, as opposed to the cup final, but I wasn't entirely sure. (T2 includes real footage of George Best in action for Hibs against Celtic, so what's not to like there?) Liam Henderson also received an invite, but if he was there I didn't see him. Then again, maybe his former captain told him to avoid the slavering arsehole with the ponytail and very red eyes at all costs. At least I had the good sense – *just* – to leave Neil Lennon in peace...

The Hibs gaffer may have wanted to forget all about the cup for a while, but the draw for the next round which had taken place just before we all piled into the pictures couldn't have escaped his attention. Hopefully away to Raith Rovers for the Hibees (which would virtually ensure that they lifted the thing again, as the last four winners had all defeated the Kirkcaldy club on their way to the final.) But just possibly the jambos at the PBS... This was as a consequence of the 1-1 draw between the sides that afternoon, setting up a potential re-run of the previous year's tie. During a particularly purple patch for the home team in the second half, one numpty in blue and white missed a sitter of staggering proportions, blasting a shot off the crossbar from all of three yards.

"How the fuck did he miss *that?*" wailed a Hibbie mate via a text message just after the incident.

"Easy – he must have studied footage of Jason's similar fuck-up there last season," I replied, involuntarily shuddering at the memory. (The one where he leapt joyously towards the Hibs fans to celebrate, before belatedly realising that he hadn't actually scored.)

In fact, Neil's most pressing immediate concern would be searching yet again for a back-up keeper, as it was revealed that Marciano had sustained a suspected cracked rib in the clash at Tynie. Talk about a Rocky road to recovery… Subsequently, it turned out to be not as serious as that, but he was still looking at another spell on the sidelines. Typical bad timing – just when they'd waved goodbye to Virtanen too, although he'd never looked like a long-term solution. Plus, third choice Maciej Dabrowski was out with a dislocated thumb. Was Neil fully able to concentrate on the antics of Renton, Sick Boy, Spud and Begbie on the silver screen at Cineworld, or was he feverishly thinking, "Choose life. Choose a goalkeeper. Choose one who won't immediately get injured, panic under pressure or lose a goal within thirteen seconds in Europe. Choose another Zibi the Hibbie, Ole the Goalie or Ma-Kalamity at my peril…"

The last week of January found Jordon Forster in reflective mood, as he looked back somewhat ruefully on his decision the previous season to seek a fresh start elsewhere. Frustrated at the lack of regular playing opportunities, he'd hightailed it to Plymouth and although the deal was of the 'loan' variety, not a few Hibbies were surprised to see him return. It wasn't the first time that Jordon had pondered thus, but in light of what had occurred with the Big Cup bonanza, he'd come close to admitting that it had been a mistake of sorts.

"I missed something that was so massive for the club, winning the Scottish Cup. Those boys are legends now and part of me thinks if I hadn't left, "What if…?" I feel I am a bit closer to playing than last year. We have a great chance to win the League and take the club back to where it should be – and I want to be part of that."

He'd certainly played his part at the PBS – a *goal-scoring* one no less, but it was largely down to Paul Hanlon's absence that he'd got the chance to make an appearance. With the generally excellent form of the usual defensive set-up, he must have been aware after re-signing that he wouldn't necessarily find it any easier to make a decisive breakthrough this time around.

"I was aware of the strength in depth we have at centre-back," he acknowledged. "Outside Celtic I think we have the strongest defence, so I knew it was always going to be difficult. Paul and Daz are the preferred pairing and Fonts plays in the three. It is frustrating, but I have been training well in my opinion and that's a big thing."

Jordon was one of the many in green who'd found the Gorgie gap-site a happy hunting ground in the past – four years ago he'd been on the winning side in his Hibs' debut, as Ross Caldwell's solitary goal sunk the scumbos.

"It's not our stadium, but it's an enjoyable one to play in. The Hibs fans took it over on Saturday and it was good to give them a good showing. It may have been against a lesser team but there are still eleven men trying to stop you."

Events at the PBS on the Wednesday then ensured that it would be a return there on Scottish Cup duty for Hibs after all, as Hearts overcame Raith Rovers at the second time of asking. It was far from convincing however, the jambos coming from behind and needing an extra half-hour in which to defeat the plucky Fifers, despite being awarded two penalties which they duly converted. Neil Lennon had probably been resigned to that outcome, revealing that he'd had a feeling that the cup draw would pan out in such a manner. It would be a first for him at any rate, as he'd never even attended an Edinburgh derby before, but there was no doubt he'd enjoyed his last two visits to Gorgie immensely. The teams he was in charge of managed to rack up a total of *fifteen* goals, as his Celtic side had previously inflicted the mythical 7-0 defeat on the hapless home side.

"These are slightly different circumstances," he conceded. "It would be nice to get another seven or eight but I'm not sure that will be feasible. I like the ground, I like the atmosphere and I'm sure this will be as raucous as anything I've experienced before."

The manager had now eased his goalkeeping worries, as he snapped up Scott Gallacher, who had just had his contract terminated by mutual agreement with his last employer, St. Mirren. Previously with both Hearts and Rangers, he was at Easter Road until the end of the season at least. So yet again Neil found himself attempting to put the cup on the back burner for the time being and focus on the matter in hand.

"I'm more concerned about how we get on against Queen of the South and Ayr United the week after. It's really important we keep winning games in the League, far more important than any cup-tie at the minute."

"Promotion is our priority," concurred Darren McGregor, "so Queen of the South takes precedence. We are well aware that they are on a good run and have players who can hurt you. Of course the Hearts game will be at the back of our minds, but that's where it will stay for the moment."

The Dumfries men were something of a rejuvenated force, having emerged from a dreadful twelve game sequence of no wins to flourish under new gaffer Gary Naysmith. They were now sitting comfortably in the middle of the table, having lost only once in seven outings.

On the day of the match, an in-depth interview with Neil appeared in The Scotsman, in which he discussed Trainspotting, team training, depression, meditation and the benefits of learning Portuguese with that paper's resident diehard Hibbie, Aidan Smith. His assertion that the challenge of managing Hibs was greater than that of managing Celtic must have raised a few eyebrows.

"The attention to detail required here is greater than I had at my previous clubs," he explained. "At Celtic you got to the point where the team played in a rhythm. Plus, these were international players. This is different. Although we have the biggest budget in the Championship there isn't such a gulf between the teams."

He added that although he didn't view it as an absolute necessity, he'd still like to bring Kris Commons back. But in an ideal world, he'd settle for filling the team with eleven Darren McGregors.

"That would make my job the easiest in the world. I admire his attitude, bravery, leadership, will to win – he's a fabulous player."

Daz lined up in his usual slot on the plastic pitch at Palmerston Park, again missing his stalwart sidekick Paul Hanlon, who now looked to be facing a longer period absent than had been thought originally. That aside, Hibs had the similarly settled aspect that they'd enjoyed of late, with Holt and Cummings leading the charge up front, Fontaine filling in at the back again, but no room this time for Chris Humphrey. That maybe came as something of a surprise, but then again the narrow strip of fake greenery that passed for a playing surface was hardly conducive to wingers racing down the flanks. With that in mind, Neil also opted to start without Boyle either, although he at least made an appearance late on. The visitors were certainly the dominant force in the first half with Queens creating zilch up front, ex-Hibee Stephen Dobbie ploughing a lonely and fruitless furrow on his own as solitary front-man.

However, Hibs moved up a gear right after the interval, gaining their first corner of the afternoon on the fifty-second minute. It was text book stuff as James Keatings picked out John McGinn, who lashed it into the net with some help from a deflection.

"I think they read it, but it was too late," opined Super. "It was such a great ball from Keats that all I had to do was get my body over it and it took a wee nick on the way in."

Wee Nick was certainly unhappy with his unintended contribution, unlike the Hibs gaffer.

"It was really well executed, a great ball from Keatings and John timed his run to perfection," enthused Neil.

He stated that although he was never comfortable with a mere 1-0 margin (nor are we, Nellie!) and would have liked a more decisive scoreline, he was pleased with the overall performance. Hibs totally ran the show after Super's sizzler with chances going a-begging from cross-balls which *just* failed to pick out their intended targets and they seemed well in command. You're never relaxed with that solitary goal lead, sure, but up against a side incapable of mounting any sustained attacking forays throughout, there's a fair chance that'll be enough on the day. So it proved, with Neil leaving it late before giving his substitute trio of Boyle, Forster and Graham their head, but it wasn't really necessary from a match-winning point of view. Barring some utterly unforeseen fluke favouring Queens, they'd done enough.

"We're playing well and creating chances," remarked the sole scorer. "We're on a good run of form and momentum is key at this stage of the season. There's certainly more to come. In the final third we had a lot of the ball and I think we can score more goals. Jason and Holty are still to hit their peak and there's Martin and Brian too."

He was also pleased and very relieved to have been back in action so soon, as the two month period of absence might well have been extended by an extra third, to aid recovery.

"I'm pleased I got the surgery when I did. I feel as though I am fit. It doesn't feel like I was out for that length of time."

His manager would have been pleased on perusing the other results, to see that Dundee United were continuing to huff and puff and make heavy weather of things. A 1-1 draw away to Dunfermline meant that they now lay eight points adrift, with a vastly inferior goal difference.

"We can only look after what we do. If we can extend the lead, then great. It's a hard League – nothing is given to you. I said that to the players, that we have to earn the right to get out of this League. We don't have a divine right. We are in a good spell with five wins in a row, but we are not getting carried away."

He had every reason to be satisfied, as his team had enjoyed a one hundred per cent record for the first month of the year and had significantly increased the gap between themselves and the rest of the pack. They were far better off than they'd been at the fag-end of 2016 and the onus was now on the other teams to attempt to play catch-up. With the best will in the world, there didn't look much imminent danger of that. In fact, Morton – fresh from a terrific 4-1 victory away from home against Ayr United – were for the moment the most likely looking, but they were eleven points off the pace with a game in hand. Dundee United's form had been erratic – they'd started badly before rallying admirably as new players bedded in, but were now in the throes of another slump. To some degree, their pursuit of Hibs was akin to Hibs' pursuit of Rangers during the previous campaign. They'd done well to come from behind once, but did they have it within them to do it twice? Time would tell...

The wee team finished the month on a high too, beating Falkirk 4-1 away, to send themselves four points clear at the top of the Development League. Danny Handling, making his second appearance after injury got the fourth one, with both Murrays (Fraser and Innes) netting, as well as Bradley Donaldson. Dylan McGeouch also featured from the off, which would give Neil hope that he might not be too far away from consideration for a first team return. Well, at least until his next injury...

8.

FEBRUARY: WE NEED TO TALK ABOUT SEVEN

The shortest month arrived, with – as expected – no last minute manoeuvring by Neil in the transfer market. It was always a long shot that Kris Commons would return, given the complications over wage structure etc., and Brendan Rodgers had more or less nixed it by suggesting he was now likely to feature in his future plans at Parkhead. So none in, but one out though, as Lewis Allan went out on loan to the second side in the Capital. Edinburgh City gaffer Gary Jardine was understandably delighted to land him, revealing that he'd sought to acquire his services before, but that had proved impossible at the time due to the player's health issues.

At this stage of the campaign, you certainly weren't likely to find any current employees of Hibernian F.C. making claims for the ultimate goal being achieved, but one former player was not exhibiting any such reticence. Citing the fact that the interminable length of the previous season must have taken its toll on the Hibees to some degree, Tam McManus was a lot more optimistic this time around.

"Chasing Rangers also put them under pressure, going into every game trying to claw their way back," reckoned Tam. "To be honest, I can now see Hibs winning the League comfortably. There's no Hearts or Rangers this season and I think Hibs have really gone for it, they've been in this League far too long and can't afford another year in it. They are also so flexible, players capable of playing anywhere and in any system, which makes them unpredictable."

Well, he was right there, regarding them playing anywhere. Lewis would be doing so at Meadowbank (or possibly Pilton once they bulldozed the creaking London Road eyesore), Kris at Parkhead and Jason was currently playing in the sandpit at East Mains. Makes it a lot harder for the opposition to man mark them when they're that spread out, at least.

Glancing through the 'deadline day' transfer list, I then shuddered involuntarily at coming across the following: 'Bury to AFC Wimbledon – Tom Soares.' If ever there was a man who failed to live up to his surname... It could only have been more inappropriate if they'd added a 'c' after the capital 'S'. Still, I suppose Terrible Tom was just joining a select band of historical Hibees with the wrong handle. We've had Barry (who wasn't), Cannon (he never had a shot), Duguid (do bad more like, he wasn't even registered and played under an assumed name against the jambos in 1906), Power (he often switched off), Price (didn't cost anything) and Ward (should have been confined to one instead.) And whilst we're on the subject, spare a thought for the careless commentator in ye olden days when Cox, Dick and Flucker were all still playing. The fact that the latter was allegedly nicknamed 'Mother' only made the situation worse. Thank God P. Ness had already been transferred by then.

By midweek, cup final hero Stokesy found himself in Dublin again, for the latest instalment of his legal circus, stemming from assaulting an Elvis impersonator in that fair city back in 2013. It was down at the end of Leeson Street...at Buck Whalley's nightclub. OK, it hadn't got quite the same ring to it as Heartbreak Hotel admittedly, but facts are facts. I've already made my feelings clear about these jumpsuited jiving jackasses in my previous book, but what threw me was the report that the assault had occurred in the VIP area of said establishment. What the flying fuck was an Elvis impersonator doing in that hallowed conclave, unless the letters now stand for 'Very Idiotic Person'? Possibly anticipating a spot of compulsory Jailhouse Rock, Anthony was relieved when the judge gave him a choice – firstly, a heavy fine, or secondly, straight to Kilmainham nick.

"So it's one for the money...?" queried Anthony, curling his lip and swivelling his hips suggestively in the dock.

He was still All Shook Up when the wooden-hearted beak sideswiped him with a thirty thousand euro penalty though and even that might not be the end of the matter. The injured Hound Dog in question had upped the ante and a further hearing in lieu of damages being awarded would likely take place at a later date in Ireland's High Court. They should have awarded Stokesy damages for being pestered by the burger-guzzling fat rhinestoned oaf in the first place. He'd only knocked out some of his teeth after all, practically doing him a favour in the long run. He could now hang up his blue suede shoes and retrain as a Shane MacGowan impersonator instead.

But hand on heart, who amongst us *hasn't* beaten up an Elvis impersonator at one time or another? I know that I certainly have. On one occasion I kicked the shit out of a weedy little guy who was annoying me with his crap rendition of 'Oliver's Army'. Of course, he turned out to be an Elvis *Costello* impersonator, but you've got to start somewhere...

Neil Lennon then revealed that he'd actually tried to get Stokesy back to Easter Road for the third time, even as the transfer window was slithering shut, but a proposed loan deal with Blackburn Rovers had come to naught. The gaffer didn't appear too downcast though, as he deservedly picked up the Ladbrokes' Championship Manager of the Month award for January, saying, "It's been a great month and I just hope February is the same. I do think we can score more goals. I think we *should* score more goals for the chances we create and the amount of possession we have. That would be my only criticism of what we have been doing this season. Defensively we have been excellent."

The last man in through the green door, Chris Humphrey, remarked, "You look around and I don't think we really need to get someone in. I'm sure the club would have done so if needed, but there was no need to just go out and panic buy. I was on the bench at Palmerston Park and I looked to my left and then my right and all I could see was very good players – and very good players already out there on the pitch. The boys have been brilliant. After training with them for three days it was like I'd known them for five or six years. It really opens your eyes to the quality we have here."

Scotland gaffer Gordon Strachan dropped in at East Mains to see his former club captain from Celtic days and his charges and was impressed by the atmosphere of happy positivity he found there. From an international perspective, he was delighted at John McGinn's return to fitness, revealing that he'd bestowed yet *another* nickname on the player, who already had Super, The Sponge or The Meatball to choose from. Apparently when representing his country, John evolves into 'The Radiator', which sounds more like the world of American Football to me. But to Strachs it was fitting, as, "He walks in the room and the place radiates." Which room is that then, Gordon? The control room at Chernobyl Nuclear Power Station? But it would be fair to say that if The Radiator hadn't exactly sprung a leak, he was somewhat off the boil in the first half against Ayr United, as were the rest of his team-mates. For unfortunately, this was likely the grimmest opening period I'd seen from Hibs yet this season.

They got off to the worst possible start, conceding a goal within four minutes as Rab Crawford waltzed virtually unimpeded through the defence before hitting a low shot which eluded the grasp of Ross Laidlaw. The back-line had been rightly praised for their general performances throughout the season, but they were found wanting here. Liam Fontaine had the sort of game he'd wish to obliterate from memory as soon as possible and signally failed to close the Ayr man down. Our keeper might have done better too and also seemed uncharacteristically out of sorts, frequently launching clumsy clearances which threatened to decapitate innocent spectators as the ball flew into the stands. The first half-hour in particular was almost unremittingly woeful, although the home team did have chances to draw level. Keatings wasn't far away with a free-kick and Martin Boyle was denied by goalkeeper Fleming almost on the line, before Shinnie wasted an opportunity by heading over the bar. Ayr looked well-organised if unadventurous; having unexpectedly taken such an early lead they seemed content to hold on to what they'd got. Certainly, they bore little resemblance to the hapless lot who'd been so comprehensively turned over by Morton the previous weekend.

Lennon then threw Holty on for the ineffectual Humphrey right at the start of the second half and the big man's presence did seem to at last galvanise his team-mates. He had the closest shout of the lot, right at the death, when his effort was cleared off the line. The *sixth* occasion this season in which he'd been denied in such a manner, he later lamented. But Hibs looked a lot better than they'd done before the break – they could scarcely have been any worse – and the long overdue appearance of Jason Cummings on the hour mark gave them some fresh impetus. Neil Lennon had made clear his reasons for leaving him out earlier in the campaign, but you had to wonder at his decision to do so here. Saving him for the forthcoming cup-tie at Tynecastle? Well, possibly – but a lone James Keatings up front in the first period had not looked like overly troubling Ayr. A spot of Jason spontaneity might have done the trick on an off-day for his compatriots, but it was he who finally broke the deadlock on the seventy-fifth minute. He got his head on the end of a Keatings cross and a sense of relief rippled around the stadium at long last. Neil then threw on Brian Graham in a last-ditch bid to salvage the full three points, but it wasn't to be.

That old bugaboo called inconsistency; no wonder it drives managers up the wall. You could scarcely believe that this was largely the same lot who'd turned in that superb sparkling performance against the Arabs just under a month ago and then won three on the trot after that. This game was a low point alright, but thank goodness there had been precious few of them of late. The fans tried to console themselves with the standard fall-back of 'getting the bad game out of the road' before the big one against the jambos the following weekend. Hearts' assistant gaffer had been reported as being at Easter Road 'on a spying mission' – so Austin MacPhee now thinks he's Austin Powers?? Shagadelic, baby! He wouldn't have been too worried by what he'd witnessed on this day, although he'd be aware that it was hardly indicative of Hibs' form overall.

"Awful," said Lennon afterwards. Then, just in case anyone missed the vehemence of his assessment, he repeated the word another three times. "We backed off and had we backed off any further we'd have been in among the Ayr supporters in the away end. I just don't think we looked ourselves."

"It wasn't our greatest performance," agreed The Radiator, with some degree of understatement. "But all credit to Ayr. They made it difficult for us, it was tough to break them down. We didn't get the break of the ball. Holty had a header cleared off the line that could have won us the game. To be fair to Ayr, they defended well and they had a couple of chances towards the end. They are fighting for their lives."

Post-match analysis in Middleton's was aided by a trio of understandably jubilant Ayr supporters, who had now seen their team take four points off Hibs away from home and but for Jason it might have been six. They were rather kinder in their rating of the home team than most of the Hibbies present – on at least the second half showing – but they could afford to be magnanimous after such a result. One of them had just ordered a round of drinks and was extolling the virtues of Darren McGregor to me.

"Aye, it's just as well you're saying nice things about DARREN McGREGOR in here," I replied, loudly upping my tone for the benefit of the barmaid.

"Eh...why's that?" he asked, looking a trifle worried.

"Because his sister's just pouring your pint now," I pointed out.

Ah well, have to just put this one down to a bad day at the office. And it might have been worse... It was still another point on the board, although Dundee United went on to predictably beat Raith Rovers quite convincingly, narrowing the gap at the top to six. The League was the most important consideration, no two ways about that, even more so than it had been the previous season if that were possible. Neil had rightly sought to emphasise that at every opportunity, but now the focus would switch back to the Big Cup, at least for a week or so.

Unfortunately, the jambos had recently turned the corner under Cathy, who had been signing new players at a dizzying rate. When I last saw the wee hobbit on the telly he appeared to have suddenly developed Gordon Ramsay-type furrows on his forehead as a result of all the strain, thereby achieving the difficult trick of somehow managing to look both incredibly ancient and ridiculously young at the same time. But the generally grim run of results that had heralded his introduction to the Hearts hot-seat had been magically transformed over the previous week.

I'd forgotten that they were playing the huns on the Wednesday evening and was at home cranking up Lady Gaga's 'Born This Way', only to be reminded when a mate sent me a text on the subject. I fired one back enquiring as to the score which he'd failed to mention and wasn't overly surprised to receive a reply of "4-1."

"Well, that'll be the hobbit getting handed a one-way ticket back to The Shire then," I responded.

"No – it's 4-1 to *Hearts!*" came the scarcely believable follow-up.

Suddenly I felt like I was going gaga myself. I was that surprised the can of Export fell from my nerveless fingers immediately.

Mind you, they'd been largely aided by a dire Rangers performance with some utterly schoolboy defending thrown into the mix, but had then gone on to beat Motherwell 3-0 away, before Hibs and Ayr had even kicked off. However, that scoreline was deceptive as an outrageous deflection gifted them the opener and Motherwell (reduced to ten men for nearly the entire second half) could still have turned the tables before new boy Goncalves got a late double in the last five minutes. So they'd certainly be in a confident mood for the cup-tie and undeniably had a more satisfactory run-up to it than Hibs had attained. Still, we we could all fall back on that other favoured comforting cliché (after "getting the bad game out of the way") of sagely observing that the form book generally goes out of the window where derbies are concerned. It bloody better – if they turned up at Tynie and started playing like they'd just done against Ayr I'd be going oot the windae myself.

I must have been getting a tad desperate though, as Sunday evening found me in The Diggers viewing the Africa Cup of Nations Final on Eurosport. Naturally, this was principally in the hope that Arnaud Djoum would be grievously injured at some point, thus ruling him out of the PBS showdown seven days later. Well he wasn't, but one of his Cameroonian compadres wasn't so fortunate. The whole pub winced in unison as the poor felly collapsed on the deck, frantically caressing his crushed crown jewels. The camera homed in unerringly as he lay there writhing in agony, legs wide akimbo. Outside of a full-scale porno production I don't think I've ever seen such searingly intimate focus of the genital region on the screen before. (Not that I'm in the habit of watching gay porn, you understand.) I could hardly bear to look if truth be told, especially when a trainer helpfully sprayed the damaged area with some sort of aerosol, causing a pseudo smoke-like effect and giving off the impression that his baws were actually on fire. Still thinking about this grisly spectacle at closing time, I found myself walking home subconsciously cross-legged – which was far from easy.

By the start of the following week, the opening salvo of the pre cup-tie 'war of words' commenced, when haggard old jambo icon Gary Mackay somehow prized open his coffin lid from the inside to declare, "I've always felt we would beat Hibs, but I think that's down to that I *always* expect us to beat Hibs, regardless of circumstances." Oh yeah? That viewpoint might have been justified once upon a time and long long ago, Gaz, but Robbo's actually hung his boots up, in case you hadn't noticed.

"It's been pretty even between the clubs these last couple of seasons," countered James Keatings. "Everyone says there is a massive gap between the Premiership and the Championship – there isn't. I personally think that this is a Premiership squad and it's up to us on the day to go and show our class and see where it takes us."

He also alluded to his talismanic team-mate who had scored in each of the last four derbies and usually made a habit of notching at least one at Tynecastle. He'd done the business against Ayr and assuming Neil actually played him from the off there was every hope that he'd do it again, come Sunday.

"Jason was at Hearts, so he probably feels he always has a point to prove. He wants to score in every game he plays, but probably more so against the club that let him go."

So it worked both ways regarding the PBS new boys who would be unfamiliar to their opponents; but equally they'd be unaware of just how much of a threat oor Jase might pose.

Another player well up for it and with experience of a whole plethora of derbies under his belt was Grant Holt. Still a hero to the denizens of Norfolk after once scoring a hat-trick for Norwich against Ipswich, the big veteran couldn't wait for Sunday.

"We know we are as good as anyone in the Premier League when we are on it. The pressure is all on them. We are only a Championship team supposedly – well, that's what I keep hearing – so we will see what happens."

Chris Humphrey – one of the many who'd been less than effective against Ayr – featured in the Development Squad's match against Rangers at East Mains, with the Wee Hibs suffering a very rare defeat. In true hun fashion, the bluenoses won it with the last kick of the game, to triumph 2-1, after Oli Shaw had equalised for the home side. Chris was the only senior player to appear for Hibs though, while the Rangers side included Joe Dodoo – who opened the scoring after missing an earlier penalty – Harry Forrester and Danny Wilson.

One player who made an exceedingly timely and somewhat overlooked contribution to Hibs' tenacity in digging out that 2-2 draw at Tynie last season was Kevin Thomson. He prevented what would almost certainly have been a late winning goal for Hearts when he cleared off the line, shortly after we'd all had kittens as Gunarsson almost gifted them an own goal. But Kev was perhaps more qualified than most to offer an opinion on the upcoming tussle, in which he hoped that Neil would go with Holty and Jason up front.

"I will put my neck on the line and say if Jason Cummings and Grant Holt do not start then it will be a difficult afternoon for my old club Hibernian."

He went on to praise "my old team-mate and friend" Jason for having a nose for goal, whilst hinting that he'd hoped other aspects of his game would have become more apparent by now.

"He has the tools to be whatever he wants. I just hope he does not reach the age of twenty-eight as still 'just' the guy who puts the ball in the net. It sounds strange, but it has to be about more than that."

I wondered if there was any point in seeking consolation in 'lies, damned lies and statistics' ahead of the game and, in an idle moment, found myself rummaging through the bottom of the wardrobe to locate my personal Hibernian journal. This comprises screeds of ancient sheets of paper covered in unmentionable stains and drunken doodles, documenting all the matches I have ever attended. After perusing this record for about half-an-hour, I came up with the following – of the seventy-one derbies I'd so far witnessed *in the flesh* (as opposed to peeping through my fingers at on Sky TV), Hibs had won twenty-four, Hearts had won seventeen and an incredible *thirty* had ended in draws. Of that number, *ten* had been of the scoreless variety. I tried to put a positive spin on this by working out that Hearts had therefore won less than a quarter of them, so that would do me for the time being. But I could well be resorting to lies and damned lies yet, before Sunday rolled around...

What follows here sounds like a damn lie alright – but it is entirely genuine and a factoid you may wish to try out on a belligerent Celtic fan of your own choosing sometime soon. Just ask them to cast their minds back to 1985 / 86 season, during which Hibs scored *eighteen* goals against the 'Tic at Easter Road, then sit back and absorb their howls of disbelief and denial. But it's perfectly true, popping up happily before my jaundiced eye as I trawled through the interminable 'Hibs 0, Hearts 0' stats on the aforementioned list. Firstly, the teams drew 4-4 with extra time played in a thrilling League Cup tie, which then progressed to a penalty decider. Even with that, it seemed the adversaries could not be separated, but Hibs eventually clinched it 8-7 on spot-kicks. Celtic got their revenge with a 5-0 tanking of Hibs in a League game not long after, but the second home Premier fixture saw a 2-2 draw, before another absolute beezer of a cup-tie (Scottish, this time) saw Hibs edge out their Glasgow rivals by 4-3. I recall celebrating that one in the long defunct 'Clan' bar – a.k.a. Ma Wilson's – on Albert Street, where the man who scored the winning goal, Eddie May, joined the happy Hibbie masses for a snifter or two.

Coming up fast behind me in the derby day stakes was Lewis Stevenson, looking forward to playing in his thirty-first such encounter and lamenting that he felt much older than his actual years due to this. No wonder, at first glance it seemed improbable, until you remembered just how long he'd been with Hibs and the regularity with which he'd played.

"They are the best games to play in if you win and the worst if you are beaten," he said. "There's no middle ground. You are on a real high or a real downer. When the draw was made some people were saying we were favourites – we were flying and they were struggling a bit. They've picked up recently while we had a poor result at the weekend which has levelled things a bit, probably brought a few people down to earth as they realise how tough it is going to be."

There was just time for a spot of alternative comedy before we got down to the nitty gritty, with the news breaking that Warby and his management team had tendered their resignations from Fort Ibrox. Or had they? Well, mibbe ayes, mibbe naw. When 'Reporting Scotland' phoned the crusty one for a comment they were tersely told that it was the first he'd heard of it. So – *no*, he *hadn't* resigned.

"But Dave King says that you have," persisted RS.

"Dave King?" snapped Warby. "Never heard of him. I answer to one King only and his name's Billy. Hallo Hallo! In any case, I was appointed to this position by Willie Waddell himself and I'll be staying here until I put paid to Jock Stein's 'nine in a row' attempt at Parkhead, I can assure you of that. God save the Queen. Thank you and goodnight. Wibble wibble."

I mean, I've undergone many confusing moments in my own working life, but on past occasions when I've either been sacked from various jobs or chosen to leave of my own accord, I'm pretty sure I've always remembered which were which. So luckily I'd thus far avoided that awkward situation whereby you greet your boss heartily with a cheery "Good morning!" first thing on a Monday, only to be asked what the fuck you were doing there, as you told the same man to stick his fucking job up his fat arse when you got pissed at lunchtime the previous Friday. But this apparently was the scenario that Warby now found himself in.

There was a general consensus that the matter wouldn't be fully resolved until it was dragged kicking and screaming through the courts – well, *that'll* signal a major departure from the way Rangers usually conduct their business won't it? Er, *not*. It wasn't that long ago that the judiciary informed all feuding parties within the corrupt Govan empire to stop clogging up the legal system with their interminable nonsense. They should just tow the whole festering edifice down the Clyde on a rusty barge and set sail for Guantanamo Bay as soon as possible. Warby would look great in one of those orange jumpsuits, no doubt about that. Go well with his vagina-themed headgear.

So, "Here we go, two in a row," and off to the PBS on February 12th. Although judging by the state of the pitch, you might have been forgiven for thinking you'd wound up at Gorgie Farm by mistake. It was in a dreadful condition and any faint hope that we'd be treated to a spectacle worthy of the more skilful players on show was firmly extinguished. Derbies are seldom classics though and the Edinburgh ones in particular seem more renowned for producing blood and thunder one hundred miles per hour physical contests than most. That was certainly the case here but the pleasing aspect of it was that Hibs ably matched their rivals in this department, whereas in the past they'd often lacked the muscular edge. No danger of that with big Holty up front to partner Jason as expected and Marvin Bartley outstanding in midfield. Any tentative Hearts' attacks were more often than not broken up decisively by Marv, winning nearly every challenge and using the ball intelligently once he'd done so. Rocky returned in goal – making *another* recall from injury at the same venue and luckily this time around he wasn't forced to almost immediately hobble off again. He too turned in a very assured performance and was well up to keeping the maroon hordes at bay on the few occasions they strung a cohesive attack together. There was precious little of that from either side though and the game was littered with stoppages, caused by the on-going industrial tackles on the atrocious surface. With Gollum muttering, "My precious, my precious," as he fondled his pack of shiny new cards, you doubted that there would still be twenty-two players left on the park at half-time, let alone at the end of the ninety minutes, but for once he exhibited considerable restraint. When silly Willie starts flashing the yellows and reds he seldom knows when to stop, so it was just as well. Hibs' best chance fell just before half-time, when Holty suddenly burst through the centre, scattering maroon shirts like ninepins and picking out Jason with a pass. However, a rather jittery Hamilton in the Hearts' goal snuffed it out at the second attempt.

Hibs had the bulk of the play throughout the first period, but the home team made a bright enough start to the second half, causing a few nervous ripples in the Roseburn Stand. A notorious time for the Hibees to slip up, but they held firm ultimately and soon turned the tables on their opponents. You could tell that the free-running Jason had them rattled (as he seldom knows what he's going to do next himself, how can they?) and James Keatings' corner kicks were of top-drawer Liam Hendersonesque quality. However, despite this, there weren't that many clear-cut chances in Hamilton's goal area. At the other end, the resolute rock that is Darren McGregor ensured that there would seldom be any way through for the jambos and it has to be said that their much heralded raft of new boys didn't overly impress. Neil sensibly opted to keep things pretty much the same as his team didn't look troubled, leaving it until ten minutes from the end to swap Holty for Brian Graham, but to little discernible effect. The game had 0-0 written all over it long before that – so my personal derby stats hadn't lied overall – and although there was always the chance a late slip by either side would gift the game to their opponents, that was how it finished. Not a pretty picture by any means, but Hibs would be far happier with the draw than the jambos, particularly with the previous year's memorable double-header still fresh in the memory.

"I think we can play better," observed Grant Holt. "We couldn't pass the ball as well as we would like, it was a scrappy game. I thought we probably edged it, but a draw was fair. I don't think the pitch is designed to play good football on – there was sand everywhere. There were times we were trying to play passes and it was getting stuck under our feet. We have John McGinn and James Keatings who like to run with the ball and you can't do that."

"I thought we were very strong," said his manager approvingly. "It was impossible to play any kind of cohesive football on the pitch so we had to play the pitch the right way and we did. We were strong defensively, so we could have taken care of the ball a little bit better in the final third, but I thought we were excellent."

The subsequent draw for the next round then threw up a home tie for whoever triumphed in the replay, against either Ayr United or Clyde. Not that any additional incentive should be necessary, but suddenly the Edinburgh sides would see a possible semi-final already on the horizon. Not that I'd fancy watching another home game against the men from Rabbie Burns' country if it did come to that mind you, but surely Hibs couldn't flop for a third time in succession?

They also received another major boost in Championship terms, as Dundee United were thumped 3-0 by Falkirk on Saturday, leaving Hibs still six points ahead of them but now with a vital game in hand. However, that result propelled the Bairns up and over Morton to reclaim third spot and all at Hibs would be keeping a wary eye on Houston's hucksters' progress, in light of what happened at the conclusion of last year's League race. But for the time being they still looked a long way off – nine points behind Hibs with an extra game played and vastly inferior goal difference.

Another area in which Hibs decidedly wielded the upper hand during the derby was the unstinting backing they received from the oft-overlooked 'twelfth man', i.e. their fans. They drowned out the scarf-twirlers from before start to finish and even although the 'two in a row' and '1902' songs were doing my head in long before the end, it was great to be part of such an exuberant atmosphere.

"I thought our fans were amazing," acknowledged Rocky. "I don't have words to describe it. I'm happy for them. It's a privilege to play for them. I think everyone was happy because we performed well. It wasn't a great game of football but it was a fight and everyone could see we fought. That's the most important thing in these games and I think we won every battle."

Remarkably, the keeper revealed that he was far from over the effects of the accidental clash with team-mate Liam Fontaine which had cut short his comeback against Bonnyrigg, as it certainly wasn't reflected in his consummate performance.

"I'm not fully fit, I'm still feeling pain because the area is still damaged. It's like having a dead leg in the ribs," he explained eloquently.

Well, better there than in the Dead Sea Scrolls, as the poor Cameroonian boy could have testified the previous Sunday.

"It's not a nice injury. It was one that was very sore. I had painkillers before the game but in an atmosphere like that you forget everything."

The keeper had been honest regarding his condition, so Neil had taken a bit of a risk playing him and must have been relieved and delighted at how he had acquitted himself. But he now had a bit of a worry over Jordon Forster, who'd limped off with a hamstring problem just after half-time. With Raith Rovers away in the Championship next, followed by the cup replay, he'd be hoping that Paul Hanlon might be ready for a return before then.

As previously mentioned, my ugly mug had occasionally been known to pop up uninvited on telly during Hibernian-related coverage and I was reminded on Monday the 13th of another occasion when that had occurred. This was during the 2013 Scottish Cup Final where the cameras had picked out myself and companion on the day, Colin Dobson, both looking rather glum due to the way events were unfolding. Coincidentally, we were sitting almost exactly where I'd viewed the 2001 final from and also the 1972 League Cup climax (although there was no seating in what was commonly referred to as 'the Rangers end' then of course.) But now I unexpectedly found myself attending Colin's funeral, after he'd died suddenly aged only forty-five. He'd defiantly selected the Hibees as his team of choice, despite coming from what was very much a 'Hearts' family and it was a poignant moment when he was finally laid to rest to the strains of 'Sunshine on Leith.'

Moving from that weather condition swiftly to 'Nimbus Clouds on North Berwick', as former Hibee Gary O'Connor was up in court – again. It never rains but it pours where Gaz is concerned, forever trying to out-do his old buddy Derek Riordan in appearances before the beak. This time he was fined £200 for nicking gear out of Harvey Nichols. His case wasn't improved by the court being told that after being apprehended he'd cunningly given his name as 'Nicol Harvey' to a store detective. The latter instantly smelt a rat, which wasn't surprising, as Gaz had also pocketed a valuable albino rodent from the exclusive pet shop on the top floor. The judge explained that he was going to fine him a double-ton so as 'to be commensurate with the value of the goods stolen.' Noting that prices in the posh peoples' paradise were towards the high end of the scale, the jury were still shocked to learn that Gaz had in fact nicked a whole pair of socks. He'd initially half-inched only one, but was caught when he foolishly returned to the shop to swipe the other one. Gaz explained that he'd briefly forgotten he had two feet, but thought he was entitled anyway and submitted his swipe card in evidence. But sadly the judge ruled that he hadn't got a leg to stand on and socked him with the appropriate penalty.

His rap sheet was certainly now looking quite impressive, as he could add shoplifting to crashing cars, allegedly making a false insurance claim (for which he was later cleared), possession of cocaine, giving a false name to the polis, failing to turn up for compulsory work shifts imposed under a Community Order and driving under the influence of an unknown substance. During that time he'd been charged under the following aliases – Johnston, Johnson, Johnstone, John Stone, Joss Stone, John's son, St. Johnstone and Johnston Terrace. The judge refused to believe that he was, as earlier claimed, Nicol Harvey and he was finally sentenced under the name of Mr Primark Matalan, 7 Devil Gate Drive, North Berwick.

There were rumours that the authorities were now thinking of establishing a permanent court, solely to deal with the misdemeanours of Hibees past and present. No sooner had Gaz been financially filleted than Marvin Bartley was up in the dock, for allegedly putting the frighteners on his ex-girlfriend. Meanwhile in Dublin, Stokesy's pressing Presley problems finally reached their zenith when he was ordered to fork over an extra 230,000 euros on top of the original 30,000 he'd already coughed up. Glory Glory Hallelujah!

One man still keeping a beady eye on developments at Easter Road was John Doolan, comparing where Hibs now stood to their position of one year ago. He pointed out that it was a lot better to be sitting on top of the pile and having other teams chasing you, than to be the ones doing the chasing.

"That means when you do have a set-back like we did, it can knock you out of your stride."

He was no doubt thinking of that totally unexpected disintegration at home to Morton where the visitors won 3-0, signalling the wheels coming off the green bandwagon big time. But as to the current Championship race, John harboured no doubts about the resolve of his old charges this time around.

"I think they'll get it done. Look at the characters in that dressing-room. They're not going to crumble, no chance. The fact the majority of them have won silverware recently means they won't be intimidated when the finishing line comes into view."

With Dundee United engaged in Diddy Cup business, the visit to Raith – with a newly-installed Yogi in the hot-seat – now gave Hibs a great chance to considerably bolster their lead at the top.

"A nine point lead rather than six is a big difference," contended Martin Boyle. "But it doesn't mean a start to the League being over. I'm sure there will be a lot of twists and turns to come before it's all over. It's not been hard to focus on the game, despite everyone talking about the cup replay with Hearts. The League is our priority – it has been all season."

Yogi certainly seemed to have wrested control of the Rovers' ship even as it threatened to sink altogether – from a team which had reached the Play-Off stage last season they had now plummeted into the relegation zone. They hadn't won a game for nearly four months (which extended to fourteen matches) and hadn't had a shut-out in the last nine. Additionally, they hadn't won a single game all season in which they'd conceded a goal first. However, Neil Lennon wouldn't have to remind his players that they were still above Ayr United in the table, a side who'd proved to be such troublesome opponents, particularly at Easter Road.

Unfortunately, it turned into practically a re-run of the latest game against the Honest Men, particularly for the first hour or so. In short, for the majority of their second League game in a row, Hibs were absolutely dire. As borne out by the statistics, Rovers were on a dire enough run themselves, but still looked a better side than their disjointed visitors throughout the first half. There was absolutely nothing to write home about here and Hibs were somewhat fortunate to go in at the interval still on level terms.

That wasn't to remain the case for long however, as the second half got under way. Only eight minutes had elapsed before the Indian ink splattered ex-jambo nippy sweetie Ryan Stevenson belted an impressive volley past Marciano from some distance. The manager would have been relieved that he'd seen fit to give Cummings a start in this one and it was the irrepressible live-wire who cancelled that out with a superb free-kick on the hour mark. An hour in which his team had been largely dreadful, but they did improve after that boost, if only slightly. However, the gradual introduction of substitutes Humphrey, Boyle and Holt throughout had little overall impact and they seldom looked like adding to their tally. On a day when it was hard to identify any positives, only yet another assured performance from the Mr Dependable of defence, Darren McGregor, gave any cause for satisfaction.

Lennon was incandescent at this showing and lost no time in verbally ripping into his hapless charges afterwards. Once again due to the vagaries of the fixture list Hibs had squandered an excellent chance to put themselves virtually out of sight at the top and the gaffer had every right to be annoyed.

"It was a disgrace. It was embarrassing, no, not embarrassing, it was insipid, disrespectful to the opposition and ordinary. Everything we had last week (against Hearts) was missing from the first hour. We've given a goal and an hour's start to a team that hadn't won in fourteen games. I don't want to see that ever again. I've defended them all season but I can't defend that."

He added that he'd consider playing kids from the Development Squad in the cup replay and although that was probably uttered in the heat of the moment, it was a measure of his level of frustration. It would have been of little consolation that the jambos had a similar afternoon of it at the PBS, being obliged to likewise come from behind against the bottom team in the Premiership – Inverness C.T. – to salvage a draw.

A photograph of Neil's face that accompanied match reports in the Press following the game was genuinely frightening – scarcely recognisable even as a human being, it looked like the visage of an exceptionally angry alien creature out of Dr Who whose planet had just been invaded by pesky Earthlings. You'd hope that the incentive of not seeing *that* bearing down on you again would be enough to gee up his players for Wednesday night beneath the floodlights.

But if the pressure was getting to oor Nellie, it was as nothing compared to what it was doing to Rangers' stand-in gaffer Graeme Murty. At one point during his team's defeat by Dundee he emerged from the dugout and proceeded to *stand on his head* on the touchline. I daresay watching the huns upsides-down was something of an improvement, but it was hardly dignified behaviour. You could scarcely imagine former managers like Walter Smith suddenly deciding that performing circus acrobatics during a match you were losing was the most appropriate response. John Greig neither – although he was fairly adept at standing on other peoples' heads when still playing for the bluenoses. The way things were going, there was every chance though that Murty would soon be acclaimed as the greatest Rangers manager since Kenny McDowall.

One player who wouldn't be losing *too* much sleep before gaining another notch on his derby belt was Lewis Stevenson, or at least not as much as he'd forego through nerves when a lot younger. He confessed that back then he wouldn't sleep properly for about a week before, but nowadays he looked forward more with excitement than apprehension. Mind you, he was still a bit jealous of the current crop of young whippersnappers who didn't know what a defeat by the jambos felt like.

"I heard John McGinn say he's unbeaten at Tynecastle and I am envious. I'm past the stage I can say that!"

Lewis was well on track to eventually becoming the Hibs player with most appearances against our city rivals to his name. He was one game behind Pat Stanton, three behind Pat McGinlay, five behind Gordon Hunter and nine behind the peerless Gordon Smith. There had certainly been some ups and downs throughout with the odd barren spell along the way, but nothing compared to that endured by his illustrious predecessor sitting on thirty-six appearances. I was in the old enclosure in front of the main stand at Tynie in 1994, when Geebsy notched the solitary goal of the game, finally bringing the curtain down on a horrendous run of twenty-two consecutive games without victory over the Gorgie boys. The man largely responsible for that – John Robertson – was way out in front in the derby day appearance charts, with fifty-five matches to his credit, spread over seventeen years.

Robbo was an almighty thorn in Hibs' side alright, but a guy I'd always respected, due in no small part to the way he stood up at the Usher Hall 'Hands off Hibs' rally in 1990, to denounce the despicable Wallace Mercer a.k.a. Wallet Mercenary and his 'merger' plans (i.e. to put Hibs out of business for good.) He was still playing for the jambos then and it took a lot of guts to do what he did, as his club chairman could – and did – proceed to make things difficult for him afterwards.

When I was in Dublin for the Hibs pre-season tour in 2005, I was beaten to McDaid's bar every morning by a strangely familiar looking Hibs supporter, resplendent in the replica top of the day. No matter *how* early I shuddered into the legendary howff once patronised by literary luminaries such as Brendan Behan, Flann O'Brien and Patrick Kavanagh, this joker was always already there, perched on his favourite stool. After he'd introduced himself as 'George', I confessed that I was pretty sure I hadn't met him before, but that he sure as hell reminded me of *someone,* but I was damned if I could think of who it was. He smiled resignedly, as if he'd been in this situation before.

"You're maybe thinking of my brother," he remarked. "You'll certainly have seen *him* before – unfortunately."

"Who's your brother?" I naturally asked, now completely scoobied.

"John Robertson of Hearts," he admitted, gargling back his breakfast Guinness in record time.

I almost fell off my stool. I couldn't really see it at the time, but it must have been a subliminal recognition on my part. When I got my photographs developed on return – which included one the barmaid had taken of the pair of us – the resemblance to his sibling was indeed uncanny.

Ten years later I was in 'The Radical Road', dropping off copies of my Hibs book, 'Growing Up in Green', which mine host Martin Mitchell had kindly volunteered to punt from behind the bar. After a while, I noticed a guy sitting on his own supping a pint at a table near the door, scribbling furiously in a notebook. *Deja-vu!* I did a quick double-take, before consulting Martin as to his identity, just to make absolutely sure.

"Aye, that's George the Poet," he smirked. "What a bam. How do you know *him?*"

"Hibs on tour, class of 2005 – and I've not seen him since," I explained, before striding over to reacquaint myself.

I then had to have an extra two pints to kill time, whilst he wrote me a poem to mark the auspicious occasion of our original meeting. 'Twas a cracker too. Any man that can confidently rhyme 'McDaid's' with 'Shades' is at the very least worthy of Poet Laureate status in my book...

Back to the present and some carnivorous controversy in the F.A. Cup down Englandshire way. A hoo-hah developed after Sutton United's home game with Arsenal, when footage emerged of their reserve goalkeeper apparently stuffing a huge pie into his face on the bench. When I first saw it I thought it was Conrad Logan, before quickly reappraising the situation. No way was Conrad ever *that* big. Jesus, this boy made our cup final hero look like Twiggy suffering from anorexia. In mitigation, he claimed that he was only responding to the Sutton fans' on-going renditions of 'Who Ate All The Pies?' whenever he made an appearance, saying that in any case he hadn't been scranning a pie, but a pastie instead. This explanation wasn't good enough for the authorities however, who suspected that money had been wagered at the bookies on the chances of such a gastronomic spectacle occurring. Personally, I couldn't see what all the fuss was about. He was only the *reserve* goalkeeper after all. Christian Nade once demolished a full three-course meal during a match, followed by an extensive cheeseboard, all washed down with a fine selection of sparkling wines. But the difference was that he was actually *playing* at the time.

'Twas a dark and stormy night in Leith... Well, it wasn't really, I'm just employing some dramatic license there. Obviously it was dark – dark as the soul of Wallace Mercer residing in the bowels of Hell – but the much anticipated storm with a silly name was still twelve hours away. It was cold and clear, but before long the jambos were being buffeted by the far more lethal force of Hurricane Hibernian, which was going to wreak a lot more damage on them than Doris would, a day later.

Neil's super-strength hairdryer blast following the Raith game must have done the trick, because each and every one of his players looked up for the cup replay challenge right from the off. But his careful planning was put to the test almost immediately, as with the game barely under way Chris Humphrey hit the deck clutching his calf. It became obvious right away that he wouldn't be able to continue and after some protracted treatment on the pitch he hobbled off in evident pain. That was a body blow and no mistake, but happily his unexpected early replacement Andrew Shinnie went on to have a great game, which included notching a goal. The biggest crowd at Easter Road in twenty-three years sensed that the Hibees meant business here and kept up a formidable barrage of noise throughout, as their team almost instantly assumed total domination. John McGinn was in the thick of the action and unlucky not to be awarded a penalty after a clash with

Avlonitis – you certainly don't want to catch a dose of *that* – and the same player saved the jambos' bacon shortly after, with a clearance from a Boyle cross. Martin's sizzling pace caused the defence endless problems and if Humphrey hadn't been injured you'd imagine his similarly lightning sprints down the opposite flank would have stretched them beyond breaking point. Hearts had no real answer to the pressure, a solitary ball across the goal from Struna being their only response during the first fifteen minutes and even that was ably dealt with by Darren McGregor who moved quickly to block Goncalves from getting on the end of it. There wasn't long until the breakthrough now, as five more minutes elapsed before Shinnie split the defence with a terrific pass to Jason. Up against his old club again, there was no chance that JC was going to miss from there, which must have been crystal clear to the maroon hordes behind the goal, as soon as Shinnie released the ball. The scorer was rapidly becoming a bane on the jambos' lives, equivalent to what John Robertson had once been where the Hibees were concerned.

Within the next quarter-of-an-hour the home side could easily have been four up, with a trio of great opportunities. A dangerous free-kick from the on-form Cummings looked like picking out either Fontaine or McGregor at the back post, but unfortunately both were too keen and got in each-other's road! Liam headed over and almost immediately Hearts had another scare, when McGinn came close and although goalkeeper Hamilton did well to block his effort, the rebound fell for Shinnie. His shot came off Kitchen for a corner, but unfortunately the blind man in the black inexplicably chose to award a goal-kick instead. Hibs were absolutely on fire at this stage and it was really only a matter of time before they added to their tally. That moment duly arrived eight minutes before the interval, when Jason slipped a clever pass through to big Holty in plenty space, with the defence wrong-footed. As they vainly looked for a non-existent 'offside', the veteran striker easily slotted it away. The jambos trooped off the pitch at the interval, well aware that they had a mountain to climb and it could well have been an even higher one. A re-run of January 1st, 1973 in the half-time scoreline stakes hadn't seemed that far away at all.

Cathy opted for installing a Kitchen replacement in the second half, as the original American model was clearly not fit for purpose. The hobbit had watched a rusty Kitchen sink for long enough before pulling the plug and sending on Sam Nicholson and Rory Currie, as Malaury Martin also left the field. It made little difference to the green onslaught though, as Shinnie yet again came agonisingly close. Hamilton blocked his initial shot but Andrew could well have followed through if the ball hadn't taken a kindly bounce for the jambos, ricocheting off a defender into the keeper's arms. Hearts enjoyed a brief spell where they succeeded in holding onto the ball and tipping the possession balance in their favour, but it was no more than a brief respite. They'd utterly failed to create any significant openings, underlined when Jamie Walker wildly blasted a half-chance into Row Z of the South Stand. You couldn't even recall the last time anything had remotely troubled Rocky in the Hibs goal before that.

But with just under half-an-hour remaining it really was all over and there's precious few times you could make that statement regarding a derby outcome. Shinnie broke through again and struck a shot which Hamilton looked to have covered, but the young keeper allowed it to squirm through his outstretched fingers. 3-0 to Hibs and already a sizeable number of scarf-twirlers had seen enough. They were chucking themselves off the Bothwell Street bridge by the time their team were handed an undeserved lifeline as a penalty award followed a Daz doorstep challenge on Goncalves. He opted to take it himself but hit it without much apparent confidence and Rocky kept it out. He did exceptionally well to do likewise with a second attempt by the same player and there was an element of farce about it when the striker finally somehow managed to bundle the ball over the line at the third time of asking. There shouldn't have been any cause for concern, but Hibbies with longish memories would no doubt be recalling a two-goal lead over the jambos at the PBS suddenly being cancelled out in the dying seconds, during the famous 4-4 fuck-up. It didn't look on the cards here, but you're always going to be a tad nervous where the jambos are concerned. One lucky break and they might still be in contention for at least a draw. It wasn't long before we thought a bulleted header from Daz into the net had put it out of sight at 4-1, from another fine Cummings free-kick. That was flagged offside, but thankfully it didn't matter too much now. Hibs were cruising and realistically they'd done so comfortably throughout the ninety minutes. The scoreline might not have accurately reflected it, but this was their most comprehensive win over Hearts since 6-2; a tremendous team effort all round and proof that they were capable of coming good in the really big games. There was no denying the recent League wobble, but this was a performance to rank alongside their 3-0 demolition of Dundee United. Hearts were poor, but Hibs never gave them a chance to get going and a visiting stranger would certainly have left with the impression that the winning side must be the ones lying fourth in the Premiership, as opposed to the Championship contenders.

Neil Lennon had been quick to rip into his players after the dismal showing in Kirkcaldy, but now he was just as effusive in his plaudits.

"As a manager you couldn't have asked for more. You could see what it meant to the supporters, the build up, the anticipation. The players were ferocious, absolutely ferocious. I felt it could have been more, it could have been four or five. I couldn't see Hearts scoring. I was delighted for the players. If we could play all our games under the floodlights, I would be delighted. The players rose to the occasion."

"I think we wanted it more than them," stated Jason Cummings, who'd taken his usual care to appropriately celebrate his goal in front of the Hearts fans – just for the benefit of his jambo relations, of course. "We have a lot of players who know about Edinburgh derbies, who know what it means to the fans. But you look at their team-sheet and perhaps they didn't know what it meant. I didn't think for a moment we were going to lose. I enjoy these games, I was really buzzing. I was playing with a smile."

Seven unbeaten in a row against the jambos now, here we go! No wonder he had a grin broader than a Cheshire cat's.

"Everything went wrong," was Cathy's glum assessment from the enemy camp. "We were outfought, we were outplayed. It is sad to say – but it's the truth and it's not good enough."

The songs were soon belting out in Robbie's and in most other bars in the vicinity too, I daresay. There are few feelings in this sorry world so pleasant as that warm glow of euphoric satisfaction that accompanies a fine victory in the post-match pub celebrations, surrounded by shiny happy people. I then *just* managed to catch a last bus westwards and was pleased to discover half a bottle of Pinot Grigio looking frightfully lonely on the kitchen shelf when I arrived home. Well...it would be rude not to, I thought. Here we go, Grigio, here we go... Sometime later while channel-hopping, I came across a music video compilation on one of those weird Freeview stations which seem to infect my telly in the wee sma' 'oors. Before my eyes was the twerking daughter of old Mullet-Heid himself, Billy Ray Cyrus, swinging back and forth in her knickers on that infamous wrecking ball. Soon I was inadvertently singing her dad's famous irritating ditty which directly gave birth to the Super John McGinn song, but with a slight change to the original.

"Oh don't break my Hearts, my achy-breaky Hearts..."

Hibs came in like a wrecking ball alright and smashed their achy-breaky hearts into little pieces. Ha! Sorrow, sorrow, *their* hearts were broken... I gargled back the rest of the vino, glancing one last time at the screen as the twerker continued in motion, like some sort of under-dressed half-starved stick insect on a pendulum.

"GIE THE BAW TAE MILEY!" I cried aloud, before stumbling off to my kip and some very sweet dreams indeed.

It was certainly the sort of night for spouting drunken gibberish in the privacy of your own home. A mate who'd rolled in rather merry was given a severe dressing-down by his wife the following morning, who demanded to know why he'd woken her up by repeatedly singing "that stupid song about tuna rolls." At first he couldn't figure out what she was on about, particularly as he had little recollection of it, until the penny finally dropped. When it did, he didn't have the heart to correct her. Altogether now – "Here we go, tuna roll, here we go, tuna roll..."

The following day, The Evening News announced that they were teaming up with Utilita Energy to offer readers a chance to win a day out at Easter Road with the person who'd brought them into this world. Aw, bless! Iron Maiden notoriously advised their listeners to "Bring Your Daughter To The Slaughter" in their first No.1 hit, so now Hibs were effectively saying, "Bring Yer Maw Tae Watch A Draw"? To be in with a chance of success, you were required to send them a photo of yourself and your mum, with a spiel about why she deserved it. This seemed a trifle unfair to us poor little orphans whose mothers were no longer with us, but I suppose you could get someone to impersonate her in order to score a three-course meal and free drink. While I was pondering who might fit the bill there, my eye caught details of the alternative competition sponsored by Hearts, namely to win a day out at Tynecastle with a person of your choice from Tranent. "Bring Your Belter To The Pink Bus Shelter" - you'd better believe it...

Sir David Gray now had his eye firmly fixed on the Dunfermline game, coming hard on the heels of the cup replay with only two clear days in between. He was well aware that to avoid another Lennon lambasting they'd all have to seek to maintain the high standards set on Wednesday night.

"Derbies are different – the atmosphere and the occasion takes care of itself," observed the club captain. "The manager said he wasn't worried about the Hearts game because he knew that would take care of itself. The big one now is Dunfermline and we need to make sure we're up for it. Obviously it's great to be in the Scottish Cup quarter-final but now we're back to business against Dunfermline. That now becomes our biggest game of the season."

The manager might not have been worried about his team's ability to raise their game when up against the jambos, but he'd taken the precaution of saying in advance that it would be difficult to scale such heights again, a mere three days later. It turned out to be not so much difficult as just plain impossible, but no-one was to suspect that after a very bright opening. However, the main talking point in the stadium after the first twenty minutes or so was this – exactly how much LSD have those responsible for the West Stand catering been putting in the Bovril? The songs had been coming thick and fast, from the 'Super' one – no, not in praise of John McGinn, but Joe Joe super Joe (as in Tortolano), not to mention that old chestnut concerning flying over Ibrox tomorrow...TO SHITE ON THE BASTARDS BELOW (below). I don't think I've heard *that* one reverberating around the holy ground for a couple of decades or so. In a most unusual turn of events, the tunes were actually originating in the West, rather than gradually spreading from the East, as they tend to do on occasion of high drama and electric atmosphere such as Wednesday night. The West was on fire for sure; indeed they were pretty much the only ones left with a song in their hearts long before half-time, which wasn't surprising in light of what developed.

For Hibs got off to the best start imaginable, when with only five minutes played a clever cross from Cummings picked out Martin Boyle, who slammed it home decisively. It looked as if they were simply going to carry on from where they'd left off against Hearts and a quick follow-up goal seemed already on the cards. The East Stand was soon joining their musical compatriots and likely contenders for 'The Voice' opposite in song, but in general sticking to the more modern, er, 'classics', if indeed that's the appropriate term. "ONE, TWO, THREE, FOUR – Hibs, Hibs, whoa-oh-oh-oh, Hibs, Hibs, whoa-oh-oh-oh..." Truly the crack cocaine of football chants. You guiltily suspect deep down that it's terrible and bad for you, but once you start it's just *so* damned addictive. Sure enough, we didn't have long to wait until the scorer was upended in the box and referee John Beaton immediately pointed to the penalty spot. Jason strode up to take it – just don't think and *please* don't dink, went up the silent prayer – but it wasn't necessary, as he stuck it away confidently.

Pars' midfielder Kallum Higginbotham (what a pity his dad didn't have a spellcheck to hand when he went to register his birth) later confirmed that he feared his team were going to get done over big style at that point and pretty much everyone else in the now bouncing stadium thought the same. As I nipped to the toilet the bloke next to me remarked, "We're on easy street already, eh?" and it was hard to disagree with that impression. "I'll settle for five," he continued optimistically. "Oh aye?" retorted a flustered looking guy who'd just come in. "Well, you'll have to settle for 5-1 then, cos they've just scored!" Surely not? I dashed out, just in time to watch David Gray's fresh air kick howler being shown again on the monitor. He missed the through ball from Nicky Clark altogether and Paul McMullan was happy to accept the free gift, running on to stick it past Rocky. Well, that was an unexpected turn of events, but hopefully it was only a blip and normal service would be restored as soon as possible. That was emphatically not what transpired however. By the time Fontaine had limped off to be replaced by Marvin Bartley, the Pars looked well up for it, clearly hugely reinvigorated by McMullan's strike. Unlike virtually every other team who'd come to Easter Road and simply sat tight in defence hoping for an isolated breakaway goal at best, they showed that they weren't going to settle for that approach. It was up and at 'em and suddenly Hibs' perceived 'easy street' was looking more like a rocky road instead.

Immediately after the interval a cross from Michael Moffat picked out Higginbotham and he smashed his angled drive gleefully into the net, to bring matters level at 2-2.

"We got a goal soon after they scored their second and for the rest of the first half I thought we were on top – and we were miles better in the second half," he said later.

There was no arguing with that assessment, as it was all Dunfermline for a goodly chunk of time following that and Hibs could thank their lucky stars that Rocky was in such fine form. The Israeli internationalist made a string of superb saves, including a 'double' which almost defied belief as he first managed to turn a Moffat effort onto the bar. That bounced out to Clark however, who looked certain to score, but the keeper somehow managed to beat that away as well.

Hibs were toiling in the middle of the park and such was the dearth of alternatives available, Lennon opted to throw young Callum Crane into an unfamiliar position after the largely anonymous Fraser Fyvie departed the field. He also put on Keatings, but far too late to make any difference, as there were then only two minutes of regulation time left. A substitution that should have taken place a hell of a lot earlier in my opinion, as he replaced Shinnie, who'd had a fairly bad day at the office. Ditto Grant Holt and Super John McGinn was for once anything but, having probably his worst game yet in a Hibs jersey. He passed the ball to opposition players so often you wondered if he was labouring under the delusion that he was still playing for St. Mirren, hence the desire to obligingly give the ball to someone in black and white. But these failings should not take anything away from Dunfermline, who deserve a lot of credit for their performance, the best by any visiting team over the season so far. It ended 2-2, but four or five for the opposition would not have been an injustice. Hibs had one man to thank for the fact that they didn't achieve that, Ofir Marciano.

"He had a fantastic game," acknowledged the scorer of the Pars' equaliser, "and we're disappointed that we've not won."

As for Hibs' undisputed Man of the Match – well, undisputed except by the corporate crew who voted for Boyle – the keeper sought to address the issue of possible fatigue in the wake of that great cup win taking effect.

"If you want to reach a high level, play in the Premiership and dominate in the cup, we need to handle that. It's not easy to go from a derby against Hearts with 20,000 people and that atmosphere to playing against Dunfermline. But that is how big teams measure themselves. As professionals, we have to do better. We looked a bit tired."

"Mentally and physically they were tired," concurred Neil Lennon. "I knew Wednesday night would take a lot out of them, so I'm pleased with a point."

That, ultimately, was the over-riding feeling, once we'd got over the initial disappointment and frustration at the loss of two points and yet another draw. Hibs' pursuers had not gained any ground at least, as Dundee United and Morton also drew, in what Arabs' gaffer Ray McKinnon described as "a horrible game." Falkirk drew as well – with Dumbarton – so to put an optimistic spin on it you'd have to rationalise that our main challengers now had one game less in which to close the gap.

February had not been the greatest of months at all, with four draws and one win and naturally it would be the latter which would linger longest in the memory. The string of draws was not indicative of Championship-winning form in the usual scheme of things; however, the dog-eat-dog nature of the second tier struggle had worked in Hibs' favour to a significant extent. Plus, unlike the previous season, this time they weren't reduced to playing catch-up. A spate of injuries had befallen them at an unfortunate time though and the looming fixture list was looking rather congested. Rather than a sleek cheetah-like sprint to the title as had been hoped for, there were elements of a wounded elephant shot through with arrows lumbering painfully towards the finishing line. But at least the old green and white pachyderm had a thick hide and was still leading the charge.

9.

MARCH: HAND OF GOD? THE SILLY SOD

The month opened with the happy news that season ticket prices would be frozen for another campaign at least and Iron Rod was feeling the deep financial freeze already. Of course, those who had purchased well in advance for season 2014 / 15 received an unpleasant surprise when it transpired they effectively wouldn't be getting what they thought they'd paid for (i.e. Premier League football), so hopefully this time around they *might* strike lucky.

On the playing front, Neil Lennon had moved extremely swiftly after the Pars game and the subsequent news that Liam Fontaine would be out of action for some time; to swoop for Efe Ambrose on an emergency loan deal. I didn't see that one coming, I must admit. Like many observing from afar I hadn't exactly been impressed by the Nigerian's performances in the hoops before he dropped out of Brendan Rodgers' first team plans at Parkhead. But with Paul Hanlon's return now delayed due to additional nerve damage and Darren McGregor's looming suspension, there was no doubt that Neil had to get someone on board *fast*. However, he knew the player well from his own time at Celtic Park and was well aware of the possibly rather unfair reputation he'd garnered of late.

"People always talk about the mistakes he's made, the high profile ones. But we have all made them. I think the first four years of his time at Celtic must have been deleted, the way people talk about him now."

He went on to reel off the names of top strikers on the European stage whose threat had been nullified after coming up against the big defender, during his honeymoon period in the east end of Glasgow.

As to the emergency loan system, the manager quite understandably was getting hot under the collar at some of the petty sniping by jealous parties who seemed to think it was somehow 'unfair'.

"It is there to be used – we haven't broken a single rule or law," he pointed out. "I could moan about clubs going out and signing nine players in the transfer window, but I don't. If people are unhappy about it they can write to the SFA and ask them to scrap it. It's an advantage to anyone who wants to use it – so shut up!"

(or "Efe off!" in other words.)

Also snapped up was free agent Brian McLean, who'd previously played for Motherwell and had now just been released by DPPM Brunei who compete in Singapore's 'S' League. Another defender, which was all to the good under the circumstances. At this stage there was no word of a possible return for McGeouch either, although Forster would hopefully be available again soon. Hibs' defence had been great for the most part, but it was going to be hard to maintain standards if the whole bloody lot of them were either injured or suspended! With the Championship race entering a crucial phase, it was no time for dithering and Neil should be commended for seeking to rectify the problem so quickly.

Another man without his problems to seek and the latest ex-Hibee to be found 'courting disaster', so to speak, was Islam Feruz. The last anyone had heard of dizzy Izzy was when he'd disappeared into thin air in Turkey, after running away from the latest club foolish enough to offer him a trial, but it seemed he'd somehow found his way back to these shores. It appeared that he'd come up the Clyde on a banana boat, whereupon he quickly transferred to a Porsche valued at £80,000 which he then proceeded to race at high speeds through the streets of Glasgow. The beak wasn't amused as Izzy was disqualified from driving anyway, hadn't turned up for the last hearing and had 'given a false name' when apprehended, according to the prosecution. Luckily he opted for 'Garry O'Connor' there, as opposed to 'Anthony Stokes' – he was fined three grand, but if he'd identified himself as the latter they'd probably have bumped it up a hundred-fold.

As expected, Efe – who hadn't played first team football in eight months – was pitched straight into the mix against St. Mirren in Paisley on the 2nd, with McLean being confined to the bench. It was hard to get an overview of the much-maligned defender's worth on this outing however, as Hibs were simply woeful throughout. They were in fact lucky not to have already been two or three down by the time Saints did score on the thirty-fifth minute, as firstly Stephen Mallan and then Kyle Magennis went close. The latter then saw an even better chance come to naught, as his header bounced back off the crossbar with Rocky for once stranded. The visitors' sole opening came when a McGinn cross missed Ambrose's head by a fraction, forcing a very rare save from Billy O'Brien. It took a defender to eventually score at the other end as Demetriou showed how it should be done, evading David Gray to strike a good effort past Rocky into the corner of the net.

The Cypriot doubled his tally immediately after the break, as for the second time within a week Hibs failed to waken up properly after the interval, yet again conceding in this notorious goal-leaking time segment. They had no discernible shape about them and were all at sea as Saints came within a whisker of grabbing a third through Smith. Lennon replaced Bartley with Holt on the hour mark and the big man's presence alone did seem to rally the troops slightly as it had done before, although his direct impact wasn't particularly evident. However, he wasn't fully fit, the manager revealed later, which was one reason he hadn't selected him from the start. Hibs' best opportunity saw the ball rebound off him into O'Brien's hands after the keeper had made a terrific save from Boyle. But there had been precious few of them – a whole *two* throughout – and by then the Saints could well have increased their lead anyway. Yes, the Easter Road men had been diminished by the recent raft of injuries and increasingly hectic fixture schedule, but this was still a dreadful performance against a team who were lying at the bottom of the division by some distance.

"We were poor," said Lennon, seeming uncharacteristically reticent after his recent post-match outburst, but he probably realised the futility of having a verbal go at them again. "It's our first defeat in three months and while we have not won in four games in the League, I'm not going to be too hard on them. It was a poor night, the better team won."

Only three points had now been accrued out of a possible twelve throughout this run, but as this was the only midweek Championship fixture, the gap at the top remained the same. It could only give succour to Dundee United, Morton and Falkirk, who on the recent showings must have been wondering how on earth the Hibees had built up such a lead. They looked far from title contenders for the time being and now had to considerably raise their game with a cup quarter-final just up ahead.

There was sad news the following day, with the passing of Tommy Gemmell, in the fiftieth anniversary year of Celtic's greatest triumph, lifting the European Cup in 1967. It was the full-back with the thunderous shot who equalised, after Celtic fell behind to Inter Milan in the final and he became the first player to score in *two* European Cup finals, also netting against Feyenoord three years later. My favourite memory of Tommy comes from that same year, as Celtic suffered their first defeat of the season at Easter Road. They went down 2-0 to a rampant Hibs with Joe McBride scoring twice, one of them an absolute cracker. He took receipt of a pass from Johnny Hamilton who looked to have hit it a trifle high, but Joe lashed the ball from around shoulder height past the startled Evan Williams into the Celtic net.

In those days, the polis would be ranged almost shoulder-to-shoulder across the front of 'The Cave' (on the site of the Famous Five Stand) and its notorious singing section, facing the crowd. As this would be roughly split down the middle between both sets of fans, exchanges of missiles and fisticuffs were not uncommon, as there was no physical barrier of segregation to divide the opposing factions.

"Standing on the corner swinging my chain / Along came an Orangeman and called me a name / I kicked him in the balls and I kicked him in the head / And now that Orangeman is dead / With a na na na na na na na..."

At some point, Gemmell chose to unleash one of his 70 m.p.h. piledrivers, which, luckily for Hibs, screamed past the wrong side of Gordon Marshall's post. Unluckily for a particular polisman though, who caught the full ferocious force of Tommy's attempt in the small of his back. The impact pitched him forward and he came perilously close to falling head first into the teeming masses who were laughing their heads off at his misfortune. Almost immediately another classic ditty of the day was ringing forth:-

"Who's that man with the helmet on / Dixon, Dixon / Who's that man with the helmet on / Dixon of Dock Green / On the beat all day / On the wife all night / Who's that man with the helmet on / Dixon of Dock Green."

Of course, unlike the fictional cop played by Jack Warner in the TV series, Scottish bobbies didn't wear helmets, but now this one didn't have his hat either. My personal match statistics reveal that the attendance was 37,000 and that *seventy-eight* people were forcibly ejected from the ground by the overworked cops for various misdemeanours before the game had even kicked off. This wasn't as a result of a mass 'pagger' on the terracing either, but individuals hauled out one by one, generally three sheets to the wind and exhibiting extreme difficulty in walking unaided. Incredible as that may seem today, this was quite standard for a big match and scarcely warranted a mention in the press.

So, to cup business again and a visit from Ian McCall's awkward squad from Ayrshire. Despite registering their biggest away win in the League so far at Somerset Park, the Hibees had inexplicably failed to overcome the same team at Easter Road. However, notice was very swiftly served that this time around it was surely going to be different. Only seven minutes had elapsed when Super John McG completed a move he'd instigated in the first place, sending a lovely curling twenty-yarder past George Fleming in the Ayr goal. This was followed up by another five minutes later, when a speeding Martin Boyle was brought crashing to earth by Darryl Meggatt, just inside the box. Jason stepped up in his usual confident manner to take the resulting penalty, which he duly converted. Hibs looked to be coasting for the next twenty minutes, but that changed when Craig McGuffie suddenly put the visitors right back in it. He hit a tremendous swerving left-foot shot from some distance which gave Rocky no chance and Hibs' lead wasn't looking quite so unassailable. 2-1 was how it stood at the interval and deja-vu feelings with regard to how the Dunfermline game had evolved were only too evident. Hibs had looked out of sight fairly early doors in that one too, but ended up lucky to salvage a point.

Ayr weren't able to convincingly mount counter-attacks the way the Pars had done however, but they still proved a stuffy, tenacious lot to break down. They were a man short too, as McKenna had been instantly red-carded for a shocking waist-high challenge on McGinn just before half-time. But, as so often happens, that perceived advantage to the team with the full complement of players wasn't particularly obvious. The visitors had a half-hearted shout for a penalty themselves, but any handball contact by Ambrose was clearly accidental. Efe seemed to grow into his role as the game progressed, striking up a good partnership with Marvin Bartley at the back and proving that a lot of the criticism which had come his way was unfounded. Hibs were still in the ascendancy, although there was some frustration at their inability to kill off the Honest Men decisively. But then Lennon made one of his shrewd substitutions, which had so often paid instant dividends throughout the campaign. James Keatings entered the fray on the seventy-seventh minute and almost immediately directed a fine header over Fleming to put the tie beyond doubt. The sponsors went for Shinnie as Man of the Match (making it a family affair, as his brother received a similar accolade with Aberdeen twenty-four hours later!) but for me the stand-out man was McGinn. He'd been far from super in the previous two games, so it was great to see him absolutely back to his best, scoring a sublime goal and exhibiting a wealth of creativity and tireless endeavour throughout.

"It could have been five or six," claimed the delighted gaffer afterwards. "We turned in a dreadful performance last Wednesday, but we were emphatic, head and shoulders above Ayr, who were a tough nut to crack."

The draw for the semi-finals took place the day after and the conspiracy theorists who'd always suspected the whole shebang was a fix had their views seemingly validated by Richard Gordon on Radio Scotland.

"As soon as the first one comes out, you know what the next one is going to be," he stated, as the rumbling sound in the background indicated the drum was spinning and we were under way.

So was he talking balls...or was he talking balls?? As the ugly sisters from Weedjieland were paired together for the second year in a row it appeared that he was. An outcome that used to occur very seldom, but was now becoming the norm. The silly bint on the STV News then tried to confuse everyone further by announcing that, "Rangers will play Celtic in the semi-final of the Scottish Cup." Almost as an afterthought she added, "Hibs will play Aberdeen in the next round." *What??* Still, it was as good as we could have hoped for really. The Sheep clawed their way through by scraping past Partick Thistle in a generally dire slog televised live on BBC 1, just before the draw took place. Meanwhile, a nice man from the Lodge officiating at Ibrox immeasurably aided the huns' passage to the semi, while St. Mirren gave Celtic a hell of a fright by taking the lead at Parkhead and holding onto it for a considerable time. Somewhat inevitably though, the home team's superiority prevailed convincingly in the end.

Hibs had now reached the penultimate stage of the Big Cup five times in six seasons, which was a worthy achievement in itself. The semis were scheduled for a full seven weeks in the future, which meant that every ounce of concentration could now be refocused on the League, with the manager admitting that the disparity in form his team had lately displayed in the respective competitions was driving him 'mental'. Well, we're the mental Hibees, Neil, you should have taken heed of the old song lyric before you joined up. But at this same stage the previous year the focus had naturally all been directed towards the upcoming League Cup final, which was no longer a distraction in the current campaign. They also had the Big Cup replay against ICT to deal with and – with pre-season friendlies included – had already played forty games. No matter how much Stubbsy had tried to ensure that the main prize of promotion remained of paramount importance, the players would hardly have been human if their thoughts hadn't been side-tracked by the lure of the silverware. It was towards the end of February that the wheels really came off the Championship challenge, but this time there could be no excuses at their attention being diverted from the main task. They'd done supremely well in 'The Scottish' so far, but they could now forget all about that for the time being.

"The focus is on the League, one hundred per cent," confirmed a fit again Jordon Forster. "The semi-final will take care of itself. We've got a big chance to win the Scottish Cup, to retain it and regardless of who we'd got people will look on us now as underdogs, although we know what we can do."

He had a point there, as the semis comprised the three leading sides in the Premiership – plus the 'wee' team from the Championship. It was unlikely though that Aberdeen under the canny tutelage of Derek MacInnes would be in any way underestimating the cup-holders.

There would certainly be no need for Neil Lennon to reiterate the importance of the next game to his players, as the clock started ticking down towards Friday evening's vital away fixture at Tannadice. Hopefully the first team would take a leaf out of the book of their Under-20 counterparts, who had just defeated the Arabs' wee team 2-1 at Station Park. The young Hibees scored through the on-form Oli Shaw and Fraser Murray, consolidating their lead at the top of the Development league.

"If we get a victory it's game on, isn't it?" said Tangerines' top dog, Ray McKinnon. "We have had our blip hopefully, they (Hibs) have gone through their wee blip. Everybody has their wee periods in the season where you are not at your best. We're just delighted we are still in it."

Meanwhile, the man who effectively kick-started the careers of McGinn at St. Mirren and McGregor at Cowdenbeath, former Hibee Danny Lennon, predicted that, "If Hibs keep those two fit, they should be strong enough to win the Championship. Wee McGinn for me is one of the top players in Scotland for his age. When he plays well, Hibs play well. There's no doubt about that. I was at the cup replay against Hearts and John and Darren were outstanding."

Danny was equally effusive about the latter's sterling contribution to the Hibs cause of late.

"It doesn't surprise me that he's had such a big impact at Hibs. Every set of fans that Darren has played for will appreciate him because he always gives a hundred per cent on and off the pitch. He's an intelligent footballer both on the pitch and in terms of knowing the right things to do off it. He's got such a tremendous appetite for the game. He's such a positive person with a tremendous attitude that rubs off on other people around him."

As to the calls for a possible upgrade to the international stage, Hibs' former utility player had no doubt that Daz was well qualified, due to the consistency of his performances.

"If he was given the opportunity he would rise to the challenge."

Doubtless, but would he rise to the challenge of Grant Holt taking the piss? According to the Press, Holty was jesting that it was about time someone made a movie of the Daz story – from clothes shop worker aged twenty-four to Scottish Cup winner aged thirty. Maybe something combining the two ends of the spectrum would suffice – 'How The Vest Was Won' perhaps? But Grant wants to watch his step, as Daz could easily retaliate by in turn suggesting that the big man up front could feature in a remake of a Simon Pegg flick. 'Run, Fatboy, Run'? Aye, you're ahead of me there...

"It has been frustrating that we haven't opened up a bigger gap," admitted Neil Lennon, ahead of the potentially season-defining clash with Dundee United. "But nothing is given to you, you have to earn it and we haven't done that. The intensity and quality of the cup performances has far outweighed the recent League performances. So I know what this team is capable of. It's just a case of transferring that mind-set for the League and getting that consistency. I don't think that we are far away from putting a string of very good performances together."

There would certainly never be a better time to start. A victory would send Hibs a massive ten points clear of United, while a win for them would peg it back to four, plus they also had a game in hand. No-one would be forgetting either that Falkirk had now split the Friday evening opponents at the top of the table, although they had actually played a game more than Hibs.

Events got under way at Tannadice, with the visitors being roared on by a packed-out Shed housing two and a half thousand Hibbies. As expected, Darren McGregor returned, displacing Forster, although the latter did come on for the last few minutes. A free-kick from Daz had the home side rattled early on, as Paul Dixon made a wild clearance to propel the ball over the bar, but it could just as easily have sneaked underneath it. That was swiftly followed by Cummings intercepting a weak pass-back, but the angle was just too tight and keeper Cammy Bell saved his shot. United went through a spell where they dominated in terms of possession, but they lacked the imagination to create any viable chances and make it count in their favour. It was a tousy affair, United going 2-1 up on bookings halfway through the first forty-five, one of them for Toshney, who had been shooting his mouth off a little bit too much in the run-up to the game. He could have absolutely no complaint when he added to his first offence against Andrew Shinnie with an even worse one on the same player and was promptly red-carded. Just back from injury himself, he seemed overly keen to injure someone else as quickly as possible. The game swung back in Hibs' favour and eight minutes after that Shinnie took possession of a flick from Holt. He knocked it out left to Cummings, who smashed a truly wonderful volley with his favoured left peg past Bell. He left the field at the interval protesting to referee Robertson over the lack of a penalty award just before the whistle blew, as he went to ground under a challenge by Edjenguele. The latter was his usual bruising self and was yellow-carded later for a spot of unseemly all-in wrestling with Holt, who was also booked.

Hibs started the second half on fire, seemingly determined to kill the game off as soon as possible. United were forced back right from the off and remained utterly incapable of countering with anything of note. Martin Boyle should have doubled the tally when Holt picked him out at the back post, but he hurried his shot and sclaffed it high over the bar. He redeemed himself shortly afterwards by finding Shinnie with a neat ball, but Andrew's subsequent shot was blocked by Durnan. The bookings continued to register at rather an alarming rate (ten in all), including one for Jason who reacted petulantly after being adjudged offside. Not the first time he'd received a yellow for that sort of behaviour of course and he really should have known better – but that was as nothing in comparison to his next act of stupidity. I fully expected Lennon to hook him right away after the original booking but the manager didn't do so, which might have proved costly in light of what followed. A mere three minutes later he expertly redirected a David Gray cross into the net, but unfortunately chose to use his hand to do so.

"He scores one goal like Neymar – and another like bloody Maradona!" groaned my mate in disbelief, as Mr Robertson inevitably reached for the second red card of the evening. I suppose it's possible that Jason had been watching footage of the burly Argentinian's 'Hand of God' against England thirty-one years ago and didn't realise that you weren't allowed to handle it – after all, that goal was allowed to stand, was it not? - before executing his own 'Hand of Fraud'. Well either that, or he was just acting the goat – again. (Sigh.) There was still nearly twenty minutes left and as usual he was extremely lucky that another moment of daftness (a certain dinked penalty against the same team at Hampden the year before springs to mind) would be forgiven, as his team would go on to win. Shinnie – who turned in an excellent performance for the second week in row – nearly wrapped it up decisively on the eightieth minute, but Cammy Bell made a tremendous point-blank save to deny him.

There were a couple of minor scares at the other end in the closing minutes, but Marciano only had one solitary save of any note to make and any tentative United moves were nipped in the bud by the very impressive Ambrose. Efe made two terrific tackles to snuff out any late threat and already seemed to have found his niche amongst his new team-mates. Hibs held on for a richly deserved three points, proving yet again that when the chips were down they were not to be found wanting. Big game, big *big* performance.

"Jason was stupid and he knows it, he's feeling remorseful," claimed his manager afterwards, which seemed a tad unlikely. As Neil had been sent to the stand himself for persistently venturing out-with the technical area, he was hardly in a position to lambast Jason though! Not the first time he's been guilty of that charge either. Like player, like manager... "But he's won me the game," added the gaffer. "He's a young lad and he has to learn, but he's a great talent. He's a big game player. A few people in the game have said we have been on a bad run, but we're ten points clear of our biggest rivals and we're in a Scottish Cup semi-final. I played it down during the week but we know how massive it was psychologically to win here tonight and we've done it."

Less than twenty-four hours later, the top of the Championship had a very different look about it, as a result of Saturday's fixtures. Falkirk had consolidated second spot after thumping Ayr United 4-1 away from home and Morton had now also vaulted over the Arabs by defeating Queen of the South.

At Fort Ibrox, the poisoned chalice had finally been passed to Pedro Caixinha, a man the media informed us was 'a trained bullfighter'. He'd soon have to evolve into a trained bull*shiter* instead, if he wanted to survive spraffing a load of convincing convoluted claptrap to the salivating Press regularly, which formed a large part of the hun management job description. Presumably he didn't look too closely at the fate of any of the recent incumbents, before taking on the gig. Super Ally aged about ten years, put on three stone in weight and lost most of his hair before being placed on indefinite gardening leave, Kenny McDowall ran away and was never seen or heard of again, Warby threw a warbler every time Stubbsy opened his mouth and quickly became psychiatrically unhinged and Graeme Murty reacted to defeat by standing on his head. Pedro's gonna have to go some to top *that* little lot. Still, making his debut wearing a silly spangly outfit in the dug-out and waving a red rag at the opposition will do for starters, I suppose.

In Fife, an old jambo flop was sliding down the tables faster than diners on the Herald of Free Enterprise. Raith decided it was time to change the Locke for security reasons – to prevent any more points going missing – and he'd pitched up at Cowdenbeath, who were firmly mired at the foot of the second division. It was possible that he'd been misled about his destination, however. Rovers cunningly got rid of him by telling him he'd scored a free trip to Central Park, causing Gaz to erroneously assume he'd won a holiday in New York.

At the PBS, a purely Academical result led Cathy to boast that he was delighted "to have convincingly beaten Hamilton." One glance at the extensive cuts and bruises covering his goalkeeper from head to foot testified that he'd done a thorough job. Poor Jack looked like he'd been hit by a car into the bargain. It later transpired that he had, as the hobbit had also reversed over him in his Austin MacPhee. Changed days though – in Budgie's era it was goalkeepers battering their managers, rather than the other way round.

Over to Falkirk, where the bellyaching baldy was perhaps indulging in mild mind games by seeming to suggest that he'd be happy with a second place finish in the Championship.

"I would much rather be in Hibs' position than ours, but we will keep battling away," said Houston. "Finishing second would mean two less games. But we will try and hang on to the coat-tails of Hibs."

Mickey Weir was quick to voice his opinion though that the Bairns would definitely be the ones to watch in the run-in. He reckoned that Dundee United were now out of it in terms of winning the League outright, but Houston's lot had the experience of being in this situation before. It certainly added an extra edge to the upcoming showdown against them at Easter Road, just under a fortnight away.

Before that, Hibs would have to negotiate a home game against Dumbarton, who had just thumped Raith Rovers 4-0. In this they were hugely aided by on-loan Sam Stanton who was at the centre of everything, but at least the 'conflict of interest' angle would rule him out of facing his parent club. Yogi's Kirkcaldy crew now looked to be the ones in freefall, as the other teams grouped towards the bottom of the table all seemed to have undergone mini revivals of late. Hibs' biggest win of the previous campaign had come against the Sons at Easter Road, also by 4-0, with James Keatings notching a hat-trick, but they wouldn't be taking anything for granted this time around.

"Just because we have beaten Dundee United doesn't mean they are dead and buried," cautioned Martin Boyle, just prior to the Arabs' midweek game in hand away to St. Mirren. "We still have a tough task on our hands as others have crept up behind us. Falkirk have been on a great run and Morton have a fantastic home record – unbeaten at Cappielow in almost a year – so it is no surprise to find decent teams like that holding their own."

Martin was right to exercise caution of course, but shortly afterwards it seemed as if Mickey Weir's assessment of the collapse of the Arab Spring was proving correct. A 3-2 defeat in Paisley saw United remain a full ten points behind Hibs with the same number of games played. They'd only won once in their last nine outings and the overly niggly physical approach they'd displayed the previous Friday worked against them here. Two of St. Mirren's goals came from free-kicks, the first following a typically needless foul by Edjenguele.

Two days later saw a notable anniversary, as exactly ten years ago the Hibees had emphatically seized the day to win the League Cup in a sizzling 5-1 victory over Kilmarnock. The fact that the latter was managed by a certain glum-faced ex-jambo just made it all the sweeter. Altogether now – "Cheer up Jimmy Jefferies, oh what can it mean..." I'd become somewhat disillusioned with Hibs after the demise of Tony Mowbray's sparkling 'young guns' and hadn't been attending that many games at this time. In fact I'd probably subliminally generated a situation which would lead me to avoiding Easter Road that season, as a result of jacking in my job and setting off on an approximately ten thousand mile vaguely round trip of Europe, which lasted several months. As I chose to travel solo and didn't have a mobile phone back then, I was blissfully unaware of events back in Scotland, Hibernian-related or otherwise. However, certain dates on the footballing calendar are of course hard-wired into all our Hibbie brains and by the time I'd pitched up in a cheap doss-house in Budapest, I rather reluctantly thought I'd better utilise the pay-phone there.

"You'll have to come back!" yelled the floozy I'd elected to call. "Hibs are in some sort of cup final!"

Well, that was any idle thought of extending the trip into the Baltic States snookered then, I wearily realised. Now – just how long will it take to hitch-hike home from Hungary...?

But it turned out to be worth returning for, as John Collins' team brought the League Cup home in some style, for the first time since 1991.

"We had a lot of confidence in going into that game," recalled the man the fans called 'Boozy' (as a corruption of his surname, rather than a reference to any intemperate habits, I hasten to add.) Currently assistant manager at Hamilton Accies, Guillaume Beuzelin was also a vital cog in J.C's well-oiled machine and couldn't believe a decade had gone by since then.

"We had everything a good team needs," he went on. "We had a big dominant centre-half, two offensive full-backs (Whittaker and David Murphy), Fletch, who was good in the air, Ivan (Sproule), who was quick and Benji (Benjelloun) who was a goal-scorer. On top of that, you had myself alongside Scott Brown and Lewis Stevenson, who were running machines in midfield. Everything was there for us to win that game. The fact that we won it in style makes it even better. We played really well."

How about the big cup then, Boozy, what are your thoughts on that?

"The fans are singing 'two in a row', so why not?"

Hibs would be without Cummings and Fyvie for the visit from Dumbarton due to suspension, but a potentially greater loss loomed on the horizon with regard to the Falkirk fixture one week hence. That would see both McGinn and Marciano almost certainly ruled out due to international commitments, doubtless a source of major irritation to Neil Lennon. Not that any right-thinking person would want to derail either player's chance of doing a job for their country, but that could only be accomplished if they were actually selected in the first place. Super's last international travel jaunt was a complete waste of time as he didn't play at all and Rocky was injured in a training session before Israel had even kicked off. With a vitally important game now imminent, Hibs could well have done without this distraction.

The Dumbarton game turned out to be a carbon copy of so many other games played at Easter Road over the campaign, where a 'NOT GOOD ENOUGH' sticker stamped on the contents would have been appropriate. Hibs huffed and puffed throughout the ninety minutes against a team content to defend in depth, signally failing to get the better of them despite a host of chances. In recent games they'd similarly struggled, but had at least managed to get goals on the board early on. That didn't happen here though and there was an air of inevitability about it when Marvin Bartley needlessly fouled McRorie on the edge of the penalty box. I was sitting in the East Stand for a change so didn't get a clear enough view of it, but although Marv definitely made contact it was debatable whether the challenge took place just inside or just outside the area. The latter, according to my source in the West stand, but the ref pointed to the spot regardless and equally predictably Christian Nade trundled forth to put it away. It was hard to conceive the Sons scoring by any other method given their stuffy performance up until then, but they went in with their noses in front at half-time.

Hibs were back in it twelve minutes after the restart, as Lewis Stevenson picked McGinn out with a long ball down the touchline. Super struck it forcefully from an angle – was it a direct shot or was it a cross? – hard to tell, but the visitors' defence seemed equally unsure. Left back Harvie slid in to try to avert the danger, but only succeeded in putting through his own net. A touch of luck for the Hibees, but John had done well, whatever his intentions. This would surely give the home team a much-needed fillip, but just the opposite transpired as only four minutes later Thomson put the Sons back in front with a good finish from the edge of the box. So Hibs had a mountain to climb all over again and were thrown another lifeline when Darren Barr yanked big Holty down from the back in the goalmouth. Keatings – on from the start due to the absence of Cummings – failed to convert the resulting penalty, with goalkeeper Martin having a last second change of mind as to which way to dive. He called it right and had an excellent game throughout, denying Hibs on numerous occasions, but luckily his one slip proved to be a costly one. Under pressure from substitute Brian Graham he failed to secure the ball as Martin Boyle quickly nipped in to propel it forward with his head. The outcome was hardly decisive though, as it seemed to take forever to roll agonisingly towards the line. It did finally cross it which was a major relief, but with only seven minutes remaining, Hibs had little time left to put the game to bed once and for all. Dumbarton hung on grimly and the boos ringing out at the conclusion indicated the crowd's quite understandable level of dissatisfaction.

"We missed chances, we missed the penalty and that summed up our day," sighed the manager. "I was really frustrated with the first half performance, it was not acceptable. I'm sick of them doing this and I'm sick of us dropping points at home for not approaching games the right way. I was pleased with the second half, we got ourselves back into the game early but then we switched off again and they score. It's not the end of the world and we thoroughly deserved to win the game but we have to stop being sloppy."

Frustrating though it was to yet again squander valuable points, the Hibees could take solace from the fact that their fellow challengers were making equally heavy weather of it. Except for Morton that is, who beat Falkirk 1-0 away to emerge as possibly the biggest imminent threat. Certainly, there were few who had seen *that* one coming. But Dundee United crashed to another defeat, losing to Raith Rovers, and now looked to be well out of the running. A draw between the Bairns and Morton would probably have been the best result for Hibs, but not many of those in the Iona watching the late kick-off on the telly were too downcast at the final outcome. After the conclusion to the previous season, anything that pegged back Houston's henchmen at this stage was to be welcomed, although it undoubtedly left the Greenock men in a much enhanced position. They lay seven points behind Hibs, tied with Falkirk on the forty-eight point mark, but had two games in hand over them. Coincidentally, Hibs next faced both sides at Easter Road within a five day spell and the task at hand was at least crystal clear. Win those two and surely to God...

Up at Pittodrie, there was much speculation about just who exactly was picking the Hearts team, as TV footage zoomed in on a hapless message boy running betwixt dug-out and stand throughout. This was in order to pass on a series of notes to Cathy, being issued by the evil puppet-master / director of football watching from on high. There's always been something sinister about Levein's appearance – that blank humourless unsmiling four-eyed face, complete with movie baddie wee goatee clinging to his chin like a distressed stoat – it was little wonder the message laddie looked terrified. The first missive issued to Cathy ordered him to immediately change the team formation to 8-1-1, in a damage limitation exercise after Logan netted for the Sheep. But when they went two up, Craig decided to throw caution to the winds and despatched another note telling Cathy to switch it to 1-1-8 instead and go for glory. That failed to turn the tide however and with a quick malicious pull of the strings the puppet-master soon had the hobbit doing a strange little dance of distress along the touchline. At a news conference later, the manager vehemently denied that he was in any way being manipulated by the director of football – which might have carried more conviction if he hadn't been sitting on Craig's lap with the latter's hand working him from the back at the time.

"Gottle of geer, gottle of geer," jabbered Cathy manically through gritted teeth, to the general bemusement of the media hounds in attendance.

Meanwhile, John McGinn was temporarily removing his Hibee head to replace it with his Scotland one, in anticipation of hopefully getting a run-out in the friendly against Canada in midweek. At least he wouldn't be fucked around with travel trauma this time, as the game would be played at Easter Road.

"If I get the chance to show what I can do, then I want to stake a claim for the Slovenia game," stated Super, as the World Cup qualifier against the boys from the Balkans would follow three days later.

"Johnny be good," I muttered involuntarily, taking in the sad news about rock 'n' roll pioneer Chuck Berry's death at the same time as I was perusing Super's comments. (Or should that read 'The Radiator's comments', his usual international alias according to Strachan?) I then raised a toast to the dear departed Chuck, before digging out and playing my three favourite cover versions of his timeless songs. 'Johnny B. Goode' by Jimi Hendrix (the live version from 'Hendrix in the West'), 'Memphis, Tennessee' by The Faces and 'Back in the USA' by The MC5, a record of such exuberantly authentic brilliance that a reviewer once raved that you could practically *smell* the hamburgers sizzle on the open grill, just by listening to it at high volume.

"Well oh well I feel so good today…"

And in the event of a McGinn call-up – go, Johnny, go!

It wasn't only the Hibs' first team that would have to put up with possible international absentees though, as Oli Shaw looked to turn out for the Dark Blue Under-19s against Austria. Oli had emerged as the Jason Cummings equivalent of the Hibees' young 'uns, with twenty-two goals to his credit so far this season, a tally which included two hat-tricks.

"He's a stand-out at that level," enthused Neil Lennon. "At times he looks head and shoulders above the opposition. That's all well and good at Development level but the gap between that and the first team is huge. He needs to bridge that gap but I'm sure he will. If he wasn't out on loan at Stenhousemuir he'd be in the squad now."

Scotland duly kicked off against Canada on an utterly filthy night weather-wise at Easter Road, with no sign of Super. He did however come on with only fourteen minutes left, rendering the whole exercise pretty much as pointless for him as it was for the rest of the team. What on earth can be gained by playing a friendly against a team ranked 117th by FIFA completely eludes me. Strachan talks a load of bollocks at the best of times and defiantly claimed that arranging to take on the Canadians was "one of the better decisions" he had made as Scotland manager. Yeah, right. Beforehand it looked as if this one was heading for the record books by being the worst *ever* attended international game – that was in 1902 appropriately enough, given the venue – and although the crowd was 'officially' a few thousand higher than that total of 5,284, many of the tickets had been given away for free. Those without their snouts in the SFA trough were obliged to cough up £22, a ridiculous price to view the equivalent of a kick-about in the Meadows, for a game that was live on the telly anyway. In the event, Scotland were lucky to scrape a 1-1 draw against a country ranked fifty places below them, although that apparent gulf certainly wasn't evident on this performance.

Super remained with the international squad, unfortunately for Hibs, with Lennon remarking – probably through gritted teeth – "It's a bit of a surreal situation, really, that we have to go ahead with a game – a really important game – with two of our most important players going away with their country. I'm not sure if you would call it punishment, but it is definitely a hindrance." If a third player had been selected for international duty Hibs would have been entitled to seek postponement of the Falkirk game, but as England surprisingly decided against calling on the services of Grant Holt to face Lithuania, that wasn't an option. But at least the suspended duo of Cummings and Fyvie would be available, along with Dylan McGeouch. The manager had gained something too from subjecting himself to viewing Wednesday night's underwhelming showing in person – advance warning of a potential threat from the Bairns' midfield.

"Fraser Aird was excellent," noted Neil. "He was certainly Canada's best player. He was a threat the whole night and I was very impressed. It definitely gave me some food for thought. There will be a confidence and familiarity for him going into the game tomorrow."

Luckily, the player made nowhere near the impact for his club that he'd done for his country, but Lennon had already concluded that his domestic performances hadn't been at a consistently exalted level. Backed by a big crowd on a beautifully warm, sunny day, Hibs were certainly the dominant force throughout the first half, without creating too much in the way of clear-cut chances. A Cummings free-kick which curled just outside the Bairns' goalpost with keeper Thomson well beaten was as close as they came, but Martin Boyle's explosive bursts of pace were putting a strain on the visitors' backline. They generally held firm though, as the player's final ball was often a bit of a hit or miss affair and at half-time it wouldn't have been overly surprising if a no-scoring draw would be the result at the end of the ninety minutes. You always expect a close game against Falkirk and this one looked no different in that respect.

Both teams considerably upped the ante after the interval though, with Falkirk's usual niggly foul-strewn approach well to the fore. The referee seemed overly lenient in only booking four of them and failed to react to a blatant push in the back which saw Cummings sprawled over in the penalty box on the fifty-fifth minute. Hibs had another couple of shouts for possible spot-kick awards which also went unheeded, but that was the most obvious one. Boyle made his most penetrating run yet, storming through the Bairns' defence and unleashing a shot which unluckily was deflected away from its route to goal. Falkirk had their chances too at the other end, with both Baird and Wednesday night's Canadian kingpin Aird coming close, the latter's effort being blocked for a corner. But for all that the tempo had picked up a lot, there still weren't a multitude of opportunities and it was going to take something special to break the deadlock. That came along with fifteen minutes left, when Ambrose got on the end of a Keatings free-kick and absolutely bulleted it into the back of the net with his head. Almost as easy on the eye was his multi-somersaulted goal celebration which followed, but the joy for Hibbies was short-lived. Their opponents equalised almost immediately, after Ross Laidlaw erred by pushing an awkward through ball over the bar, when it was heading that way anyway of its own volition. In the lavvy for a quick 'comfort break' after Efe's stoater, I heard that ominous distant roar clearly emanating from the away end, which signalled a goal for the opposition. Having needlessly conceded a corner, Hibs were then punished when Craig Sibbald nipped in to convert at the near post. In fairness, Ross had usually acquitted himself well when deputising for Rocky, but it might have proved a costly blip. Happily however, in the dying seconds Keatings took possession of substitute Brian Graham's flick and immediately homed in on goal. He then struck a curling right-footed cracker past Thomson into the corner of the net and the Hibees had deservedly clinched it right at the death.

Most of us had probably resigned ourselves to yet another home draw by this stage, which in the event wouldn't have been a bad thing. Morton slipped up at home, losing there for the first time this season to Dunfermline, who had shown on their last visit to Easter Road that on their day they were quite capable of beating anyone in the Championship. But given Morton's excellent recent run it was still an unexpected result and one which certainly suited Hibs. The Greenock men were now a full ten points behind them, albeit with a game in hand, sitting alongside Falkirk (who had played a game more) on the forty-eight point mark. Dundee United were otherwise engaged on Mickey Mouse Irn Bru Fizzy Juice Made in Scotland fae Girders Cup business, but lay a further four points behind them and were now so far off the pace they had no realistic chance of overtaking the table-toppers. Once again, when the chips were down and the stakes raised, the Hibees had admirably risen to the challenge and emerged victorious.

"I'm delighted. Absolutely delighted," declared Neil Lennon. "It's in our hands. There's no question of that and even if Morton win their game in hand there's still a significant gap. We still have a bit of work to do, but I think psychologically it was huge for us after dropping points last week. It was a good win, really important – and with Morton losing it could be a pivotal day in the run-in."

"We've got to focus on second now," concurred Falkirk midfielder Mark Kerr. "It's Hibs to throw away."

The following evening Scotland dug out a last-gasp victory over an off-colour Slovenian side in a depressingly half-empty Hampden; no surprise really, given the national side's current form. Equally unsurprising was the non-appearance of John McGinn, but at least

Lennon wouldn't have to worry about him getting needlessly injured. Before scoring two minutes from time, Chris Martin had come as substitute only to be roundly booed – well, that's what you get for fronting up a crap band like Coldplay, I'm afraid. Strachan said that was a positive thing though, as in the past the fans had also booed the likes of Kenny Dalglish. Trust wee Gordy to put such a peculiar spin on events. If Martin had been shot dead instead like that poor Colombian boy who made an on-field howler some years back, I suppose that would have been the ultimate accolade in his manager's eyes. Strachs even played Griffiths from the start – young Leigh must have sprouted a few inches recently, as not long ago he was deemed 'too small' for requirements. A case of the pot calling the kettle black there, surely. Did Gordy never wonder how he used to get picked for Scotland himself, despite being a short-arse who couldn't even get a leg over an advertising hoarding to celebrate a goal?

Neil Lennon was now fully focused on the midweek showdown with Morton, conceding, "That will be it," as far as the title was concerned, if another three points were gained. But in light of the way the previous weekend's results had panned out, Hibs at last had some leeway in the run-in.

"We'd need to lose four games on the bounce and they'd need to win all their games as well," pointed out the manager. "These two games were the biggest of the season and we've come out of the first one with three points."

He also took time out to praise the scorer of the opener against Falkirk, who had been so maligned in the recent past. (I shamefully confess I was guilty of making cheap jokes about him in my last book, unfortunately – but fair dos, he *was* still playing for Celtic then.) However, my own lazy assumptions about his perceived defensive shortcomings based on little more than picky Press-related put-downs were happily proved to be wide of the mark.

"You could see what it means to him to be back playing football and the Hibs public have seen what a class player he is," enthused Neil. "Efe isn't a bona-fide right back but I can trust him in that position. (His role against the Bairns, due to David Gray's absence through injury.) As a centre-half he's been superb. It's been good for both parties and excellent for Efe to get his profile back in a positive manner. He's shown the people of Scotland, Britain, Europe and back home in Nigeria what a class act he is. It's been a great bit of business and he's really enjoying the moment."

Indeed it had, and all credit to the Hibs' gaffer for moving so quickly to make it happen.

Neil selected both international returnees for the Morton game as expected, with Paul Hanlon also making his welcome return after nearly three months on the sidelines. It was McGinn who came within a whisker of putting his team one up well within the first minute, only to see his firmly-struck shot crash off the post. It was a fitting response to the opposition, who had chosen to punt a long ball straight at Marciano from kick-off, probably hoping he was still jet-lagged. That caused no problems however and the keeper gathered it easily, but he certainly had a busier ninety minutes than he was generally used to, on domestic duty. Hibs looked a bit nervy in the opening spell and the visitors were quick to capitalise, pushing forward in numbers and forcing a string of corners. They went close with an O'Ware header which fizzled just over the bar, but although they exerted plenty of pressure the final ball all too often let them down. For their part, the home team found it hard to cohesively put anything together as far too many passes went astray. Martin Boyle again caused untold problems with his electric pace, but unfortunately his team-mates failed to capitalise on his ensuing crosses.

You'd imagine that Neil would have been none too happy about the carelessness and given them a rocket at half-time, but equally Jim Duffy would have been less than ecstatic about his forwards' finishing. As the second half progressed it didn't look like getting any better. Hibs had a good chance with a free-kick on the edge of the box, but Cummings – who appeared out of sorts throughout – sent his shot curling over the bar. His striking partner Holt singularly failed to impress and was replaced by Brian Graham twenty minutes in. It was the tall substitute who then had the best opportunity of the lot as a Stevenson cross picked him out, but his header sailed *just* the wrong side of the post. However, the pivotal moment came when Morton keeper Gaston clearly handled the ball outside the box as Boyle closed in and inexplicably neither referee Walsh or his assistant O'Neill sought fit to take any action. It was hard to believe that both somehow missed the incident and the thunderous howls of protest which spontaneously erupted from the stands surely must have indicated to them that something was amiss. The keeper should have been sent off and Hibs should have been awarded a penalty, simple as that. Morton continued to push forward and harry at the other end, clearly aware that the onus was on them to try to seize the three points. Given the yawning gap at the top of the Championship, they needed a win more than Hibs did. But just when we were all resigning ourselves to it ending in a draw, all hell suddenly broke loose.

Morton substitute Kudus Oyenuga had been on the park for all of five minutes when he chose to commit a horrendous challenge on Jordon Forster, who had been on the pitch for even less time. It was a disgraceful foul, highly dangerous and quite rightly described by Neil Lennon as "a leg-breaker." The fact that that mercifully wasn't the outcome did little to dilute the fury from the Hibs bench and players, who instantly surrounded the culprit. He then compounded his initial crime by going down like a ton of bricks, when confronted by Hibs' captain for the night, Darren McGregor. Daz never touched him but the inept referee was easily conned and red-carded both players. They were swiftly joined by both managers who'd also participated in the free-for-all argy-bargy, with Lennon asserting that Duffy had offered him a square-go. ("Come and have a go with the Greenock aggro!") It was certainly a lively ending to what had been a distinctly underwhelming performance and naturally would be the main talking-point afterwards. Neil Lennon for one was not holding back.

"Here's my take on it. The guy tried to break my player's leg. Darren goes over and he feigns a head-butt, he goes down holding his face but Darren did not make any contact. The next thing I have got is the Morton manager asking me for a square-go, which is fair enough, I'm not going to back down. I didn't react any differently to the way any other manager would have reacted to a tackle like that. It's disgraceful, the boy's behaviour was embarrassing. Not only has he tried to break my player's leg, he's got my captain sent off as well in an act of cowardice and I have to take that?"

Neil later somewhat retracted his 'square-go' assertion, claiming that he meant it 'metaphorically', but in a highly-charged Press Conference two days later he showed that his anger had not diminished one iota. "An incredible tirade" was how Moira Gordon of 'The Scotsman' described it. One reason for the manager's wrath was the apparent flippancy with which his opposite number had played down the incident afterwards, even seeing fit to make a joke about it. Thumping the table for emphasis, Neil stressed that he found it very far from funny and questioned whether Duffy would have been quite so dismissive if Jordon had indeed suffered a broken leg, which was quite possible given the recklessness of Oyenuga's assault. He was also furious about the Morton substitute's play-acting which got McGregor sent off and that no-one from the opposition bench had showed any concern for his player, choosing instead to involve themselves in the large-scale pitch-side rammy which then ensued.

So once all the dust had settled (only *slightly,* mind you), it was a case of 'as you were' at the top of the table, the ten point gap still intact.

With the exception of the defeat away to St. Mirren on the very first day, March had been a pretty good month for the Hibees overall. A couple of rather disappointing home draws had been balanced out by the fact that they'd faced down their three principal adversaries and emerged unbeaten – winning two and drawing one – and they'd also had a fine quarter-final win in the Scottish Cup under their belts. They had the semi against Aberdeen to look forward to as a result of that and the main aim now was to wrap the title up before then, the sooner the better!

10.

APRIL: EASTER RISING

All the hoo-hah emanating from the Morton match had rather obscured the fact that another game was coming up hard on its heels – away to Dunfermline on April Fools' Day. That's the one day of the year above all others that Neil knows he has to keep an even closer eye on Jason than usual. But with the manager's blood pressure still soaring after Wednesday night's events, the player probably sensed that hands of God, dinked penalties, swapping the referee's can of foam with one of hairspray and placing a whoopee cushion on Neil's chair would not be a good idea at East End Park. The latter had quite enough on his plate, being forced to alter his original plans yet again, as Paul Hanlon had to pull out at the last minute. That was due to a recurrence of the nerve problem which had developed in the later part of his recent lay-off and of course Jordon Forster was now also crocked. A shoulder injury had been one result of Oyenuga's shocking lunge and it would be of little consolation to Jordon that it might have been a hell of a lot worse. So Brian Mclean got his first run-out with the big boys, slotting in alongside Darren McGregor in central defence and doing a very competent job for the most part. A superb strike from McGinn on the twelfth minute put the Hibees ahead, a lead that they held fairly comfortably until half-time. Still, the old problem of not turning enough chances into goals remained, a point that Lennon must have been tired of reiterating to his charges.

"We've got to score goals. Jason has done brilliantly, Martin has chipped in, but the rest need to look to themselves and ask, 'have I done enough?'"

Although Hibs had by far the best defensive record in the Championship, realistically their overall superiority should have been reflected by a far larger number in the 'Goals For' column. (Dumbarton, lying twenty-six points behind them in seventh place, had only scored six less!)

This failing was punished by the opposition (as it had been throughout the season) not long after half-time, but in rather debatable circumstances. The official saw fit to award a penalty as the ball appeared to clip Lewis Stevenson's hand. There didn't seem to be any intent to handle, but Aitken pointed to the spot and Kallum Higginbotham converted to bring the Pars back on level terms. They gave a good account of themselves against the Hibees again though, but the bulk of the chances and the possession was in the visitors' favour. Brian Graham, on from the start as a replacement for Holt, missed a sitter and had that gone in you'd have fancied Hibs to snatch the full three points. As it was, they had to settle for yet another draw – their *twelfth* of the campaign (as it was for the Pars), but you'd expect League challengers to be doing a lot better than that.

"We are well aware of the number of games we have drawn," said Darren McGregor. "But actions speak louder than words. It's up to us to go into these games and get the three points as opposed to drawing. We are well aware we could be doing better in the goals department."

"I was disappointed not to have won the game – we were in total control," lamented his manager. "We're closer to the title. We are dragging it out but we will keep going."

Fortunately, Morton lost 1-0 to Dumbarton, causing Falkirk to vault back over them to reclaim second spot, after a similar scoreline in their favour over Raith Rovers. The Bairns were now nine points adrift of Hibs and Dundee United were a further four points behind them, going down again, this time losing 4-2 at Queen of the South.

The next day at the PBS, the jambos crashed to their heaviest League defeat since Alan Gordon made it number seven on January 1st, 1973, as Celtic finally wrapped up the Premier title.

"The scoreline was not an accurate reflection of the game," claimed Cathy.

Too bloody right, it should have been ten nil rather than only five. And that was Celtic without Dembele and Griffiths too, God knows what it might have been if they'd been on the park. Eagle-eyed observers were quick to spot the evil puppet-master with a face like thunder despatching a note via the message boy to the dug-out as soon as Scott Sinclair struck home the fifth. Cathy opened the heavy envelope with trembling fingers to find a small Derringer pistol with a single bullet in the chamber and a note reading 'FOR CHRIST'S SAKE DO THE DECENT THING AND DO IT QUICKLY.' Lacking the courage to do the deed himself, the hobbit shakily passed the gun to Jamie Walker who had just been subbed and instructed him to do it instead. Glowering down from the stand above, Levein was then furious to see Walker take aim at Cathy's head, before firing wildly and hitting Austin MacPhee by mistake – it certainly wasn't the first simple shot he'd missed that afternoon either.

Elsewhere on Planet Football, the violence and mayhem continued to rage unchecked like an out of control forest fire, making the Lennon / Duffy square-go spat look like a spot of ineffectual dinky handbags between two old ladies at a church social. Take St. Johnstone for instance... No, *you* take St. Johnstone, if you think you're hard enough. No need really, as the Saints were quite capable of taking themselves. Danny Swanson or Richard Foster, which one is better? "Only one way to find out," as Harry Hill used to say on his TV show, "FIIIIIIGHT!!" The team-'mates' decided to knock lumps out of each-other just after the half-time whistle blew in their away match at Hamilton, which – as at Easter Road the previous week – soon dragged in all manner of other miscreants. Hamilton assistant Boozy for one, who was immediately sent to the stand in classic Lennonesque style. The harassed man in black had initially upset the fiery Frenchman by yellow-carding Accies' midfielder Ali Crawford, before it all kicked off in the tunnel. When Boozy demanded to know why he'd been booked, the ref explained it was for spelling his Christian name like a big girl, which was punishable under Sexist Injunction No. 007 in the Blazers' Disciplinary Handbook. He then added insult to injury by red-carding Guillaume, for the crime of having a silly nickname. Swanson and Foster were then also showed the same colour from the referee's rapidly diminishing pack, which was hardly surprising.

In Sunderland, David Moyes went one better – and threatened a female reporter with a slap if she had the cheek to ask him annoying questions ever again, such as, "Do you think you'll get the sack for being a shite manager?" Davie Boy went on to prove that there was only one bitter old slapper in the room and it certainly wasn't her. He was later forced to say sorry – not sorry for threatening to assault a woman for doing her job, but sorry that he was caught on camera doing it. Oops! In fairness, that was the impression you might have gleaned from the initial over the top media coverage, but footage of the incident which surfaced later showed that it had been blown out of all proportion.

Moyes has always come across as a decent sort actually and it was clear that the remarks had been uttered in a light-hearted fashion and accepted as such by the reporter at the time. The 'banter' may seem a bit robust to the more sensitive feminists amongst us, but that's really all it was.

The first week of the month opened with someone else making an April Fool of himself, in this case SFA Compliance Officer, Tony McGlennan. He'd reviewed footage of the Oyenuga incident and deemed in his wisdom that there was not enough evidence to charge the player with contravening the rule regarding feigning injury, which caused an official to make an incorrect decision (i.e. sending off McGregor). Plenty evidence though that Tony needed to make an appointment with his optician pronto.

Meanwhile, Brian McLean revealed that he'd only found out an hour before kick-off against the Pars that Paul Hanlon was toiling a bit, having resigned himself to spending the afternoon on the bench.

"The team sheets were already out but football can change in a heartbeat. Hopefully Paul will be OK, but I was delighted to get on the pitch."

He might not have featured before then, but Brian was as caught up with the race for the Championship as keenly as his more established team-mates were.

"It's been quite a long, drawn-out affair. We want it wrapped up as quickly as possible, but nothing is given to you on a plate. Football in general is full of frustrations, the highs and lows, and it is important you take the highs when they do come. It's important we do get that high we want – promotion."

By the middle of the week Hibs were happy to report that the positive fall-out from events on May 21st the previous year had contributed to roughly a thousand season tickets per week being snapped up in the five weeks since the 'Early Bird' offer for next season had been launched. This meant that they were well on course to exceed the current campaign's take-up and at this rate there was every chance that the record figure of 11,500 might be surpassed too.

At Ibrox, the Portuguese matador was displaying that he'd already mastered the art of managing the Currant Buns in the correct manner, by effortlessly evolving from bullfighter to bullshiter overnight. You've gotta love the way these foreign dudes act when they pitch up in Scotland and instantly start spouting wild-eyed nonsense, whereas your traditional dour Scottish gaffer is too savvy / pessimistic to say anything which might come back and bite him later. Pedro had airily announced that Rangers could still overhaul Aberdeen to finish in runners-up spot, which might have seemed feasible when you considered that they were only one place behind them in the League. However, a closer examination of the Premier table showed that – with seven games to go – the Dons were *twelve* points ahead of the huns with a goal difference of *plus thirty-seven*, as opposed to the Bluenoses' paltry nine. What on earth was he planning to do in the forthcoming games against the men from the north? Run onto the park in his sparkly red, white and blue cape and stick big pointy spears in their guts? Someone should have told him that killing off sheep is a lot harder than killing off bulls. And on that subject, in the immortal words of Jim Royle, "Bullfighting my arse." If you think you're so tough why not go up against something that can actually fight back, you sadistic jackass? Like a sabre-toothed tiger for example.

But as already stated, Pedro was only following a long line of foreigners whose brain-cells had been fatally compromised by exposure to the ghastly Scottish climate and shock diet of deep-fried Mars Bars washed down with buckets of Tennents' Super. Mad Vlad had famously promised that he was going to win the Champions League with the jambos of course, Ronny Deila at Celtic had grandly said, "Judge me on Europe!" when his team would have had a better chance of success if they'd participated in the Eurovision Song Contest instead, that Italian radge and major fraudster Giovanni de Stefano at Dundee proudly remarked that he was a close personal friend of the notorious Serbian war criminal 'Arkan', who he described as "a very nice man", and Ivan Golac assured everyone that his Dundee United would *definitely* win the Scottish Cup. At that point, the Arabs' record in finals was almost as bad as Hibs had been and his remarks were generally greeted with howls of derision. However, that one actually came to pass, although he was soon shown the door for the crime of being too optimistic and successful, thus undermining the whole dreary dreich damp grey fabric of Scotch fitba' at its most suffocatingly soul-destroying.

In Perth, the jambos floundered to yet another defeat, losing 1-0 to St. Johnstone, in a game marred by splatterings of saliva. This was the fault of the puppet-master, who became irritated at Sam Nicholson's performance, reckoning that he would be far more effective playing out wide. He quickly despatched a note via the usual message laddie, instructing him to hold it up from the dug-out as soon as Nicholson hove into view. 'GO TO THE LINE, MAN!' was Craig's terse command. Unfortunately Sam was running past at such a pace he misread it as 'GOB AT THE LINESMAN!' and promptly directed a fusillade of toxic spittle at the hapless official. He was unsurprisingly rewarded with a red card, which had the hobbit spitting feathers into the bargain. The jambos were now five points behind the Saints with only two games left before the split and fifth place was looking like the best they could hope for now. Maybe not even that either, as Partick Thistle were snapping at their heels from just below.

In a break from tradition, the Blazers then showed some measure of common sense (well, there's always a first time) by downgrading the red card issued to Daz during Square-go-Gate to a yellow. That, presumably, for merely squaring up to the assailant, meaning that the decision a few days earlier to find Oyenuga not guilty of cheating made no sense at all, but that's the SFA for you. Darren's former Buddies' buddy was quick to jump to his captain on the day's defence.

"He's gone over to protect his team-mate," pointed out John McGinn. "No-one was more mortified than I when I saw the red card. I've played with Darren for a long time and I knew it was not a red card and I was delighted to see common sense prevail. Darren has been a big player for us this season."

In an unfortunate twist of fate and the fixture list, Hibs now faced Morton again, at Cappielow this time on April 8th and it was fair to assume that the fall-out from the previous encounter would likely carry on into this one to some degree. Tempers hadn't cooled much, if at all in Neil Lennon's case. The gaffer had further reasons for irritation with the authorities too, as he'd been summoned to a disciplinary hearing regarding his own behaviour (along with Jim Duffy) on April 20th, i.e. two days before the Scottish Cup semi-final. Understandably, the manager was at a loss as to the inexplicable delay, particularly as the players involved had already been dealt with. Any sanction could therefore count him out on the day against Aberdeen and he now had the worry of that outcome hanging over him in the build-up to a huge game. You can never second-guess the Blazers' motives though – was the scheduling down to their usual incompetence, or was it something more malicious? God only knows.

However, there was a conciliatory exchange between the gaffers before the game got under way and it seemed like we were in for another blood and thunder contest in a suitable sequel to the recent Easter Road clash. Always likely to be close, it turned out to be a match of two penalties – one awarded, the other inexplicably not. That of course was the one Hibs *should* have got, as just after the halfway stage of the first period, Martin Boyle picked up a pass from McGinn and sped towards goal. He hit his shot firmly, with intent to evade Morton's Mark Russell, who promptly opted to block it by raising both arms as if he'd suddenly been confronted by a bank robber wielded a sawn-off shotgun, yelling "HANDS UP!" It was as clear-cut a spot-kick as you were likely to see, but referee Madden denied it. Yet another baffling decision by an official and one which might prove costly in such an evenly balanced game, where the stakes were high. But Hibs had their tails up after such an injustice and within ten minutes they'd taken the lead anyway. Cummings again proved how valuable he was by astutely anticipating a long ball hoofed upfield by Darren McGregor, dodging the attentions of defender Tom O'Ware and slotting it into the net beyond Gaston.

The second penalty incident occurred twenty minutes after the interval and unfortunately the hitherto blind Bobby Madden's eyesight had improved sufficiently for him to see Daz clumsily lunge in on Morton substitute Jamie McDonagh, who had just come on. Shankland made no mistake with the spot-kick as Rocky dived the wrong way and it was back to level pegging. Morton had shown at Easter Road how effective they could be in stifling opposition attacks, but even so, the visitors should still have been capable of pressing home their superiority. Martin Boyle had one good chance and then Brian Graham, guilty of similar laxity the previous week, also failed to convert. So it finished all square (but with no square-go, thankfully) which wouldn't have come as a huge surprise to many. Hibs had now amassed a mind-boggling *thirteen* draws over the campaign, more than anyone else in the Championship and Morton were only two behind that total.

That naturally didn't please Neil Lennon, who said bluntly, "It's not good enough. As a team we're not ruthless enough, that's the bottom line. I don't like criticising the players but if there's one (criticism) it's that we could easily have won ten of our thirteen draws. Maybe I haven't brought the right players in, I don't know." But the manager reserved most of his wrath for the maddening Madden and his sidekicks and quite rightly so. "Their player used two hands to block a goal-bound shot. I just don't understand it. I've no qualms with the penalty Morton got, but everyone could see what happened with the other incident. I need an explanation but I'll not get one."

So the Hibees continued their long limp towards the finishing line and the fans certainly weren't counting their chickens just yet. No-one was likely to be celebrating, until it became mathematically impossible for them to be overhauled, but with Dundee United and Falkirk also seeing out a draw, the green machine were moving painstakingly just that little bit closer.

A few days later, Neil was still sounding off about the men in black, with dark references to some sort of anti-Hibs 'agenda', which was unlikely to find favour with the Blazerati. But it would be hard for even them to deny he had a point regarding refereeing standards, as shown by the red cards flashed in his players' direction recently. Three of the five had been rescinded on appeal, which surely flagged up some sort of disconnect between the whistlers and the game's adjudicators. Neil was as unequivocal as ever as to where the problem lay.

"That's maybe because the officials are not good enough. I have worked at a high level as a player and a manager and I have not seen as bad as this."

Morton's game in hand rolled around in midweek, where they were comprehensively thumped 4-1 at home by a determinedly resurgent St. Mirren in the Renfrewshire derby. That left them now eleven points behind Hibs with the same number of games played, while a win by Dundee United over Dunfermline saw them leaping over Duffy's men, one point to the good. So – in theory – it was mathematically possible for those two (and Falkirk) to still pip Hibs for the title, but highly unlikely. Indeed, if the Hibees defeated Queen of the South in their next fixture then surely *that was it*, no matter what the pedants might claim. Falkirk could conceivably draw level on points by the end but even in the event of a catastrophic Hibs' collapse their superior goal difference rendered that scenario virtually impossible. Still, as they'd drawn as many games at Easter Road as they'd won, a victory over the Dumfries men couldn't be taken for granted.

The injury situation wasn't helping in enabling the manager to plan too far ahead, although he was hopeful that Humphrey might be available for selection, while he intimated that Paul Hanlon *might* return before the end of the season. But unfortunately that seemed to be a tricky one in medical terms and you could only feel for the player being forced to view from the sidelines as the campaign built to a climax. Danny Handling had gone out on loan – to Raith Rovers, explaining that, "I was more than happy to go because I wanted games and I'm not sure I'd have got that at Hibs the way things were going. It was looking like I wasn't going to play this season, so the opportunity to go out and get games was one I couldn't refuse. Neil Lennon was really supportive. He's been understanding of my position."

Rovers certainly needed all the extra help they could get, having plummeted down the table to second bottom place and looked in grave danger of dropping out of the second tier altogether.

One player that Neil was delighted with was Efe Ambrose, his decision to bring him to Easter Road being fully vindicated as the big man scooped the Championship Player of the Month Award for March.

"He has been through the wringer," pointed out his current gaffer. "Sometimes players at clubs can be made a scapegoat and Efe certainly came into that bracket, but that doesn't mean he's a bad player. It's no disgrace not to get into that Celtic team at the moment. They are setting the bar really high. He has come to Hibs and done exactly what I thought he'd do."

"Winning the medal is not the most important thing," said Efe, adding that whilst it was a great feeling, he was looking at the bigger picture, out-with his own personal achievement. "The most important thing is for Hibs to get out of this League. It would be nice to win the Championship and give something back to everybody who has put everything into this club, to take them back into the Premiership, where they deserve to be."

Well, no sooner said than done, Efe – *almost*. For within thirteen minutes of kicking off against Queen of the South, Hibs were one up, courtesy of Darren McGregor finishing off a pin-point perfect free-kick from John McGinn. The manager had emphasised that he aimed to fully concentrate on his own team's actions, without being distracted by thoughts of what might be unfolding at the Falkirk Stadium. However, the crescendo of noise reverberating around the stands must have alerted him to the fact that St. Mirren had already taken an early lead there. Anything other than full points would be useless in terms of the Bairns snatching the Championship title – as long as Hibs won, of course. And they did look on course from fairly early on, despite the usual failing of passing up some good chances to increase their lead. It was the same defender to yet again show his forwards how it *should* be done, as Daz doubled his tally after a neat pass from Jason found him in a good position. Two up before half-time and although news filtered through that Falkirk had pulled one back against Saints, that did little to dampen the mood. Despite some fine performances lately, Queens never looked like finding a way back from the first half deficit and ex-Hibee scoring sensation Stephen Dobbie was a lot quieter than usual.

The game had barely resumed when David Gray soared above everyone else to bullet home the third with a stonking header and even the most cautious observer in green and white could surely now relax and prepare to get the party started. There had been something of a strange atmosphere crowd-wise up until this point, as they'd been fairly quiet for spells in between the upsurge of noise that accompanied reports of St. Mirren's two goals against Falkirk. But that sense of middling anxiety was quite understandable if you were a diehard Hibbie of long-standing! It seemed impossible that they could blow it now, but equally it had seemed impossible that they could surrender a two-goal first leg advantage over Hamilton in the Play-Off, to plunge out of the Premiership three seasons before. Even Neil appeared laid-back enough to give all the substitutes a run-out in what would prove to be a definitive match, introducing Alex Harris in place of Andrew Shinnie on the sixty-fifth minute and also adding Keatings and Bartley to the fray. On another day he might have been complaining that once more his team could and should have scored more, but in the absence of any real threat from the opposition, three goals were clearly going to be enough. Thirty miles to the west the Bairns had drawn level again, but it mattered little now.

The noise from the stands continued to grow as the ninety minutes drew to a close, with general hilarity at the sight of the stewards dragging flimsy looking wee barriers in front of the East, some attached to others with thin tendrils of coloured sticky stuff. "Oh no, not the red tape!" gasped the masses in horror (or, more accurately, "What the fucking hell is *that?*") In the event of a pitch invasion, they were likely to be about as much deterrent as those G4S clowns had been at Hampden back on 21 / 05 / 16. However, that didn't transpire after pleas over the tannoy were heeded, although there were still a few minutes left at the conclusion, before confirmation of the draw at Falkirk came through. Cue 'I'm On My Way' and 'Sunshine On Leith' blasting out, as CHAMPIONEES status was finally achieved, accompanied by a celebratory quadruple somersault from Efe Ambrose, Neil Lennon being hoisted aloft by his charges and Jason Cummings with a scarf tied round his napper cuddling kit-man Tam McCourt. It had been a *very* long time coming, three years since that nightmare capitulation against Hamilton at the same venue and the ensuing agonies of missing out on promotion twice since then. But the job was done and the title safely wrapped up before the Cup semi-final, which would come as a huge relief to fans and players alike. Many, many congratulations to Neil Lennon and his tenacious team. They'd risen to the task over Easter weekend and Premiership resurrection was the ultimate reward.

"The big games at a club like this take care of themselves, but it was the other games that mattered," observed the gaffer. "The other thing was that if we couldn't win, don't lose it. We did have a few more draws than we would have liked, but each point was important going forward. Now we are in the Premiership I don't think there will be so much inconsistency. The expectation will be less, but there will still be expectation to finish in the top six, I would imagine. I think the players need Premier League football."

Man of the Match Darren McGregor was "on cloud nine. To play for the club I've supported and get promoted. I'm trying to take it all in. I've such a hunger and desire to do well for the club and the fans. It's not just me, my family and friends are all Hibs fans. The buzz I get playing for Hibs is far better than anything else I've experienced for any other team. Sometimes it can be too much. When we are not playing well or I'm not performing then I can beat myself up about it."

Chief Executive Leeann Dempster addressed the fans directly, saying, "Through it all you continued to turn out and support your team in increasing numbers. Thank you. Winning the Championship is dedicated to you and your families who have kept this club going throughout the years. I'd like to congratulate Neil Lennon and his coaching staff and of course the players, for working hard to win the Championship. They have worked incredibly hard, dealt with pressure and there is no arguing that they have deserved to win the League."

Although he never stuck around to finish what he started, Alan Stubbs also played his part in the revival and deserves a lot of credit for his input – eight of the team who defeated QoS were regulars in his usual squad. One of those, Lewis Stevenson, was of course a grizzled veteran in terms of his personal Hibernian longevity and the only first team player apart from Jason Cummings still left over from the 2014 second leg debacle against Hamilton (although Harris and Forster were both on the bench that dark day).

"It's only been three years but it does feel a lot longer than that," ruminated Lewis, a sentiment doubtless shared by a large chunk of the support. "But if you'd told me we'd come down, win the Scottish Cup and get back in the third year I would probably have taken that."

What was described as 'a small celebration' followed, which featured Jason Cummings unsuccessfully trying to boil and poach his Easter eggs, before going out to roll them down Smoky Brae. (In the old days the tradition used to take place on the Easter Road pitch, before the famous slope was mysteriously stolen overnight.) The champagne was soon flowing in The Iona afterwards, although Irvine Welsh opted for a nice wee cup of tea instead, as the rallying cry of "We're gonna party like it's 1902 / 2016," echoed forth from the hostelries of Leith and beyond. Posing for selfies in Fingers Piano Bar much later on, actor Woody Harrelson looked somewhat lost for words when a green and white bedecked reveller asked him if he was in town to sign for Hibs. Not a question he was ever obliged to answer, when working behind the bar in 'Cheers', that was for sure. Woody wasn't saying, but 'Natural Born Hibees' could be on the cards yet...

So now the focus could switch whole-heartedly to the upcoming semi-final, with former Dons' dude Fraser Fyvie well in the mood to face down his old club.

"We go there full of confidence after winning the League. We're going back up to the Premiership, which is fantastic. The pressure is probably off because we don't have to worry about the League any more. We still want to win our last League games but going into Saturday, I think that it's fair to say there's less pressure because we're back up."

Since swapping the Northern Lights of Old Aberdeen for Northern Soul at Wigan Athletic in 2012, he'd never played against the Dons, as he'd been injured for the previous season's terrific League Cup victory over the then Premiership leaders at Easter Road. Fraser confirmed that he'd have back-up of sorts at Hampden – although not all his personal followers would be hoping for a Hibs victory.

"Pretty much all of my family will be in the Aberdeen end, bar my mum and dad who'll be in the Hibs end. My uncle did say, "I'm getting to a final either way," but I think he'd rather Aberdeen got there."

The same applied to another man with a solid Sheep-ish background, Martin Boyle, who confirmed that all his pals would be in the Aberdeen end, but at least his fiancée would be on his side.

"My dad's a Hearts fan so he won't care," revealed Martin. "My mum's going along, she'll cheer me on. I've got a lot of uncles who are Aberdeen fans. If we win they'll be happy for me, but if we lose they'll be happy because Aberdeen are through."

If Hibs wanted to put the frighteners on their opponents in advance, they could have done worse than send them a copy of 'The Evening News' issued two days before the match. It featured a remarkably sinister photo of Martin, with half his face cast in shadow, glaring straight at the camera with an icy stare freezing his features like some otherworldly alien. If you'd stuck him in a police line-up looking like that, any potential witnesses to a particularly gruesome murder would instantly be crying, "That's him for sure! The one wearing the green top with the No.17 on it…"

Whilst they were at it, they could also forward footage of Jason preparing for the game in his usual inimitable way, which was guaranteed to frighten the horses, let alone the Sheep. Last season he'd been sighted running around Saughton Park in his socks playing football with the bairns in a run-up to an important game, this time he was indulging in a wrestling bout with a so-called professional of that dubious sport, known as 'Grado'. (Who also writes a column for 'The Daily Record' apparently – an even more dubious activity.) Not like Jase to make a Giant Haystacks of himself of course and Lennon was probably already shuddering about how he might choose to prepare for the final, in the event of Hibs getting past Aberdeen. Fighting with sharks of the Great White variety perhaps, or freefalling out of a plane at forty thousand feet without a parachute.

Down south, Stubbsy was wishing his old charges all the best, being optimistic about their chances.

"Hibs have got nothing to lose, they've got a free shot at Aberdeen," said Alan, after praising the overall performance of Derek McInnes's side over the season. "I believe all the pressure is on Aberdeen. They're the Premiership club and realistically the main challengers to Celtic at this moment in time. Hibs will go into the game with nothing to fear. They'll be buoyed by the fact that, over the last three years, they've only lost once to a Premiership team in ninety minutes. If that doesn't give you confidence, then nothing will. Aberdeen will be confident in terms of their own form, but they'll be wary of Hibs and what they can do."

Awakening early on the morning of the 22nd, I was pleased to find no trace of the traditional feelings of grim foreboding that used to precede any trip to Glasgow for a final or semi-final. In short, I used to *hate* going to Hampden. If the absolute nadir had come in 2012, the agonising loss to Ross County in the 2016 League Cup final only prolonged the sense of utter futility in repeatedly making these soul-destroying trips for no return. But as if by magic, that glorious day in May of the same year (as well as the semi-final triumph over Dundee United) had put these negative emotions to bed, for the time being anyway. The fact that this time the Championship had been safely wrapped up counted for a lot too. Most fellow Hibbies seemed fairly philosophical about this one; i.e. it wouldn't be the end of the world if we didn't win through, as unquestionably the principal priority of the campaign had already been achieved. It'd be disappointing, sure, but I felt I could take a defeat firmly on the chin which most certainly would not have been the case in either of the Big Cup jaunts there in 2016. Amazing what finally getting the 1902 monkey off your back can do for your overall mental well-being.

However, the usual dreadful traffic bottlenecks which habitually greet the visiting fan from the east on the approaches to Glasgow were in evidence yet again – they were digging up all the fucking slip roads off the M8 when we'd been here thirteen months ago for the League Cup lamentation I recalled, and apparently they were still at it. Once through that, we were faced with the traditional irritant of having to drive right past the National Eyesore, before being forced to park the bus about halfway back towards the city centre and then partaking of a twenty-five minute walk in the opposite direction. That was enlivened by risking life and limb in the face of speeding oncoming traffic on Aikenhead Road, where motorists regard anyone being pushed off the kerb due to the sheer volume of pedestrians as legitimate targets. If you survived the attentions of pretenders to the throne of Harry the Killer Bin-Lorry Driver, you then had to negotiate the obstacle course of fucked-up fencing leading to the burger-van theme park outside the stadium, where over-zealous stewards fucked you about even further as they searched Hibbies suspected of cunningly trying to smuggle nuclear weapons in through the turnstiles. Er, did I mention that I *used* to hate going to Hampden? Well apparently I still did...

So despite leaving Edinburgh in plenty of time, we had just scaled the steps to the concourse at the east end when a distant triumphal bleating borne on the wind from the west indicated that our opponents had scored already. Straight from winning the ball back from Hibs at kick-off, they'd poured forward, aided by firstly a Bartley lapse and then a McGregor error, whereupon Rooney broke through and lashed the ball past a helpless Rocky. Still gawping in disbelief, we struggled to our seats. A mere twelve seconds had elapsed – but at least that meant there were still another five thousand, three hundred and eighty-eight left in which to rectify the situation. Or not, as the case may be...

Certainly, there was nothing in the next half-hour or so to suggest that Hibs were capable of such a feat. Buoyed up by their unexpected early gift, Aberdeen continued to make all the running, pressing high and forcing the men from the east very much onto the back foot. They just couldn't get going at all. It was little surprise when the Dons doubled their lead, but it was the manner of the goal which quite understandably had the manager fuming. After Fraser Fyvie fouled Kenny McLean, the two-man 'wall' inexplicably split as soon as Ryan Christie struck the resulting free-kick. But worse was to ensue. The player had probably surmised that Rocky was poorly positioned and succeeded in cleverly curling the ball into the net at the near-post. It was the kind of goal that simply should not be conceded and indeed such was the surprise of the Aberdeen fans at the other end of the stadium, there was a pronounced pause before they erupted in celebration. Hibs were really up against it now and it wasn't long before the gaffer took drastic action in attempting to remedy the situation, as he replaced Fyvie with Holt just after the half-hour. The former looked highly disgruntled at being taken off, but he could have no complaints. He'd stupidly given away the free-kick, been booked into the bargain and had failed to make any positive impact. But nor had many of his team-mates if truth be told. A raging Lennon later credited only Bartley and McGeouch as being up to scratch at this stage.

But then we were treated to what could only be described as a Holt from the blue. The big man scarcely had time to get warmed up when, after a fantastic jinking run, Martin Boyle picked him out with an excellent cross. Grant leapt heroically like an overweight salmon, getting above the Dons' defenders and thundered it into the net with his head. At last, a much-needed lifeline. It couldn't have come at a better time either, as Aberdeen were still very much in the ascendancy. If they'd nicked a third before then – which was quite possible – you really couldn't have seen any way back for Hibs.

The second half got under way and now they were the outfit buoyed up by their reprieve and for a while it looked like a case of the tables being completely turned. Now the Dons were being forced back and seemed somewhat hesitant as the green jerseys poured forward in numbers. You sensed that they now had it in them to press home their advantage. That moment duly arrived on the hour mark, when Dylan McGeouch raced down the flank and played a lovely one-two with Holty on the edge of the box. The latter's delightful wee touch was gratefully picked up Dylan, who struck it home beyond Lewis in the Aberdeen goal.

"Here we go, two in a row…" Well, it seemed possible in the aftermath of that, as the thunderous chanting from the now delirious Hibs support rolled around the stadium. They had the bit between their teeth and might well have taken the lead only a couple of minutes later when Cummings broke through. He was wrongly adjudged offside though, a very poor call, and that let-off gave Aberdeen the impetus to strike back at the other end. They hadn't let their heads go down in the face of Hibs' startling comeback, which surely couldn't have been foreseen in light of their woeful opening spell. But unfortunately for the plucky Championship side, there was a nasty twist in the tail just up ahead. With less than five minutes left and extra-time now on most folks' minds, Johnny Hayes hit a long-range effort towards Marciano. He didn't seem to catch it quite right, but it took a brutal deflection off Darren McGregor's knee. Even so, it looked to be heading narrowly past the post with the Hibs keeper stranded across the goal, but such was the wicked spin on it that it curled agonisingly just inside the upright instead.

A bad blow, but the Hibees weren't done just yet. The mighty long-throw ability of Ambrose was utilised and they had a good chance when McGinn reacted quickly to one such incoming missile being blocked by the defence. He hit the loose ball well enough, but there were too many bodies in the way. A more likely scenario for a fortuitous deflection than the one we'd just witnessed at the other end, perhaps, but it wasn't to be. In a last desperate throw of the dice, Rocky himself came lumbering upfield in the dying minutes, on the award of a corner to Hibs. He got on the end of it too with a powerful header, but it was aimed directly at his opposite number, Lewis, who was equal to the task. We knew that was the last gasp and so it proved. It had been a very courageous fightback and extra-time was the least that the Hibees deserved after such a valiant effort. But they'd paid the price for an inept start and you clearly couldn't expect to gift a team of Aberdeen's calibre such presents and hope to get away with it.

Lennon was, not unnaturally, focused almost wholly on that aspect of the defeat.

"They get no accolade for me. Not today. They should have won, the opportunity was there and they will have loads of regrets about the game. They can go home and watch it again. You can talk about tactics and formations, it's all nonsense. If you gift goals like that, it's got nothing to do with tactics."

Harsh words, in some way justified, but if we're talking tactics, Neil might look to himself for once. Holt made all the difference when he came on, so what impact might he have made if selected from the start? To leave Jason exposed virtually on his own against the second top side in the country was a big ask and Holty's breenging physical attributes which had proved so effective in the first cup game against the jambos also might have paid dividends here. Plus, Lennon is still guilty of speaking out in the heat of the moment and to repeat his infamous 'boy band' jibe to the Press and television about his team was uncalled for, in my view. Knowing his temperament, the media love to encourage him to sound off of course, but that was a mean-spirited remark. Not classy at all, Neil.

Despite being largely to blame for Aberdeen's second goal, Marciano had been very consistent throughout the season when fully fit and indicated he'd be happy to remain at Easter Road if a deal could be done with his parent club.

"All I can say is I'm really happy here and appreciate what the people around the club do for me, the support and the love I get. When you get so much love at a place, you want to stay, obviously."

Mmm, sounds from that like Rocky's been spending a bit too much time over the road at Scorpio Leisure, but he was only one of several players whose futures had yet to be decided. It was the time of year when contract expiry dates started to hover on the horizon and loan arrangements were drawing to a close, so it was good to hear that St. Johnstone midfielder Danny Swanson would join up on a two-year deal in time for the new season.

"The opportunity to sign for Hibernian was one I couldn't resist," said the recent Douglas Park pugilist. "I'm an Edinburgh boy and grew up supporting the Hibees. It's always been an ambition of mine to play for the club."

The gaffer no doubt had other targets in mind too, as he sought to motivate his squad towards finishing the League campaign off in style, with three such games still remaining.

"We won't rest on our laurels," promised Hibs' top man at Hampden, Grant Holt. "We want to finish with a bang, we want to end with a swagger and get as many points as we can and show everyone why we are the best team in the division and why we've won the League."

He was also hoping for a new deal, having enjoyed his time with Hibs, only regretting how long it had taken for him to attain a reasonable level of fitness after not playing regularly for a considerable while and not scoring more goals. But the green and white army had played their part in influencing his thinking too.

"To have 20,000 fans still there singing and cheering for you after you've just lost a semi-final says a lot about what type of supporters they are."

Meanwhile, Darren McGregor deservedly scooped the Player of The Year Award at the club's annual ceremony at Dynamic Earth, which would hopefully be some measure of consolation for him after events at Hampden. All players make mistakes and Daz had made far fewer than most over the season, generally being a model of reliable consistency throughout. Players' Player of The Year went to Lewis Stevenson, while Jason was voted Young Player of The Year. As for Old Player of The Year, well, there's no such category unfortunately, but surely Holty would be a shoo-in there, after his semi-final showing. Goal of The Season accolade was awarded to James Keatings for his last minute sizzler against Falkirk in March.

I was trailing up Albion Road to the boozer by the time that one hit the back of the net, a feat of stupidity I was destined to repeat, as Raith Rovers came a-calling on the last Wednesday of the month. Same player, same goal-time, same situation. Keats – will you kindly confine your scoring exploits to earlier on in the match? Thank you. But at least I saw his first one, a volley from some eight yards which followed a perfectly weighted cross from Humphrey, just a few minutes shy of half-time. Neil Lennon (relegated to the stand after being handed a two-match touchline ban by the Blazers) certainly rang the changes here – there were no less than *ten* alterations to the starting eleven which had taken the field at Hampden. If ever there was a time to give the youngsters their chance to show what they could do, then this was it. Coincidentally, Hibs' three remaining fixtures were against the three bottom teams in the division, all scrapping desperately to escape from the danger zone. But in the light of this result, St. Mirren and Ayr United could have no complaints about Hibs putting out a weakened side. Indeed, from the off they'd looked a hell of a lot livelier than the 'real' team had often done, against so-called inferior opposition.

Alex Harris returned and Fraser Murray (who scored in the Irn Bru Cup away at Turriff United) was given his big team debut in a proper game. Scott Martin also featured and it was good to see Humphrey back on the wing and Jordon Forster return from injury sustained in the notorious square-go encounter. All acquitted themselves competently. Jordon even had a pop at goal, perhaps aware that the bookies were offering generous odds of 25-1 on him scoring the opener. That was blocked by the Rovers' defence however and the best early chances fell to Shinnie, with a powerhouse drive from the edge of the box and an absolute raker from young Fraser Murray which skimmed just over the crossbar. Rovers fought back pluckily and had something of a purple patch in the latter stages of the first half, with McManus coming close via an over the bar effort following a corner. But then Brian Graham set off the move which led to Keats's opener with a cracking pass out to Humphrey motoring down the flank.

Hibs almost shot themselves in the foot for the second time in five days after the restart, as Alex Harris diverted a Barr cross marginally over his own crossbar and that narrow squeak seemed to give Rovers an extra fillip. Barr himself went close soon afterwards (with a name like that he should save himself for the Irn Bru Cup), but Efe Ambrose, the sole surviving starter from Saturday, did well to snuff that one out. However, the equaliser was only delayed for a few minutes more. The same player broke through and passed wide to the accelerating McManus, who placed his shot well beyond Ross Laidlaw into the corner of the net. Rovers continued to dominate and press for the next ten minutes or so, McManus almost netting a second, which prompted the introduction of Bartley and then Holt immediately after. And it was super-sub Grant who did the damage once more, after a clever chip from Keatings, finding him out there all on his tod. The visitors' defence froze and the big felly gratefully took the opportunity to put away his second goal within a week. Rovers weren't done yet though and clawed it back again with a late strike from substitute Ryan Hardie, who was so far offside he was practically chapping at the doors of Meadowbank. Inexplicably the officials allowed it to stand and a draw looked on the cards, before Keats's free-kick sealed it right at the death.

This was a highly entertaining game, aided no doubt by Raith having plenty to play for and it must have been a crushing blow for them to forfeit all three points in time added on. Atmosphere-wise, it had very much an 'end of season' feel about it though, but those who stayed away missed a good show from the emerging Hibee young guns. As for the man in the stand, "Very, very pleased with some of the performances," was the gaffer's take on it. All teams in the Championship had now played the same number of games, with Hibs eleven points clear of the pack. It was going to be an interesting dogfight at the other end though, as only three points separated Raith, St. Mirren and Ayr.

Neil's pleasure seemed to be short-lived however, as he went on to address what he perceived as a spot of verbal vacillating from his two Championship Player of The Year nominees. Both Jason and John McGinn had spoken vaguely of 'assessing their options' regarding the 2017 / 18 campaign and their gaffer was quick to remind them of their contractual obligations.

"They won't be going anywhere unless this club wants them to go, not unless we get an offer we deem fit for our purposes. Until that happens, they will be playing for Hibs. They are on cast-iron contracts so if anyone is interested it is going to cost them a lot of money."

In Jason's case that commitment in writing to Hibs did not expire until 2020, a year longer than Super's, although realistically the era of contracts being 'cast-iron' was effectively over. Back in the good old days Wee Jim McLean could sign up some whippersnapper of a laddie still in short trousers to play for Dundee United for a fiver a week until his knees gave way rendering him fit only for the knacker's yard twenty-five years later, but alas, no more. Apart from the raft of players whose contracts were up being offered new deals, Neil also indicated he'd be hopeful of securing the services of Efe Ambrose on a permanent basis.

"That's something we're looking into. Does he want to stay in Scotland? If so, there aren't many better clubs outside Celtic than here."

Jason's airily confident remark of, "It doesn't matter where I go or what League I play in, I know that I'll score goals," had probably irked him somewhat, but the hit-man was now going to be toiling to equal or surpass his goal tally of the previous season. That had been largely down to his playing time being curtailed as a result of managerial decisions of course, but he was also quick to credit his regular striking partner of late with abetting his scoring. Holty had contributed greatly through his unselfish approach, reckoned Jase, as well as putting in the physical leg-work – "all the stuff I hate doing, like winning headers and battering defenders." This from a man who wasn't averse to tangling with professional wrestlers in the Hibs canteen too. It wouldn't be Jason without a compliment of the back-handed sort to conclude, naturally, as he added, "He's actually been a really close mate as well – he makes me laugh for an old guy!"

The old guy and the young guy were back as the upfront double-act for the penultimate League game at Somerset Park, as the Hibs team reverted to a more conventional look. But Ross Laidlaw retained his berth in goal and Chris Humphrey again featured on the wing. The explosive pace generated by him on one side and Martin Boyle wide on the other flank were always going to trouble Ayr, battling as they were for Championship survival and looking nervy with it. Right at the start, defender Meggat's awkward back-header foxed his own goalkeeper, but Jason Cummings was unable to take full advantage. He still managed to hit the post though and was no doubt keen to take every opportunity to try and match his previous season's goal tally. He came a step closer to that halfway through the first period as a McGinn cross picked him out and he directed it past keeper Fleming with his head. Only three minutes later he had the chance to grab another, but unselfishly allowed a Holt cross to run onto the more favourably positioned Boyle. Martin skelped it high into the net and Hibs were already looking home and dry.

The Honest Men had stunned Hibs with a shock win at Easter Road near the start of the season and had also done well to secure a draw on their next visit, but here they already looked on course to suffer the same fate as they'd done on Hibs' last trip to Somerset. That one had ended 3-0 in the Hibees' favour and this occasion was shaping up to be almost a carbon copy, as substitute Keatings continued his impressive recent run with another goal midway through the second half. But with Jason even more eager than usual to rack up the goals it wasn't too surprising when the Young Player of The Year sealed in in emphatic fashion with a further decisive strike six minutes later. That was how it finished and pretty much finished off the home team's brief tenure in the second tier too, as that now left them mired three points behind Raith at the foot of the table. They'd need to beat the Fifers by a minimum of five clear goals in Kirkcaldy the following week to escape the automatic drop (although fellow strugglers St. Mirren had just thrashed them by that very margin.) Hibs could undoubtedly have gone to town further as there were still eighteen minutes left on the clock after Jason completed his double, but for once the manager seemed content with the outcome.

"We looked a very good team against Ayr. I thought we were different class. It was a really polished performance against a team that are fighting for their lives."

April had been a month of mixed emotions, including as it did the Cup disappointment, but it had also seen the Championship wrapped up with a decisive home win over Queen of the South. The Hibees had not taken their feet off the gas as some cynics suggested they would and admirably sought to round off the campaign with a flourish. Two very fine back-to-back victories had just been attained and pushed their lead at the top of the division to thirteen points. They'd now scored more goals and conceded fewer than any of their opponents and no-one could say they weren't worthy champions. The Saints would go marching into Edinburgh one week hence and then – at long last – it really would be all over.

11.

MAY: THE SENSE OF AN ENDING

One man who'd come on in leaps and bounds over the season was Martin Boyle, adding a dollop of grit and physical resilience to his undoubted Billy Whizz-on-speed attributes. He'd also bagged nine goals and was extremely keen to reach double figures. With Jason also looking to notch as many more as was humanly possible, there was no danger of St. Mirren having an easy time of it at Easter Road on the sixth day of the new month.

"We've got a good week to look forward to, finally getting our hands on the trophy, but we also want the three points as well," said Martin. "We want to win in front of our fans, in front of a sell-out crowd."

Fresh from their thumping win over Raith Rovers, St. Mirren now needed a solitary point to avoid the relegation spot. It had been a quite remarkable transformation for the Buddies of late, after looking doomed to taking the drop for much of the season. Needless to say, if they'd performed as well earlier on as they'd done recently, they could have been challenging at the other end of the table instead!

Hoping to reprise his role between the sticks again was Ross Laidlaw, seemingly on the brink of putting pen to paper which would tie him to Hibs for another couple of years. Despite being brought in very much as back-up for Rocky, he'd in fact played eighteen times for the first team, largely as a result of injuries sustained by the Israeli No. 1. The contrast at the start of his Hibs career could hardly have been greater – he'd gone from being farmed out on loan to Elgin City from then parent club Raith, to featuring against Brondby in Copenhagen in the Europa League clash, after Virtanen's blunder cost his team the first leg.

"We seemed to be waiting forever to take the title, every time we dropped points the other teams did the same," reflected Ross. "We were delighted to finally manage it. I think we've been the best team by far, we've been the most consistent and we deserve to go up."

Midweek found Hibs and Celtic fans celebrating in honour of their blessed saviour from thirty-one years ago, donning Bobby Ball-style wigs and moustaches for the duration of May 3rd. That's right, Albert Kidd Day was upon us once more. Thirty-one l-o-n-g years since *their* Hearts were broken, sorrow, sorrow, as the jambos' Premier League crown was cruelly snatched from their grasping fingers at the very last minute, thanks to a super-sub at Dens Park. In tribute to the great man, I'd just read Grant Hill's highly entertaining book on the subject, the amusingly titled 'AK-86: Two Shots in the Heart of Scottish Football'. A bizarrely irresistible story, of how one previously fairly anonymous journeyman player who might not even have played that day wrote his name into the history books forever. Awarded honorary knighthood status by Hibbies, *Sir* Albert Kidd preceded David Gray in that distinction and must be the only bloke to be voted 'Player of The Year' by a Hibs' Supporters Club, despite never actually playing for the club! He was accorded equal veneration at Parkhead of course, as his actions on that day aided Celtic in nicking the title at the death (although they still had to put St. Mirren to the sword in Paisley, a fact that jambos frequently overlook.)

Hill's book is a highly entertaining trawl through a vanished era in Scottish football, when it was still possible for someone out-with the Old Firm to realistically win the top division and serves as a reminder just how immeasurably the game has changed since those more innocent times. It brought back with crystal clarity the agonies of that season for Hibbies in particular, as there seemed no way that Hearts *wouldn't* lift the title. There appeared to be about as much chance of them blowing it as of Gary Glitter getting the janny's job in your local primary school, but blow it they did.

Sir Albert comes across as an essentially modest bloke, who became somewhat overwhelmed by the unexpected fall-out from his strikes on May 3rd, 1986, although he wasn't averse to milking it in later years either! He was even accorded an on-field reception before a match at Parkhead sixteen years after that day, receiving a standing ovation, and it is safe to say that he wouldn't have to buy a pint in any pub in Leith to this very day (assuming anyone recognised him, that is.)

Emigrating to Australia not long after his heroics, he once met Billy Connolly by chance at a hotel in Adelaide. On hearing a Scottish accent, The Big Yin stopped for a chat and asked him what he was doing in the country. Explaining that he was playing for West Adelaide at the time, Sir Albert couldn't resist adding that he'd once played for Dundee and had scored a couple of goals which were rather appreciated by Celtic fans. With that, the comedian immediately yelled "FUCKING ALBERT KIDD!!" before grabbing hold of him and jumping up and down on the spot. He proceeded to invite the player to his show in the city that evening, with full backstage access and privileges included.

"I ended up telling *him* jokes," recalled Albert.

It wasn't all sunshine and roses though – apart from receiving death threats from jambos, one maroon charmer posted him an abusive missive which he'd wiped his arse on, but Bobby Ball's stunt double took it all in his stride. A great read and a nice stroll down memory lane for Hibbies, who were so overjoyed that day they were happy to celebrate a 2-1 *defeat* by Dundee United at Easter Road, when the final scores from Dens Park and Love Street came through.

The same day (2017, not 1986) brought with it the unwelcome news that Hibs would commence their Premiership campaign without two of their most influential players – assuming they were still there of course! Bookings for Sir David Gray and Darren McGregor at Ayr took them to the one-match suspension threshold, which would give Neil some extra food for thought before a ball was even kicked in season 2017 / 18.

Better news for James Keatings in particular though, as PFA Scotland selected his last gasp winner against Falkirk on March 25th as a contender for goal of the season, an accolade it had already merited from his own club. But as he had the bad manners to wait until I'd left the stadium before executing it, I really think it should be downgraded. Why not vote for his second effort against Raith Rovers instead? Oh no, hang on, I missed that one as well...

If the manager was still unsure as to which of the current crop of out-of-contractors he'd have to work with next season, one prospect which encouraged him greatly was the possible stepping up to the big team by the cream of the Development Squad. Ryan Porteous and Oli Shaw were the names on everyone's lips, as Neil proceeded to sing their praises, as well as extolling Fraser Murray's showing against Raith Rovers. Porteous had been out on loan with Edinburgh City, whereas Shaw had been instrumental through his goal-scoring prowess in lifting Stenhousemuir off the bottom of League One. Their manager was delighted with the Hibs' youngster's progress.

"He's got the ability to go and do something spectacular," raved Warriors' warlord Ferguson. "He's definitely improved since he came to us last summer."

He'd also scored three hat-tricks over the piece for the Development Squad – which was three more than any of his first team contemporaries had managed this time around! (Keats had a couple under his belt over the 2015 / 16 campaign.)

Assistant coach Grant Murray was of the opinion that if Oli and Ryan hadn't gone out on loan they may well have already broken through to the fringes of Neil's top squad.

"They've been fantastic for the Under-20s and got themselves in the Scotland Under-19 set-up."

By the end of the week, Police Scotland finally made a breakthrough in one of the most baffling cases they'd had to deal with in many a year. I refer of course to the mysterious overnight thefts of numerous bus shelters from stances all across the west side of Edinburgh. They'd been disappearing at a regular rate over a number of months, but after a tip-off the cops attended an address in Macleod Street, Gorgie, where to their astonishment they located the missing items. Crudely welded together to form one structure, they'd been painted pink and hoisted aloft a giant crane, awaiting imminent insertion into Tynecastle Stadium. The trail soon led the tenacious sleuths to apprehend two suspects, a Ms. A. Budge and a Mr C. Levein, whose addresses were both given as c/o the current PBS, Gorgie, Edinburgh. When asked by a reporter if she was looking forward to her day in court, Annie declared defiantly, "I'm ready to take the Stand!" As for the puppet-master, well, he'd already started assembling a raft of lawyers to fight his corner. It wasn't long before he'd put together a team of legal eagles running into double figures.

"Ten men in my defence," said Craig. "And not for the first time either."

Czech, please!

Across town, the curtain was due to descend at last, as St. Mirren pitched up at Easter Road for the final game of the season. The scene was set for a green and white party whatever happened on the park and a packed stadium bathed in glorious sunshine (on Leith) welcomed the two sides who'd had very different kinds of fortune throughout the campaign. St. Mirren had plenty of impetus to take the game to the Hibees, but early reports filtering through from Kirkcaldy indicated Raith were already doing them a favour by taking the lead against Ayr. However, the home team looked more lively in the first half, but it was still level pegging at the interval.

Grant Holt was quick to take advantage from close in just after the restart, notching his third goal in four games; the big man really seemed to be on an end of season roll. Nervy times for the Saints, but Rory Loy equalised on the hour after sustained pressure from the visitors had indicated that a goal was probably on the way. Cue mass celebrations from the excellent away support numbering 1,800, which only increased in volume when it became clear that Raith had taken the lead for the second time, after Ayr had drawn level. In truth, it mattered little to Hibs, but at the end of the day it would be enough to lift the Buddies well clear of danger into seventh place in the division.

It wasn't a huge surprise when 1-1 turned out to be the final result, with both sets of fans as happy as could be. Then we witnessed the presentation of the Championship trophy on the park, followed by an emotional lap of honour for the players, their accompanying family members and the watching fans too. (Most heeded the tannoy pleas to remain in their seats, although a few young scallywags did breach the hallowed turf. Yes, Patrick Burns, I'm talking about *you*...) Credit must also go to the followers of St. Mirren who stayed back at the end to applaud the victorious Hibees. Their team's late season recovery had been a thing of wonder to behold and with a support base like that behind them you felt – like Hibs – that they really belonged in the top tier.

"I'm pleased for St. Mirren," said Neil Lennon sportingly. "They're a good club and they've played well in the second half of the season."

But there was no doubting that the day belonged to him, his players and all connected with the club from the east.

"I didn't know how I was going to feel, but it felt good," he added. "There was a real personal amount of pride for the club and people I work for and the players. It meant a hell of a lot. I was trying not to get emotional out there but I think the older you get the more it means to you. We went into the Championship as favourites but thoroughly merited the title – we won it handsomely. I have immense pride in everyone associated with the club. It's really grown on me, got under my skin. Sometimes in this job you get the chance to make a lot of people very happy and today they get to go home happy and proud."

Happy and proud alright, underpinned by a burgeoning sense of relief that finally the job had been done at the third time of asking, would be most fans' take on it, I think. Certainly, no-one wanted to go through that awful nail-biting rollercoaster of the Play-Offs yet again and we could all now relax a bit and look forward to our long-delayed return to the top table. Understandably, the frenzied euphoria that accompanied the historic cup win of a year ago was not matched by the more low-key revelling in the wake of this season's achievement, but everyone was well aware of the importance of promotion. If it had been highly desirable in the previous two campaigns, there was a feeling that it was an absolute necessity this time. A fourth tenure in the second tier really didn't bear thinking about.

So what of Neil Lennon's time in charge so far? There was no doubt that his appointment divided opinion and as I stated at the start of this book I wasn't overly keen myself, initially. I feared the worst when he was sent to the stand for blowing his top soon after coming on board too! But over the course he'd shown that he'd calmed down overall and although there was the odd rush of blood to the head (such as 'Square-Go-Gate' for example), that was the exception rather than the rule. He'd undoubtedly injected a measure of steel into the team that had perhaps been lacking somewhat under Stubbsy's tutelage and he'd moved with admirable alacrity to bring in fresh faces when the occasion warranted it. Kris Commons may not have been at Easter Road for long but he'd still made a valuable contribution and Efe Ambrose had seemingly got his career and confidence back on track by joining the ranks. Neil also appeared to have the happy knack of shrewdly bringing substitutes on at pivotal moments during games, whereupon they'd not infrequently made their presence known by notching a vital goal or two. Obviously not all his decisions or team formations would find favour with the fans unequivocally, the starting line-up for the semi-final being a case in point. But no manager can keep all of us fusspots happy all of the time, and – certainly in comparison to Stubbsy's immediate predecessors – Neil's first season in charge would surely be seen as a resounding success. Yes, his team had drawn too many games which they should have won, but they'd only lost three times in the League (second-placed Falkirk had lost eight) and won the division by a clear eleven points with a very superior goal difference to boot.

As a last hurrah to 2016 /17, John McGinn scooped the Championship Player of The Year award and although this campaign had wound up earlier than 2015 / 16 had done, the Hibernian Ladies still had their cup final to look forward to. Against Celtic – on May 21st, of all dates! Good luck to the girls with that one, as I sign off here on May 8th, looking forward to a fitba'-free couple of months at least. Then, back for the big Premiership adventure to come. No worries there though, my Hibernian compadres. Onwards – and UPWARDS!

COMPETITIVE MATCHES 2016 / 17

Competition abbreviations: E: Europa League, L: League, LC: League Cup, IBC: Irn Bru Cup, SC: Scottish Cup. Numbers or letters after indicate round of competition, i.e. QF: Quarter-Final, SF: Semi-Final, (R: Replay). This is followed by venue designation, opponents, goals scored and conceded, scorers and attendances.

14/07/16	E	H	Brondby	0-1		13,454
21/07/16	E	A	Brondby	1-0	Gray (1-1 on aggregate aet, Brondby win 5-3 on pens. Hanlon, Holt, Boyle net for Hibs)	11,548
06/08/16	L	A	Falkirk	2-1	Cummings (2)	6,458
09/08/16	LC	H	Queen of the South	1-3	Hanlon	7,646
13/08/16	L	H	Dunfermline Athletic	2-1	Richards-Everton (o.g.), Cummings	16,477
20/08/16	L	A	St Mirren	2-0	Cummings (2)	4,517
27/08/16	L	H	Morton	4-0	Shinnie, Holt, Cummings, Graham	14,508
04/09/16	IBC3	A	Turriff United	3-0	F Murray, Graham, Boyle	1,791
10/09/16	L	A	Dumbarton	1-0	Cummings (pen)	1,339
17/09/16	L	H	Ayr United	1-2	Cummings	15,056
24/09/16	L	A	Queen of the South	0-0		3,703
02/10/16	L	H	Dundee United	1-1	Keatings	15,492
08/10/16	IBC4	H	St Mirren	1-2	Harris	4,393
15/10/16	L	A	Raith Rovers	0-0		3,753
22/10/16	L	A	Dunfermline Athletic	3-1	Wedderburn (o.g.), Holt (pen), Graham	7,622
29/10/16	L	H	St Mirren	2-0	Boyle, Holt	14,485

05/11/16	L	A	Ayr United	3-0	Boyle (2), McGinn	3,100
12/11/16	L	H	Falkirk	1-1	Hanlon	14,558
19/11/16	L	H	Queen of the South	4-0	Graham, Higgins (o.g.), Gray, Boyle	14,021
02/12/16	L	A	Dundee United	0-1		10,925
10/12/16	L	H	Dumbarton	2-0	Hanlon, Graham	13,881
17/12/16	L	A	Morton	1-1	Cummings	2,156
24/12/16	L	H	Raith Rovers	1-1	Boyle	15,409
31/12/16	L	A	Falkirk	2-1	Cummings, Commons	6,747
06/01/17	L	H	Dundee United	3-0	Cummings (2), McGinn	18,785
14/01/17	L	A	Dumbarton	1-0	Commons	1,523
21/01/17	SC3	A	Bonnyrigg Rose	8-1	Shinnie, Keatings (2), Humphrey, Cummings (2), Stevenson, Forster	13,000
28/01/17	L	A	Queen of the South	1-0	McGinn	3,007
04/02/17	L	H	Ayr United	1-1	Cummings	14,349
12/02/17	SC4	A	Hearts	0-0		16,971
18/02/17	L	A	Raith Rovers	1-1	Cummings	4,172
22/02/17	SC4R	H	Hearts	3-1	Cummings, Holt, Shinnie	20,205
25/02/17	L	H	Dunfermline Athletic	2-2	Boyle, Cummings (pen)	14,437
01/03/17	L	A	St Mirren	0-2		3,441
04/03/17	SCQF	H	Ayr United	3-1	McGinn, Cummings (pen), Keatings	13,602
10/03/17	L	A	Dundee United	1-0	Cummings	9,532
18/03/17	L	H	Dumbarton	2-2	Harvie (o.g.), Boyle	14,093
25/03/17	L	H	Falkirk	2-1	Ambrose, Keatings	16,140
29/03/17	L	H	Morton	0-0		15,149
01/04/17	L	A	Dunfermline Athletic	1-1	McGinn	7,058

08/04/17	L	A	Morton	1-1	Cummings	4,229
15/04/17	L	H	Queen of the South	3-0	McGregor (2), Gray	17,054
22/04/17	SCSF	N	Aberdeen	2-3	Holt, McGeouch	31,969
26/04/17	L	H	Raith Rovers	3-2	Keatings (2), Holt	13,604
29/04/17	L	A	Ayr United	4-0	Cummings (2), Boyle, Keatings	2,157
06/05/17	L	H	St Mirren	1-1	Holt	19,764

Biggest win: 8-1, v Bonnyrigg Rose (A), Scottish Cup

Biggest defeat: 1-3, v Queen of the South (H), League Cup
0-2, v St. Mirren (A), League

Top scorer: Jason Cummings (21)

Average home attendance: 14,633 (last season: 9,913)

Average away attendance: 5,843 (last season: 8,623, which was skewed by two visits to Ibrox, if those had been excluded the average would have totalled 4,348.) This season's tally does not include Scottish Cup semi-final, as that was played at neutral venue, but does include cup-tie v Bonnyrigg, as it was drawn as an 'away' game, before being switched to Tynecastle by mutual consent.